COMPETENCE

AND CHARACTER

THROUGH LIFE

The John D. and Catherine T. MacArthur Foundation
Series on Mental Health and Development

COMPETENCE AND CHARACTER THROUGH LIFE

EDITED BY
Anne Colby, Jacquelyn James,
and Daniel Hart

THE UNIVERSITY OF CHICAGO PRESS / CHICAGO AND LONDON

Anne Colby is the director of the Henry A. Murray Research Center of Radcliffe College.
Jacquelyn James is assistant director of the Murray Research Center.
Daniel Hart is professor of psychology at Rutgers University.

The University of Chicago Press, Chicago 60637
The University of Chicago Press, Ltd., London
© 1998 by The University of Chicago
All rights reserved. Published 1998
Printed in the United States of America
07 06 05 04 03 02 01 00 99 98   5 4 3 2 1

ISBN (cloth) : 0-226-11316-7

The University of Chicago Press gratefully acknowledges a subvention from the John D.
and Catherine T. MacArthur Foundation in partial support of the costs of production of
this volume.

Library of Congress Cataloging-in-Publication Data

Competence and character through life / edited by Anne Colby,
    Jacquelyn James, and Daniel Hart.
        p.   cm. — (The John D. and Catherine T. MacArthur Foundation
    series on mental health and development)
      Includes bibliographical references and index.
      ISBN 0-226-11316-7 (hardcover : alk. paper)
      1. Character.   2. Performance.   I. Colby, Anne, 1946–   .
    II. James, Jacquelyn Boone.   III. Hart, Daniel.   IV. Series.
    BF818.C66   1998
    155.2′5—dc21   97-35198
                                                                        CIP

CONTENTS

The Development of Competence and Character through Life

ANNE COLBY, JACQUELYN JAMES,
AND DANIEL HART

This book is the product of a collaborative program of research on the development of character and competence from childhood through middle age. Competence and character are at the heart of our notions of a mature and successful adulthood, yet many questions about their nature and development remain unanswered. To focus attention on these broad developmental goals and how they can be nurtured, the Henry A. Murray Research Center of Radcliffe College initiated a new program of research, in collaboration with the Institute of Human Development (IHD) at the University of California, Berkeley, and three research networks of the John D. and Catherine T. MacArthur Foundation: The Network on Adolescent Development, the Network on Human Development and Criminal Behavior, and the Network on Successful Midlife Development. The purpose of the program was to support the use of data from the Murray Center's social-science data archive for the study of selected issues relating to these two complementary and broadly encompassing categories of developmental goals.

From the outset, the new program was committed to genuine collaboration among researchers. This emphasis was stimulated by our awareness of the success of the cosponsoring MacArthur Foundation research network. Beginning in 1982, the MacArthur Foundation's Program in Mental Health and Human Development established a number of research networks, which brought together distinguished researchers from many disciplines to address issues of normal and deviant development across the life course. Many of the other MacArthur networks have a developmental orientation and stress positive adaptation and successful development, along with the study of maladaptive development and psychopathology. In addition to pursuing these substantive research goals, the networks constitute "an experiment in scientific organization" based on sustained collaboration across disciplines and institutions.

Along with this cross-disciplinary focus, the networks represent an effort to shift the research climate toward greater openness in the scientific process, including the sharing of data as well as conclusions of research (Kahn 1993).

Because the Murray Research Center institutionalizes a related set of substantive concerns with human development across the life span, the sharing of research data, scientific openness, and a spirit of collaboration, including collaboration across disciplines, it was natural for the center to serve as the host institution for the new research program on competence and character. The Henry A. Murray Research Center of Radcliffe College was established in 1976 as a national repository for social- and behavioral-science data, focusing especially on studies from psychology, psychiatry, sociology, and education, with some additional data sets from criminology, political science, and economics.

The Murray Center's archive is unique in several ways. First, the Murray Center is the only archive that preserves the original subject records as well as coded, machine-readable data. The availability of these raw data, such as transcripts of in-depth interviews, behavioral observations, and responses to projective tests, is especially valuable for secondary analysis, allowing the application of different perspectives and new scoring procedures to the original data. This makes possible the radical restructuring of the subject records and mitigates the degree to which one is locked into the theoretical assumptions under which the data were collected.

In spite of the clear advantages of making raw data available, most data archives offer only coded computer data. Some major longitudinal studies are archived in a manner that allows access to the records by outside investigators, but in general each of these studies is housed separately. The Murray Research Center is the only repository that is designed to offer a wide range of data sets with original, qualitative records, many of which are longitudinal. The Murray Center is also unique in that samples from many of the studies it holds are available for further follow-up by the new investigator. This is, of course, very valuable in that it allows a new investigator to design the outcome measures used. Use of archival data also allows for the addition of a new cohort to a single cohort longitudinal study or the integration of two data sets into a single multicohort study.

The Murray Center currently holds 216 data sets, seventy-three of which are longitudinal. The center adds new studies to the archive each year and has recently developed a major collection of longitudinal studies of mental health. Funding from the National Institute of Mental Health and the MacArthur Foundation supported the acquisition of many key longitudinal studies for this collection, including, for example, Baumrind's Family Socialization and Developmental Competence Project, Brunswick's Harlem Longitudinal Study, Glueck and Glueck's Crime Causation Study, the Institute of Human Development's Intergenerational Studies, Terman's Life Cycle Study of Children of

High Ability, and Vaillant's Study of Adult Development (The Grant Study). With additional funding from NIMH along with a grant from the National Science Foundation, Murray Center staff moved on to another major archival project, this one designed to enhance the racial and ethnic diversity of the archive.

The issue of underuse (or waste) of data has been a concern of funders and research administrators for some time and has recently received renewed attention. As Kozlowski (1993) has pointed out, "The further one gets from a project, the greater is the chance of loss. Those details which once seemed too obvious to note become fragmented or lost." For this reason, and because grants tend not to fully cover thorough and complete analyses of complex data sets, projects are often abandoned with a great deal of valuable data unanalyzed. A central purpose of the Murray Center is to turn data that might otherwise be wasted into a rich and accessible resource for new research. In order to be an effective resource for new research and thus contribute to minimizing the waste of data, it is important not only to preserve and document data, but also to let the research community know about the availability of the data and to provide some training in how to use archival data. The latter is especially important because methods for secondary analysis, especially secondary analysis of qualitative data, are unfamiliar to many researchers and not taught in many graduate study programs.

In order to ensure the maximum usefulness of its archival data for new research, the Murray Center has offered a number of programs to support the use of the data and a series of conferences on techniques for productively reanalyzing longitudinal archival data. These conferences have resulted in several books, including *Working with Archival Data* (Elder, Pavalko, and Clipp 1993), which outlines this research team's very useful approach to the secondary analysis of qualitative data.

In 1992, the Murray Research Center adopted the theme "Character and Competence: Exploring Pathways of Development Across the Lifespan" as an organizing principle for much of its research and other programming. In using this theme, we take the position that successful human development includes the development of personal strengths and positive values, social responsibility, and social, intellectual, and emotional adaptation and competence. The theme highlights the potential for positive development and points to the possibility of multiple pathways, rather than a single universal sequence of development. The theme also assumes a life-span perspective, in which early development is understood in terms of later development and vice versa. The theme also calls for a holistic view, looking at many facets of the person as they change dynamically over time in ways that interpenetrate both one another and the social context.

In order to promote the use of the data from the center's archive for research on issues relating to this theme, we launched the Character and Competence

Research Program in November 1993. Along with the MacArthur research networks, we were joined in sponsoring the program by the Institute of Human Development at the University of California, Berkeley, which is the home of some of the most important longitudinal studies in this country, the Oakland and Berkeley Growth and Guidance Studies, collectively known as the Intergenerational Studies. In some ways the program was rather like a "mininetwork," in that it involved researchers from several disciplines and many institutions working together over time on a related set of studies.

From among those who submitted proposals, fourteen researchers from the fields of psychology, social work, criminal justice, political science, and human development were selected to participate in the program. These participants met for two days, along with Diana Baumrind of IHD and the staff of the Murray Center. A year and a half later, in April 1995, they met again to discuss the results of their research and their interpretations of what they had found. Through this process, participants gained an intensive and well-supported experience in the reanalysis of archival data, and they also generated a substantial body of empirical work. This book is a compilation of eight of the papers that resulted from those projects, along with Diana Baumrind's integration of the central themes that bind the various chapters together.

Not only do the studies reported here contribute to an understanding of the developmental trajectories of competence and character, but they serve as well to demonstrate in a concrete way a number of approaches to using archival data for new research. Therefore, the volume can be used as a source book for researchers seeking to learn more about the secondary analysis of longitudinal data, including qualitative data, as well as a source book of current research on the development of several aspects of character and competence. The range of data sets available at the Murray Center has made it possible for the book to address the development of competence and character in people from low-income as well as middle-class circumstances (about half the studies use middle-class samples, about half use poverty or working-class samples) and also to look at a broad age range, from childhood through middle age.

In thinking about the goals of human development, the broad categories of competence and character help us to organize the many dimensions that must be included in a full picture of maturity and positive adaptation. The developing individual is potentially advancing in a wide range of competencies, many of which are interrelated and overlapping. They include intellectual competencies, various self-regulatory and life-management skills, and a large number of other intrapersonal and interpersonal competencies. Character is also a multifaceted concept and includes moral and prosocial development, values and beliefs around moral, social, and political issues, as well as social commitment and responsibility in all of life's domains. The authors in this book approach these complex concepts in multiple ways. Some trace carefully the development of a single facet; others try to sketch the entire concept; while still others aim for a middle ground that combines the specific and the general. In our view, all three approaches are essential to the enterprise of understanding the acquisition of competence and character. These features of mature, successful adult life cannot be nurtured without attention to their constituent elements and to the wholes that subsume the facets.

In the opening chapter, Diana Baumrind provides a broadly inclusive context, showing how these specific studies relate to the wider landscape of competence and character. In this and other chapters, we see that the development of competence and character is multidimensional and multidirectional, that there is continual interplay among the subsystems, and that the developmental tasks, problems, and challenges that represent key dimensions of competence and character shift over the life course.

We believe, and the studies presented in this book bear out, that both competence and character must be understood contextually and in relation to opportunities. The competencies needed to cope well with one set of environmental conditions might be quite different than those needed for a different setting. We also believe, however, that in spite of the contextual definition of developmental goals and pathways, it is still possible to talk about developmental gains and losses, as several of these chapters do.

The relationship between competence and character is not entirely straightforward or easy to disentangle. As we shall see in Chapter 1, Baumrind argues that they are inextricable. In Baumrind's view, a highly competent person cannot be conceived as one who pursues bad ends well because competence must include prosocial attributes as well as an awareness that one's actions have social as well as physical consequences that in the long run affect one's effectiveness. This position seems plausible if one defines "highly competent" broadly and as necessarily including certain social and moral competencies. In this case, particular aspects of character are said to constitute competencies. However, if one thinks of competence as a multidimensional concept, it does seem clear that one could show many particular competencies without necessarily exhibiting strong character.

Baumrind also discusses at some length the important issues of self and human agency, self-efficacy, and their relation to competence and character. These issues come up in several of the later chapters as well, especially self-efficacy, which is a key component of the ability to perform competently and to take socially responsible action.

The studies of different aspects of competence begin with childhood, with Mary Gauvain and Ruth Duran Huard's focus in Chapter 2 on how families facilitate the development in their children of the ability to plan and the propensity to approach their daily lives with an orientation toward the future. These key aspects of competence, which come to include delay of gratification, organization of goals and means to those goals, and careful decision-making, are picked up in each of the other chapters in Part I as central elements in the authors' conceptions of competence. An important contribution of Gauvain and Duran Huard's initial look at the development of the ability to plan is their discussion of the process of development and explication of the family as a cultural context within which emerging competencies are coconstructed through participation in everyday practices.

Marion Underwood's chapter carries forward the theme of planning as a central aspect of competence in her attempt to explain why some teenage girls are able to avoid pregnancy and sexually transmitted diseases. The results of her analyses highlight the importance of peer relationships and future academic and vocational plans in this critical area of adolescent competence. Her chapter raises the important question of the specificity of competencies within and across domains and documents adaptive, normative development in low-income African-American adolescents.

John Laub and Robert Sampson in Chapter 4 evaluate competence in a sample of low-income adolescent boys by operationalizing Clausen's (1991) concept of planful competence using data collected many decades ago for another purpose. They are then able to use the long-term longitudinal data available on these men to show the impact of adolescent competence for adult outcomes. As we read the earlier chapters in this part, we may ask whether the proficiencies developed in childhood (as described by Gauvain and Duran Huard) and played out in adolescence (Underwood and Laub and Sampson) really make an important difference later, in early and middle adulthood. Laub and Sampson are able to use the Gluecks' powerful data set to show that planful competence in adolescence does indeed have a very significant impact on later life outcomes, though it is also possible to be diverted from a positive path or pulled back onto a better track after starting off in a bad direction.

In the final chapter on competence, Caire, Pliner, and Stoker propose a new approach to thinking about intrapersonal competence as they explore the idea that the self can be the object of implicit mental models of greater and lesser expertise, in much the same way that the game of chess, for example, can be approached with more and less expert mental models. This approach allows them to look more closely at the question of what successful functioning in adulthood means. Laub and Sampson use education and income (socio-economic achievement) to define positive adult outcomes. Especially given where the men in this sample started, the kind of social mobility Laub and Sampson are able to predict is undeniably important. But the picture of successful functioning is incomplete without some representation of the internal experience of the individual. Caire, Pliner, and Stoker's construct of implicit models of the self provides a way to look at how individuals function in their own terms and thus frees us to some extent from particular norms of success.

That is, the approach provides a way to take cultural context and opportunity into account more fully, and yields a less culturally arbitrary way of assessing life functioning.

The studies of character in Part 2 of the book focus on values and their intergenerational transmission and on aspects of late adolescent and adult social engagement and responsibility. These chapters carry forward the look at development across the life span in their investigations of what contributes to outcomes that are good not just for the individual but also for society.

Farber and Rehner Iversen use qualitative analyses to look at the connections between the home environment and educational attainment among poor African-American adolescent girls. They analyze the perceived family values about education, the ways in which the girls' families act on those values with the intention of influencing their daughters' educational outcomes, and how these practices do influence the academic and childbearing outcomes in the daughters. The authors raise the question of whether there are some core American values that appear to be shared across subcultures and provide a concrete illustration of the important distinction between professed and lived values as they play out in the lives of these families.

The section continues with two studies that emphasize the social historical context of political beliefs and behaviors. Connie Flanagan's study in Chapter 7 investigates the meaning of higher education for the development of values and character more generally, with particular emphasis on the development of an appreciation for civil liberties, human rights, and political participation and responsibility. She is concerned specifically with changes in political and moral beliefs and values that occurred during the college years for a particular cohort of youth: those attending college in the politically charged era of the 1960s.

In Chapter 8, Eric Plutzer looks at a national sample of black women, including both married and single mothers, and asks what are the factors that lead these women to make their political voices heard through regular voting. He finds that single mothers are much less likely to vote than married mothers, and also that single mothers fail to show the age trend seen in most other groups, including married African-American mothers—that is, an increasing tendency to vote as they grow older (until later life, when voting decreases again). In light of the demands on single mothers and their relative lack of resources, these results may not be especially surprising. What is more surprising is that many plausible explanations for differences in the two groups' trajectories of voting across age do not account for the differences. The analyses Plutzer uses to explore this puzzle provide an enlightening example of a statistical approach that allows one to assess alternative explanations for different age-related patterns rather than mean differences between groups. These analyses shed clarifying light on the important question of single and married mothers' political participation, indicating the importance of income and some realistic expectation of increasing income with age. The results lead Plutzer to end with a reminder of the importance of keeping hope and optimism alive in this relatively disadvantaged group of single black mothers if they are to take advantage of the opportunity to participate in the political process.

The final chapter, by MacDermid, Franz, and De Reus, takes a developmental perspective on the themes of social participation and responsibility. The authors use the Intergenerational Studies, comprising the classic longitudinal studies of two cohorts conducted at the Institute of Human Development at the University of California, Berkeley. They apply to these data a Q-sort method of assessing generativity. The success of this approach to reanalyzing data that contain no explicit measure of generativity allows them to describe both general trends in generativity over time and diverse patterns of inter-individual variability in paths through midlife. In so doing, they are able to suggest several factors that appear to be involved in developing "other-oriented, world sustaining, caring behaviors" in both men and women in their middle years.

Through establishing "competence and character" as a theme for this book and other Murray Center programs, we wish to draw attention to the importance of these two encompassing sets of developmental goals as guides for our thinking about human possibilities and about institutions whose missions include supporting and stimulating the achievement of those possibilities. We believe that the field of developmental research needs to be explicit about the set of competencies and aspects of character that a well-functioning adult needs and to understand the various ways those competencies play out in a range of circumstances and contexts. Part of the message of this book is just that—the value of framing our discussions about human development in these terms. The book also takes the next step of presenting some new empirical data on some of the key issues within each of the two broad domains.

The social and developmental issues explored in this book have all been studied elsewhere, but too often those treatments take a problem-centered approach. For each issue, we could cite numerous studies of problematic outcomes. There have been many reports of the problematic aspects of teen pregnancy, for example, and the school dropout rates among low-income teen mothers. A characteristic feature of the work presented in this book is its focus on positive developmental adaptations. Here, the successful avoidance of teen pregnancy is explored along with some of the familial factors involved in educational attainment, including active family support of homework and schedules (Farber and Rehner Iversen) and planfulness (Gauvain and Duran Huard). We have heard repeatedly of the well-worn path from delinquency to hardened criminal. Here, the relationship between a set of competencies in delinquent adolescents and positive adult outcomes is delineated (Laub and Sampson). And we have heard about crisis and gloom associated with midlife. Here, we find an exploration of the midlife opportunity for generativity and some of the factors involved in trajectories of increasing care and concern for others (MacDermid and Franz). This book explores these issues through the lens of possibility rather than defeat. We would like to suggest that there are a host of other complex problems that would benefit from this perspective. We hope that this sample of explorations will contribute to the the growing body of work on the development of competence and character as a positive approach to our conception of human possibility.

References

Clausen, John A. 1991. "Adolescent Competence and the Shaping of the Life Course." *American Journal of Sociology* 96: 805–42.

Elder, G. H., Jr., E. K. Pavalko, and E. C. Clipp. 1993. "Working with Archival Data: Studying Lives." Quantitative Applications in the Social Sciences series, 88. Newbury Park, CA: Sage Publications.

Kahn, R. 1993. "An Experiment in Scientific Organization." MacArthur Foundation Occasional Paper.

Kozlowski, L. T. 1993. "Data-Waste: The Ethical Challenge of the Underdone and Unfinished." *APA Observer* (July/August): 26–29.

CONTRIBUTORS

Diana Baumrind, Institute of Human Development, University of California
Jill Bond Caire, Department of Psychiatry, University of California, San Francisco
Anne Colby, the Henry A. Murray Research Center, Radcliffe College
Lee Ann De Reus, Department of Child Development and Family Studies, Purdue University
Naomi Farber, Graduate School of Social Work and Social Research, Bryn Mawr College
Constance Flanagan, Agricultural and Extension Education, Pennsylvania State University
Carol E. Franz, Institute of Human Development, University of California, Berkeley
Mary Gauvain, Department of Psychology, University of California at Riverside
Daniel Hart, Department of Psychology, Rutgers University
Ruth Duran Huard, Graduate School of Education, Stanford University
Roberta Rehner Iversen, School of Social Work, University of Pennsylvania
Jacquelyn James, the Henry A. Murray Research Center, Radcliffe College
John H. Laub, College of Criminal Justice, Northeastern University
Shelley MacDermid, Department of Child Development and Family Studies, Purdue University
Patricia Pliner, Department of Psychology, Erindale College, University of Toronto
Eric Plutzer, Department of Political Science, Pennsylvania State University
Robert Sampson, Department of Sociology, University of Chicago.
Sarah C. Stoker, San Francisco
Marion K. Underwood, Department of Psychology, Reed College

CHAPTER ONE

Reflections on Character and Competence

DIANA BAUMRIND

In selecting "character and competence" as a major programmatic thrust the Murray Research Center has chosen to emphasize normative and optimal functioning in social contexts throughout the life cycle, rather than to focus on dysfunctional and psychopathological behavior. The intertwined constructs of character and competence focus on positive values, abilities and proficiencies of the self in social contexts. The ensuing reflections on both were shaped by the specific research topics selected by the fellows in the Research Program.

Character

In contrast with related constructs of temperament or personality the construct of character has moral connotations. When the moral connotation is explicit, character may be thought of as personality evaluated. When its evaluative aspect is muted, character refers to the composite of salient and consequential attributes that constitute the essential nature of a person.

Character and Personality

A "character" is a type defined by the accentuation of some dominant disposition or trait that provides the organizing principle that integrates the behaviors, attitudes, and values of each member. Typologies whose organizing principle is based on inherent temperament have their origin with Hippocrates who identified the Sanguine, the Melancholic, the Choleric, and the Phlegmatic characters, each under the influence of a dominant "humor." Aristotle's pupil Theophrastus, a critic of his society, identified thirty characters, all unflattering, and each described by a dominant disposition or trait such as the flatterer, the boor, the loquacious, and the penurious man. In modern times Kretschmer identified four constitutional types that were reduced to three by Sheldon (1942)—fat (pyknic), muscular (mesomorphic), and lean (asthenic)—each with associated characteristics, such as sociability with the fat type.

Allport (1937) used characterology and personality synonymously to refer broadly to the science of the characteristics of human beings. He regarded traits as biophysical properties of individuals, influenced but not determined by genetic makeup. Allport defined personality as "the dynamic organization within the individual of those psychophysical systems that determine his unique adjustments to his environment" (48). Allport objected to the use of typologies and to the moral connotations of character, exclaiming that, "The study of personality is difficult enough without complicating it at the beginning with ethical evaluation" (252). He urged psychologists to study personality by formulating nomothetic principles illustrated by idiographic case histories. Typologies, Allport claimed, are devices that distort and dismember the individuality of the person in order to exalt the abstraction favored by its author's special interest. Unlike Allport, I regard typologies as useful prototypes.

Character typologies differ from other typologies—such as personality, behavioral, or developmental typologies—in that they purport to describe the essential nature of a person and to be exhaustive. Noncharacter typologies are employed to classify people on the basis of personality or behavioral characteristics that are not intended to be exhaustive. They claim to be valid only for a particular scientific purpose, and to embrace particular salient aspects of individuality, rather than the total individual. For example, not all parents can be classified into the four prototypes of authoritative, authoritarian, permissive, and rejecting-neglecting patterns that I identified as salient for middle-class Euro-American families (Baumrind 1971, 1978, 1989, 1991b). These prototypical patterns of parental authority, like the Ainsworth attachment categories, are intended to describe a particular parent-child relationship in historical time, not the all-embracing character of the individual parent: Thus a parent may be authoritative or securely attached with one child, and authoritarian or insecurely attached with another child. Developmental typologies such as those of Freud, Piaget, Kohlberg, Loevinger, or Erikson describe successive stages of development, and pertain to the whole person as a unit only insofar as it can be said that the person is characterized by the final stage to which he or she has progressed.

Character typologies that are nonevaluative in the sense that they allow for constructive or healthy *and* destructive or unhealthy variations are of special interest. One of the most complex and long-lived character typologies that is nonevaluative in the above sense is based on the 9-point Enneagram traditionally used by Sufi masters to guide the spiritual development of their disciples. The Enneagram claims to offer an exhaustive taxonomy of all possible lifestyles with the source of character to be found primarily in the family context in which the individual has matured. Each character has praiseworthy and blameworthy elements. For example, Type 8 in the Arica system, much like Octant 1 in the Leary (1957) interpersonal system, is a justice-maker who has a sense of potency and efficacy that can be used to rectify real wrongs, but also to exact revenge for imagined wrongs done to self or friends.

The ongoing work of A. J. Malerstein and Mary Ahern also illustrates the current use of character in the nonevaluative sense. In developing their Piagetian model (1982) they have identified three distinct character structures, each based on one of Piaget's three stages of cognitive development (intuitive, symbolic, and operational). The point of therapy in their view is not to change clients' character structures but instead to reduce their pain and improve their functioning by helping them to construct more effective coping and defensive skills consonant with their basic character structure.

By contrast Robins, John, Caspi, and colleagues (1996) have identified three personality types, one of which (resilient) is clearly positive, and the other two (overcontrollers and undercontrollers) clearly negative, although each of the latter two types has some positive characteristics. Although replicable, these types cannot be thought of as exhaustive, if only because there are more ways of being competent than the extroverted type classified as a resilient.

Character typologies, whether ancient or modern, evaluative or nonevaluative, share the assumption that individuals should be grouped on the basis of their salient and dominant attributes or dynamic organization, rather than studied by the idiographic approach Henry Murray advocated, or as representatives of the generalized human being to whom nomothetic laws apply. The salient attributes that characterize each prototype can, however, be treated nomothetically as traits, and the individual's profile of scores on those traits then used to describe or categorize that individual.

Character in Ethical Context

Character when used in its evaluative sense, rather than within the context of personality assessment, is the ethical estimate of an individual. Competency to know right from wrong and to regulate one's own actions consciously and intentionally so as to choose the right defines the human species as "the ethical animal" (Waddington 1960).

Character refers to that aspect of personality which engenders accountability, is responsible for persistence in the face of obstacles, and inhibits impulses in the service of some more remote or other-oriented goal. Character provides the structure of internal law that governs inner thoughts and volitions subject to the agent's control under the jurisdiction of conscience. Within limits imposed by their competencies (cognitive, affective, and physical), circumstances, and cultures, ethical agents are able to plan their actions and implement their plans, to examine and choose among options, to eschew certain actions in favor of others, and to structure their lives by adopting congenial habits, attitudes, and rules of conduct.

According to St. Thomas Aquinas, a virtue is a habit one develops as a result of consistently choosing and acting on the good. Choice implies self-conscious moral reflection as well as habits deeply embedded in the child's culturated and natural dispositions. Each virtue modifies the character of the one who practices it (see Cessario 1991). Character refers to such positive and cultivated habits as social responsibility, moral commitment, self-discipline and resoluteness by which constellation the whole person is judged to be deficient, adequate, or exemplary. Whereas judgments about morality, or abstract moral principles as assessed by responses to hypothetical moral dilemmas (e.g., Kohlberg 1971), are disembodied and decontextualized, character is concerned with the ethical worth of the individual, and implicates affective and physical as well as cognitive competencies.

Ethical decisions are culturally, historically, and personally relative, whereas the moral point of view—at least as viewed by Kohlberg (1971), following Rawls (1971)—requires abstracting principles from contextual, cultural, and personal considerations in order to deal solely with issues of justice, that is, with what all could will should be adhered to by everyone in similar circumstances. I will sidestep the issue of whether abstracted moral judgments are of any value except to moral philosophers, and claim only that issues of character and competence are more properly subject to neo-Aristotelian ethical considerations than to neo-Kantian deontological considerations. In this essay my concern is with the good life to which I and "we" (culturally situated) may aspire; to the practical application of concepts of justice and compassion embedded in concrete ethical life instantiated, and to criteria by which we may judge the ethical worth of individuals.

The criteria by which ethical worth is evaluated by members of a particular culture depend to a large extent on that culture's construal of the self. I refer, in the ensuing discussion, to cultural *ideals* about the self, and not to the personal experiences and operative conceptions of how individuals in the culture actually view themselves. I agree with the claim of those psychological anthropologists (for example, Geertz 1974, Markus and Kitayama 1991, Shweder and Bourne 1985) who hold that Judeo-Christian cultures differ from almost all other world cultures in their normative conception of the ego-ideal as primarily independent, unique, and autonomous, and set apart from, and often against, other individuals. In Catholic social teaching, for example, on the basis that God has imprinted upon each human being his own likeness, thus conferring essential dignity upon the person, the bounded person is central.

By contrast with this personalist view the ego-ideal of members of most Asian cultures can be said to be interdependent with the surrounding context.

What is focal and objectively real is not primarily the autonomous personality, but rather the specific configurations of the relationships with others that the self has developed. The Kantian notion that puts a premium on abstract moral judgments that must pass a universalizable test, and a categorical imperative directed to the free will of an autonomous moral agent, is peculiarly Western. By contrast the Japanese interdependent construal of the self focuses not primarily on the inner self and the concept of the person as the autonomous subject of moral decision, but upon the relationships of the person to other actors (Markus and Kitayama 1991). In such a culture, the goals of others within one's primary groups are experienced as one's own because it is assumed that other group members will be looking out for oneself in the spirit of reciprocal altruism. Although cultures differ in their emphasis on the inalienable rights of individuals as taking precedence over their responsibilities to the polity—as Spiro (1993) points out in his critique of Markus and Kitayama (1991)—in no culture do normal members lack a firm sense of self-other boundaries, or an inward experience of their own self as a relatively coherent and enduring entity that is responsible for intentions, plans, and actions; and a self that has feelings, a history, and a future.

The interdependent cultural conception of self (discussed in greater detail below) is not inherently more (or less) virtuous than the putative Western ideal. The interdependent conception of self may be exploited by patriarchal authorities to subdue subordinates who have been inculcated to regard loyalty as the cardinal moral virtue. Although in a collectivist culture the boundaries of the psychological self include members of the in-group, the subjective boundary of the in-group to whom one owes loyalty may be defined rather narrowly to exclude the welfare of the rest of humanity (Triandis 1989). Also, when the individual is regarded primarily as an element within the social organism, the autonomy needed to behave responsibly in the face of good and evil can, to the detriment of its component human parts, be subordinated completely to the operation of the socioeconomic unit as a whole.

The cardinal virtues of a culture are those which cannot be derived from one another and from which all other virtues, given the perspective of that culture, can be derived, or of which they are a part (Frankena 1963). The four cardinal virtues identified by the Greeks are: wisdom, courage, temperance, and justice—which are essentially the same as the four "human" cardinal virtues of prudence, fortitude, temperance, and justice in Christianity. Christianity added the three "theological" virtues of faith, hope, and charity. Some moralists, such as Schopenhauer, and some psychologist-philosophers, such as Kohlberg and Gilligan, reduce the cardinal virtues to two: benevolence and justice, and in some cases to *either* benevolence *or* justice.

According to Aristotle, the intellectual virtues of philosophic and practical wisdom come about through teaching, whereas the moral virtues are manifestations of a person's character and are obtained by exercising them. For Aristotle, moral virtue is a state of character concerned with choice, lying in the golden mean between two vices—one involving excess and the other deficiency. Courage or fortitude is the mean between cowardice and rashness; temperance, the mean between self-indulgence and self-denial; prudence, the mean between prodigality and niggardliness; and justice, the mean between too much and too little. Thus retributive justice seeks no more than an eye for an eye or a tooth for a tooth; distributive justice mandates that what should be given is the right gift in the right amount, and in relation both to the merit and need of the recipient, and the resources and debts of the donor.

In the Athenian polity friendship, citizenship, generosity, integrity, and courage were accepted moral virtues of free men. The exercise of virtue and the achievement of the good presupposes free will. Since neither slaves nor women were free men—and therefore did not possess free will—and virtues such as magnanimity could only be exercised by the patrician, the Aristotelian moral virtues were essentially those of affluent male citizens. The everyday virtues of humility, generosity, kindness, thrift, and conscientiousness that could be practiced by the plebeian as well as the patrician citizen were not extolled by the Athenians, whether they be Plato, Sophocles, or Aristotle.

Kohlberg derided Aristotle's "bag of virtues" in favor of the Socratic view that virtue is one and its name is Justice. But Justice and Love are not one. Justice conceived of as either equity or equality frequently is at odds with Love, in that Justice must often cause pain and withhold charity. Conversely, in the ubiquitous face of scarcity, a situation ethics that, as its touchstone, looks only to loving kindness can offer no principle of fair distribution and must often violate the claims of Justice by serving not those whose claims are most just but rather those whose needs are most vocal and immediate.

Personal integrity marks an exemplary character in Western thought. Integrity implies both honesty and wholeness. Honesty preserves trust in human relations, so that the principle of veracity requires one to avoid lies "told out of carelessness or habit or unexamined good intentions" as well as lies intended to secure personal gain (Bok 1979: 33). Wholeness means inner consistency and unity of personality. Wholeness means that a person's precepts and practices are in agreement, that the same standards are applied to means and ends, and that the dichotomy between self and other is transcended in an understanding of true self-interest. "Purity of heart is to will one thing," said Kierkegaard. This purity of heart that results in willing one thing is experienced by others in Western society as inspiring and the person of integrity as charismatic.

Although there are cultural perspectives other than the prototypical Eastern and Western perspectives, I will refer only to the prototypical Eastern perspective in order to examine the prototypical Western perspective from a vantage point external to its own frame of reference. The Eastern perspective on integrity differs from Western thought in that the self is construed as context-dependent so that its identity is allowed to change with circumstances and relationships. Therefore consistency across situations, or between private belief and public action, is not the mark of dependability, as it is in Western culture. For example, *Jen,* a cardinal Chinese virtue, is the ability to interact in a polite, decent, and sympathetic fashion, and to flexibly change one's behavior in accord with the requirements of a relationship (Hsu 1985). Thus authenticity, which requires people to focus their attention on inner feelings and convictions rather than on the reactions of others, is not considered as important as not hurting others psychologically or disrupting harmonious interactions with them. Trust is based on goodwill rather than on telling the whole truth because it is understood that how one acts is a negotiated and shared social enterprise.

Instantiated by different value hierarchies in different cultures, the cornerstone of all ethical systems is the principle of reciprocity (Baumrind 1980). The principle of reciprocity is manifest in the norm that those whom you have helped have an obligation to help you, and that you are obliged to help those who help you. Reciprocity is represented in Christian religion by the Golden Rule: "Do unto others as you would have them do unto you"—or, in its modified version, as the Silver Rule: "Do not do unto others what you would not have them do unto you." A less idealistic version of the principle of reciprocity requires people to observe the Silver or the Golden Rule initially, but then to retaliate proportionately to any intentional injury, and to do so clearly and consistently. No more and no less than an eye for an eye and a tooth for a tooth. This baser but more human norm rewards cooperation but punishes destructive behavior, thus obeying the Confucian injunction to repay kindness with kindness but evil with justice, and recognizing that karma—the sum of the ethical consequences of one's past and present actions—operates in the human sphere.

Ethical personality evolves by successive forms of reciprocity in which the capacity for treating the other as someone like oneself rather than alien from oneself develops, and the differentiation of the "part" is balanced by integration with the whole. The principle of reciprocity acknowledges the "pattern of exchange through which the mutual dependence of people, brought about by the division of labor is realized" (Gouldner 1960: 169–70). Reciprocity recognizes in the social order the underlying structure of relations described in the natural order by Piaget as reversibility. As Marx in the *Grundrisse* (1971 [1858]) put it, persons as they mature become able to understand their history as a process, and to conceive of nature as their real body: Physical nature constitutes human beings' inorganic flesh and the social environment their organic flesh. With this understanding, the distinction between pragmatic and moral considerations, based as it is on the reification of the self/other dichotomy, is transcended. Self-transcendent moments are generally experienced as illuminating, and paradoxically as self-realizing.

Subordinate to the principle of reciprocity are three ethical strategies intended conjointly to govern ethical conduct in Western society: beneficence, justice, and respect for persons. The first ethical strategy, beneficence, requires the provision of positive benefits and the avoidance of harm, thereby permitting a unilateral supply of resources for those whose dependent status precludes return in kind. The second ethical strategy, justice, requires a fair distribution of burdens and benefits such that rights and obligations are properly balanced and mutual gratification is obtained. The third principle, respect for persons, mandates that individuals be treated as autonomous agents insofar as to do so does not interfere with another's right to similar respect. These three principles embodying the norm of reciprocity are included in the Department of Health Education and Welfare (DHEW: 1978) regulations concerning the ethical treatment of human subjects.

Raising an Ethical Child

In the subsequent discussion I will focus on the contribution of adults, especially parents, in nurturing children's ethical growth. Of course the child's experiences outside the family, especially with peers and in school, contribute importantly to how children become responsible agents (Damon 1988). The earliest form of reciprocity occurs within the family and is that of reciprocity between obedience to adult authority and freedom from punishment. Parental sovereignty is traditionally authorized by the dependent status of children and by the fiduciary obligations parents incur toward their children as a consequence of this status. The reciprocal relationship between the rights and obligations of parent and child constitutes the basis of Rousseau's social contract, which he defined as follows:

> The most ancient of all societies, and the only one that is natural, is the family: and even so the children remain attached to the father only as long as they need him for their preservation. As soon as this need ceases, the natural bond is dissolved. The children, released from the obedience they owed to the father, and the father, released from the care he owed his children, return equally to independence. (1952 [1767]: 387)

In the earliest stage of reciprocity, which Piaget (1965 [1932]) terms moral realism, adult-made laws are reified as though they were absolute laws. Second-stage reciprocity consists in the literal exchange of rewards or punishment, with the goodness or badness of the act separated somewhat from the nature of the reinforcing consequences. During the preschool years, adult constraint expressed as consistent contingent reinforcement and regularity helps promote the child's sense of security and belief that the world can be a safe, predictable place. Consequently, the probability that children will repeat either prosocial or antisocial acts is determined to a very large extent by the reinforcing responses of their socializing agents. Because the preschooler's social-conventional reasoning is limited, the use of inductive disciplinary techniques that involve complex explanations may confuse the child and facilitate neither compliance nor prosocial behavior.

By the time that children have reached the stage of concrete operations they are well aware that others have perspectives that differ from their own. They actively solicit approval from adults as well as peers, and can understand the reasons for parental directives. Perceiving their peers as like themselves in status and nature, they can better extend toward them genuine concern and comprehend their antithetical position in an altercation. Childrearing practices focused on the principle of reciprocal altruism as it operates concretely in the child's own life will foster in the school-age child the ability to make inferences about how others feel, as well as provide a model of role-taking.

By Kohlberg's Stage 3, the child has a more comprehensive cognitive basis for prosocial behavior. The child recognizes, for example, that stable social relations, including those within the family, are based upon reciprocal maintenance of expectations by social partners as well as upon appropriate feelings of gratitude or malevolence. At this developmental stage, the assignment of some household responsibilities encourages internalization of the norm of reciprocal altruism, both encouraging prosocial behavior and reinforcing of the child's internal locus of control and sense of personal agency. By Kohlberg's Stage 4, the prepubescent or early adolescent child has a developed notion of social order in which social approval and respect are earned by work, and in which keeping one's word is understood to be mandated by the social contract. As youths develop formal operations they become able to acknowledge reciprocity in their relations with adults. Providing that firm parental control has been exercised in childhood, far fewer rules will be required in adolescence. If family power becomes more symmetrically distributed as the child matures, the normal adolescent will be prepared and eager to accept increased responsibility for behaving prosocially (Baumrind 1987, Baumrind and Moselle 1985).

Adolescents may appear to regress to a previous egoistic, unsocialized orientation as they become aware of the mutability of social conventions. Although at all ages a control attempt by one person toward another results in psychological forces both to comply and to resist (Brehm and Brehm 1981), by adolescence the forces to resist become an important counterforce to compliance because they reflect a stage-appropriate drive toward independence. When early adolescents adopt a pseudo-independent stance in order to compensate for still very strong feelings of helplessness, parents may mistakenly assume that their charges are as capable and desirous of substantial autonomy as they profess to be, and withdraw their own commitment and firm guidance. Firm family structure and reassuring rituals of obedience to the authority of family and tradition, however, continue to provide necessary support to the early adolescent. If accustomed parental control is withdrawn at this time of heightened stress, the adolescent may in distress turn to the peer group for support (Baumrind 1991a, 1991b, 1991c). If peer norms in turn support antisocial behavior, including the use of drugs and alcohol, the abandoned adolescent may adopt the antisocial peer norms with serious consequences. Adolescents may instead express their challenge to traditional adult norms by engaging in progressive political causes (as Connie Flanagan in this volume documents).

Moral education, according to Durkheim (1961 [1925]), requires the development of three basic elements of moral character that make for dependability: (1) discipline, (2) autonomy, and (3) attachment. Discipline consists of two character traits: (1) a preference for regularity to be developed by structure and regimen in the classroom and home; and (2) a preference for moderation, that is, respect for the impersonal rightness of moral rules over personal disposition, as this rightness is conveyed by a worthy educator. According to Durkheim, discipline, first outer and then inner, by channeling energy into pursuit of determinate and valued goals, is the precondition of freedom, happiness, and self-direction. Autonomy or self-determination develops as the rules of society are internalized by the child. For Durkheim, the moral rules are not self-chosen but, instead are the rules of the educator who rationally explains to the student the need for obeying these particular moral rules in this particular society. The moral attitude of respect for the group's authority is universal, according to Durkheim, but the group norms themselves are not, and these norms cannot be evaluated morally as better or worse. Children within a culture, however, may be judged by their respect for the norms of the group. The third aspect of moral education, according to Durkheim, is attachment to the social group through the faculty of empathy, which by identification with the pain and pleasure of others can enable the student to become altruistic and disinterested.

Socialization research suggests that children become ethcially sound by (1) internalizing adult values of kindness, fairness, and respect, (2) experiencing first empathy and then sympathy for others, and (3) forming personal standards of right and wrong conduct that result in a sense of obligation to one's fellow human beings. Parents encourage internalization of their values by offering children clear and forcefully stated rules accompanied by the principles they advocate of fairness, compassion, and respect for persons. Piaget's view that the child's unilateral respect for the parent retards the child's moral development is not supported by socialization research (for example, Baumrind 1971, 1973, 1980, 1989, 1991a). When adult exemplars practice what they preach, use reason and scaffolding, and are respectful of the child's needs and point of view, children's unilateral respect for parents should advance rather than retard their ethical development by encouraging identification with parents and internalization of their values.

Of course, children's values and motivations to act ethically grow out of their social experiences with peers as well as from guided educational encounters with adults, including parents (Damon 1988). However, parental influence, especially in the early years, is crucial in developing the child's character. Damon and Colby (1987), as well as Michael Pratt and his colleagues (1988), have proposed that one way a caregiver's social perspective can be transferred to a child is through the process called scaffolding in which the presumably ethically advanced adult leads the child to a pattern of behavior desired by both, but often for different reasons, and consistent with the different levels of development of parents and children. The adult demonstrates, persuades, assists, sanctions, and encourages role-taking and proper action with the intent of encouraging the child, through external guidance, to develop new beliefs and motives for action. Among the positive parental influences several investigators (Colby and Damon 1992, Oliner and Oliner 1988) have identified through interviews with "moral" exemplars are:

—Hands-on helping by parents in the presence of the child
—Family solidarity in which habits of hospitality, compassion, and generosity are extended to the larger community
—Direct training in role-taking
—Use of induction and reasoning in preference to power
—Observation of loved adults who manifest consistency between their beliefs, their self-perceptions, and their actions, and model compassion and courage

Authoritative parents treat the rights and duties of parents and young children as complementary rather than identical (Baumrind 1966, 1975, 1978, 1980). They remain receptive to the child's views, but take responsibility for firmly guiding the child's actions. They see the child as maturing through stages with qualitatively different features, but do not describe this maturational process as an automatic unfolding. Instead, they emphasize the importance of well-timed parental interventions. At all ages, inadequate parental involvement, even more than parental harshness, is associated with such negative outcomes as low prosocial tendencies and low self-esteem.

Aristotle claimed, and I agree, that states of character arise out of one's activities—activities that are directed by one's elders during youth. If a child can be induced to act prosocially in sufficient and varied situations, he or she will become prosocial. People become temperate by behaving with moderation, and they become just by doing just acts. People come to know their own attitudes, emotions, and other internal states by inferring them from their own overt behavior, and from others' attributions about their character based on their behavior. Aristotle's aim was to produce superior men who would be of most value to the city-state. Aristotle's virtuous character, like that of the Boy Scout, was a good citizen—brave, honest, loyal, and clean—and not necessarily an autonomous moral agent, as it is for Dewey.

Dewey's (1916) utilitarian liberal approach to education has something in common with Durkheim's and Aristotle's approaches in that all three educators believed that a primary purpose of education is to stimulate the development of ethical behavior and principles in students. For Dewey, however, in contrast to Aristotle or Durkheim, the purpose of education is to develop a free and self-directed character who refuses to subordinate itself to the social conventions or laws of the state. I agree that ethical socialization requires opportunity to dissent responsibly, and not merely to comply with parental directives.

Good-Enough vs. Exemplary Character

Persons of good-enough character need not be highly developed morally or of exemplary character. A person of good-enough character strives at least to do no harm to those who have done them no intentional harm. An ethically good-enough agent strives to avoid malfeasance, observing a negative morality. Negative morality requires one to conscientiously observe the prohibitions against killing, stealing, bearing false witness, or coveting another person's partner, and to not infringe on the rights of others, even to do them good against their will. Negative morality appeals to fair play, whereas positive morality additionally appeals to love. People who practice positive morality do good for their friends and neighbors. The culmination of positive morality by progressively embracing the stranger, thus transforming the "they" into the "we," is a relatively rare, rather than ordinary, human practice. For those few who choose this path, decentration is a lifetime journey towards enlightenment, necessarily spiritual rather than expedient, but not necessarily religious or theistic.

To my Western way of thinking integrity and arete are the personal qualities that mark an exemplary character. A person of exemplary character beneficently practices positive as well as negative morality, and does so consciously and volitionally. Moral exemplars need not be heroes but most are risk-takers in that they are willing to hazard social disapproval, as well as to accept personal discomfort, pain, and harm. Thus moral exemplars possess *arete*—that is, moral courage and valor—as well as integrity—that is, wholeness and honesty. *Agape*—or, self-transcending service and sacrifice—is a theological rather than a human virtue, and is manifested in works of supererogation—acts of love that go beyond what is required for salvation or charity. Such inspirational acts of grace have nothing to do with justice, cognitively understood, and cannot be justified by their recipient as deserved or expectable.

Agape transcends the self-other duality in action by willing sacrifice of self for others—perhaps to obtain one's reward in heaven or the next life.

The Saint of Auschwitz, Maximilian Kolbe, transcended the self-other duality by giving his sustenance and finally his life by volunteering to die in place of another man. There was nothing just about his sacrifice, for his life was, if anything, more worthy than the man in whose stead he died. Kolbe was an extraordinary man. However, even ordinary men and women in extraordinary circumstances can do the right thing at great cost, exemplified by the Christian Rescuers who, during the Holocaust, risked their children's lives as well as their own to save Jews. The reasons they gave for sheltering Jews at risk to their children's lives as well as their own were most often quite simple rather than morally justified by postconventional reasoning: "It was the right thing to do"; "When they came to my house and asked for help I couldn't refuse, although I was afraid"; "How could I face myself or my children had I refused?" And so while most remained passive or actively collaborated, a few had the courage to care. Neo-Aristotelians would say that nature gives us the capacity to receive virtue, and that this capacity is brought to its proper completion by habit. Through socialization, including explicit communication and example, adults can encourage young people to engage in prosocial risk taking behavior, and thus become exemplars to their peers.

Modern Western moralists have generally adopted the view, shared by Dewey, that human consciousness is constituted morally to the extent that actions are determined volitionally and consciously rather than by unreflective conformity to inclination or authority. Although habit more than reflection governs most ethical behavior, the resolution of complex moral dilemmas that arise in life requires self-conscious moral reflection. Morality as a cognitive structure of restraint through socialization is the process by which children come to espouse as well as conform to society's rules even when they are free from external inducements or surveillance, and is inculcated through socializing the child to reflect upon as well as to obey the laws and guidelines of the community and the family. Persons who are highly developed in their moral reflections and ethical behavior do not merely internalize the rules of society, but also construct personal moral standards to guide the conduct of their lives. Caregivers may model and nourish goodness and nobility, but the locus of control for these positive virtues is internal, and the credit for their formation and manifestations belongs to the moral agent.

Competence

Competence broadly defined is effective human functioning in attainment of desired and valued goals. It takes virtuous character to will the good, and competence to do good well. Competence is not the mere absence of psychopathology. Indeed, the presence of virtuous character, intelligence, creativity, and determination have enabled many people with serious emotional problems to make substantial contributions to society. The goals that are valued in a culture are those that enable individuals to pursue their personal objectives within the constraints imposed by the common good, and their social networks. Competence as well as good character requires both highly developed communal and agentic attributes and skills. In the short run, a person who does "bad" well may be perceived as competent. However, competence proscribes doing "bad" well because competence always includes prosocial attributes as well as awareness that one's actions have both social and material consequences that in the long run affect one's effectiveness in pursuit of personal goals.

Competence is the product of increasingly complex interactions of the developing child with socializing adults—primarily parents—who during the child's early years have the power to control these interactions. At birth there are species-specific, fixed features of the human nervous system that predispose the infant to behave in a human fashion. There are also innate dispositions, culturally shaped, that predispose the individual to possess distinctive attributes. These innate and maturational potentialities are expressed throughout the individual's entire life span in a social and physical environment that determines the form that development will actually take. The young child's development of competencies is the result neither of spontaneous maturing of inborn capacities nor of automatic adaptation to programmed stimuli. Although innate factors and maturation of the child's nervous system provide a range of opportunities for development, these opportunities can be fully realized only within a facilitating social environment that is designed by knowledgeable socializing agents.

My own studies reveal their Western origin by focusing primarily, although not exclusively, on the socialization of instrumental competence (e.g., Baumrind and Black 1967, Baumrind 1970, 1971, 1973, 1975, 1978, 1983, 1989, 1991a–c, 1993). The use of the term "instrumental competence" derives from Talcott Parsons' distinction between instrumental and expressive functions. By expressive functions Parsons refers to activities where "the primary orientation is not to the attainment of a goal anticipated for the future, but the organization of the 'flow' of gratifications (and of course the warding off of threatened deprivations)" (1951: 49). Parsons regards expressive functions (such as receptivity, nurturance, and empathy) as traditionally feminine, and instrumental functions (such as assertiveness, ambition, self-discipline, and objectivity) as traditionally masculine. Parsons designated as instrumental those functions

> oriented to the achievement of a goal which is an anticipated future
> state of affairs, the attainment of which is felt to promise gratifica-
> tion; a state of affairs which will not come about without the interven-

tion of the actor in the course of events. Such instrumental or goal-orientation introduces an element of discipline, the renunciation of certain immediately potential gratifications, including that to be derived from passively "letting things slide" and awaiting the outcome. Such immediate gratifications are renounced in the interest of the prospectively larger gains to be derived from the attainment of the goal, an attainment which is felt to be contingent on fulfillment of certain conditions at intermediate stages of the process. (ibid., 48–49)

As Parsons claimed, instrumental qualities, whether one is male or female, promote success in competitive achievements; those fittest to survive and flourish with the least dependence upon others are those who perform instrumental functions in the most competent manner. Instrumental competence as described by Parsons characterizes the ideal of the White Anglo-Saxon Protestant (WASP) male.

The unique strengths of the Euro-American bourgeois family developed to accommodate the organization of production in capitalist society. The early bourgeois family of the seventeenth century was the basic unit of society (Zaretsky 1976). The sovereignty of paternal power guaranteed the individual rights and private ambitions of the family collective. By contrast with feudalist separation of spiritual and economic life, human meaning was to be found in the secular world of production and family life. Within the family the spiritual values of personal integrity and Puritan exaltation of filial and marital love reinforced the secular values of hard work, thrift, rationality, and deferral of gratification, to produce an effective vehicle both of private ambition and social order. The rise of the factory system in the eighteenth century brought with it a schism between spiritual and secular values. The introduction of machinery required members of both the bourgeoisie and the proletariat to identify themselves with a mechanized, disciplined labor process. The individual rhythm of the family was replaced by the uniform rhythm of machines, and the working class was instructed in fulfillment of contracts on time, methodical work habits, and scrupulous attention to detail. As a free man the wage laborer had to be constrained by a stringent conscience. Thus the rise of Methodism, which preached repression, discipline, and social hierarchy. By the nineteenth century, with the imposition of industrial capitalism, both owner and worker became alienated from the economic machine that society had become. The doctrine of Malthusian overpopulation represented nature as cruel and alien to people, and vicious capitalist competition made society seem cruel and alien as well.

The cluster of values Max Weber called the Protestant Ethic arose from, and furthered, the remarkable economic growth of the nineteenth century. The simplistic utilitarianism of Bentham was balanced by a romantic exaltation of the inner life, especially of the artist. Individuals defended their subjectivity against a mechanistic social order with a romantic vision of utopian socialism. The family became the refuge of individuality and humane values, while WASP agentic competencies mitigated by communal values developed to rationalize the attainment of material advantages and social power.

During the 250 years that American mainstream character and values were shaped by requirements of capitalist production, the character and values of American blacks were forged in the crucible of slavery, poverty, and discrimination. Survival required different attributes then, and still does to some extent today. Bicultural competence remains an important socialization goal of African-American families (Harrison, Serafica, and McAdoo 1985), as well as of immigrant families. The prerequisites for bicultural competence are confidence that one can develop and sustain effective interpersonal relations in both cultures, a well-integrated sense of personal identity, and a loyalty to one's culture of origin combined with an understanding and appreciation of the majority culture. Bicultural competence includes the knowledge of the beliefs and values of both cultures, the ability to vary one's behavior (including relational skills, motivations, and coping), and the ability to communicate effectively according to the demands of the social context. The early shift from adult to peer orientation seen as necessary by many black ghetto parents encourages a linguistic pattern, identification, and socialization process often seen as antithetical to the middle-class school environment, despite its richness, complexity, and coherence within African-American poor neighborhoods (Young 1974).

The importance of a network of kin, especially of the adolescent mother's own mother to her daughter, as well as to her grandchild, has been documented in the African-American community (Furstenberg 1976, Ogbu 1981, Silverstein and Krate 1975, Stevens 1984). By inculcating obedience and conformity to the standards of in-group adults, socialization methods which by middle-class white standards may appear authoritarian, punitive, or seductive are often intended to prepare impoverished African-American adolescents to cope with the hazards of contemporary ghetto life (Kohn 1977). Parental practices that would be overly restrictive in a benign middle-class environment may provide optimum supervision in an urban ghetto (Baldwin, Baldwin, and Cole 1990, Baumrind 1972).

Implied by Koestler's (1967) metaphorical reference to the Roman god Janus is the understanding that humans must function simultaneously as autonomous, self-assertive, independent units, and as interdependent, cooperative parts of a larger unit. Agency is the dynamic expression of the individual's wholeness, and communion of its parts. Within the Cartesian dualistic tradition that characterizes the Euro-American perspective we may treat agency and communion as the two primary orthogonal drives: agency being the need for autonomous self-expression that sets the individual apart from the community; and communion being the need to be interdependent and a part of an integrated, harmonious whole. In Western psychological literature (for example, Bakan 1966), agency refers to the drive for independence, individuality, and self-aggrandizement, and in the sex-role literature (for example, Spence and Helmreich 1978) is identified as the masculine principle; communion, on the other hand, refers to the need to be of service and to be engaged with others and is identified as the feminine principle. The social dimensions of status (dominance, power) and love (solidarity, affiliation), which emerge as the two orthogonal axes from almost all factor analyses of Western human behavior (see, for example, Baumrind and Black 1967, Lonner 1980, Leary 1957, Schaefer 1959, Wiggins 1979), are manifestations of agency and communion.

In practical endeavors, the integration of the two modalities is represented by actions that resolve social conflicts in a manner that is both just and compassionate, and that promotes the interests of both one's self and one's community (Baumrind 1982). In the sex-role literature, such integration is regarded as androgynous. Optimum competence in Western societies requires a balance of highly developed agentic and communal qualities. Agency unmitigated by communion marks the sociopath who may be quite competent in the short run with regard to self-assertive outcomes, but who lacks concern for others, a deficiency that eventually results in reciprocated harm. Communion unmitigated by agency is self-abnegating and masochistic at best, and at worst characterizes cult followers who are willing to be self-destructive or destructive of outsiders in support of their group's ideological causes.

Competence Taxonomies

A discussion of personality taxonomies would not be complete without mention of the 5-factor approach (Costa and McCrae 1992), which its adherents claim is both necessary and sufficient for describing the major features of personality. These five factors (surgency, agreeableness, conscientiousness, emotional stability, and openness to experience) are said to account fully for the dimensions of normal or abnormal personality. Block (1995) has criticized the 5-factor model as based on largely atheoretical dimensions that are valid only in restricted contexts. For purposes of this discussion I have chosen to retain as orthogonal factors the older conceptualization of dominance and nurturance, or agency and communion, along which may be plotted adaptive and maladaptive variations in a circumplex model of the interpersonal circle (Schaefer 1959).

Timothy Leary (1957), before he "turned on, tuned in and dropped out," developed a useful interpersonal typology with each of eight types described by both adaptive and maladaptive variations. Each octant is determined by its position on an interpersonal circle, with dominance-submission (agency) and love-hate (communion) as the major axes. Persons are then characterized by where on the circle the preponderance of their descriptors fall. Each octant has its normal and abnormal variants. For example, Octant 1, the managerial-autocratic individual, is high on the dominance axis and somewhat lower on the love axis. When successful, an Octant 1 individual personifies the hero who wins respect and deference by energy, leadership, and planful organization. Gone awry, such a person is an autocrat who compulsively attempts to control and dominate others in order to avoid any sign of incertitude or weakness.

Whereas the love-hate axis appears in almost all interpersonal taxonomies, Leary's dominance-submission axis often takes alternate forms in other taxonomies. For example, Lorna Benjamin (1981), in order to facilitate the understanding of psychiatrically diagnosed abnormal as well as normal individuals, developed a complex psychosocial competence classification system that focuses directly on the individual's social environment. As with Leary's circle, Benjamin's horizontal axis is affiliation or love-hate. However, her vertical axis, rather than dominance-submission as in the Leary system, goes from maximum interdependence to maximum independence. The Benjamin system in comparison to the Ford taxonomy (1985) focuses more on the social control issue than on the social comparison issue along the agentic axis, or what she calls the independence axis.

Martin Ford (1985) proposed a useful taxonomy based on four defining competence issues, each issue with its agentic and communal aspects, or what Ford calls Self-Assertion and Integration. These four competence issues are (1) defining one's identity, (2) social control, (3) social comparison, and (4) resource distribution. Ford's taxonomy exemplifies the necessary link between character and competence. After summarizing Ford's discussion of each issue, I will propose for each how that issue's agentic and communal aspects may be integrated in the development of competence.

The first issue in Ford's taxonomy is identity. Its agentic component involves the development and expression of individuality—stylistically in dress, morally in nonconventional personal values, and internally in a clear and stable set of self-conceptions. But identity can also be defined by its communal component, belongingness; that is, coherent, active, self-aware efforts to construct, maintain, and enhance the social units of which one is a part. The integration of individuality and belongingness as one criterion of good character enables people to be engaged with, but not enmeshed with, significant others so that the boundaries set by the will of others are respected, and help and friendship are offered but not imposed.

The second issue in Ford's taxonomy is control, with the agentic component represented by personal agency and self-determination in social relationships, and the communal component by connectedness, or what Ford calls social responsibility. Personal agency, according to Ford, deals with perceptions of self-determination and perceptions of self-efficacy. The relevant constructs that pertain to perceived self-determination include Rotter's and Weiner's internal vs. external locus of control (Rotter 1966, Weiner 1979); deCharms's personal causation—that is, perceiving oneself as an agent or a pawn (deCharms 1968); and Deci's intrinsic or extrinsic motivational system (1980). Deci's "amotivational syndrome" results from the combined effects of perceived self-inefficacy and perceived environmental unresponsiveness. Other important constructs that pertain to perceived self-efficacy include self-esteem—for example, Coopersmith's (1967) self-esteem construct; Harter's (1982) perceived competence; and Bandura's (1989) self-efficacy construct. The corresponding communal task of the control issue, connectedness, or what Ford calls social responsibility, is represented by such attributes as dependability, trustworthiness, and integrity, and may be manifested in situations in which one has to honor a commitment, or to fulfill a role or a duty by keeping promises and accepting legitimate forms of social control. The integration of social responsibility and agency, the second criterion of competence and good character, enables people to direct their efforts toward fulfilling the needs of significant others without shortchanging their own.

The third pair of outcomes in Ford's conceptual scheme centers on the issue of social comparison. Especially in competitive situations, one may demonstrate superiority agentically through dominance, status-seeking, and leadership. However, another outcome based on social comparison processes is a communal outcome, equity, which ensures that people are treated similarly on some relevant dimension. Efforts to assure equity may focus on distribution of resources, or on more general principles of justice. Concern for equitable distribution of power and status is an important competence criterion for community leaders, employers, and social activists. A third criterion of competence and good character, the integration of superiority and equity outcomes, occurs when people use their leadership positions to assure justice for others as well as for themselves.

The last pair of categories Ford identifies in his agency/communion taxonomy concerns resource distribution. Agentic competencies enable one to acquire material and social resources that may be used only for self-aggrandizement, or else distributed in accord with the communal motive so as to enhance the well-being of others by providing them with material and social resources over which one has control. The integration of the agentic and communal aspects of resource distribution has much in common with Selye's (1980) principle of altruistic egoism. Altruistic egoism refers to the selfish hoarding of esteem, love, and respect of one's neighbors by acts of good will and compassion, with the implicit understanding that in times of need, others will reciprocate one's goodwill by extending help.

Considerations concerning the meaning and desirability of altruism, personal agency, and generativity emphasize the intrinsic relationship between character and competence contained in the ideal of "doing good well" (Baumrind 1990).

Altruism

Altruism is the uncalculated consideration of another's interests. Altruism does not imply that there is a necessary disadvantage to the self in considering the interests of the other, but merely that the motive for doing so includes genuine regard for their interests. Altruistic tendencies have their infantile origin in empathy. Empathy is an affective, nonreflective response to one's own suffering, induced by emotional identification of one's own with another's feelings. The empathic vicarious experience of the suffering of another, or projection upon another of one's own pain, provides affective support for compassionate regard of another's genuine well-being. But in order to produce benefits for others, altruistic tendencies must be a considered response to their needs based on a prior understanding of the differentiation between the interests of the self and of the other, as well as upon a sense of self-efficacy and agency. Compassion, or sympathy, a more developed response than empathy, presupposes the ability to make a prior differentiation between self and others such that the needs of others can be accurately assessed and responded to even when they differ from one's own. At higher moral-cognitive levels, the sharp self-other differentiation may be overcome and the individual bound intentionally by the principle of reciprocity: Role-taking and the coordination of the perspective of the self with that of the other can then become a stable moral enterprise rather than a primitive empathic response or a mere instrumental tactic, as implied by the concept of altruistic egoism.

Decentration should be aimed at bringing about coordination and integration of the claims of alter with ego, a realizable ideal, and not impartiality, an unrealizable ideal. Partiality to one's own interests, and those of one's intimates, is known as kin selection by evolutionary biologists, and is normative in all cultures. Just as an enlightened self-interest includes compassionate regard for others and an inclination to behave justly, so does an enlightened sense of social obligation embrace a considered view of existential obligations to oneself and a special concern for one's kith and kin. As Hillel said:

> If I am not for myself, who is for me?
> If I am only for myself, what am I?
> If not now when?

The Importance of Human Agency in Western Thinking

There has been a resurgence of interest in recent years in Western psychology in the nature and locus of human agency manifested by research concerning planfulness and self-efficacy.

Planfulness. Plans are future events represented in the present by goals that motivate and guide action. Human agency is exercised by people through their capacity to plan for the future. People plan for the future by anticipating likely consequences of their prospective actions as they set goals for themselves and chart courses of action intended to produce desired outcomes (Rogoff, Gauvain, and Gardner 1987). Future events, by being represented cognitively in the present, are converted into regulators of behavior and current motivators (Bandura 1989). In addition to accomplishing proactive control by setting challenging standards, reactive or feedback control is accomplished by subsequent adjustment of effort or goals. The agentic qualities of sustained effort and willful determination enable people who believe in their capabilities to heighten their effort when faced with obstacles, or, once convinced that the standards being pursued are beyond their power to grasp, to adjust their goals without succumbing to depressive ruminations about their self-worth. Caregivers play an important role in helping children develop planning skills through fostering cognitive growth in the zone of proximal development (Vygotsky 1978).

Clausen (1993) has developed a construct he calls planful competence that he equates with the totality of competence. Clausen operationally defined planful competence by three factors: self-confidence, dependability, and intellectual investment. Planful competence in adolescence was a strong predictor, especially for males, of occupational and family success in early adulthood. Planful competence during adolescence may be a crucial constellation of attributes needed by disadvantaged people to exit from poverty, an issue addressed by Laub and Sampson in this book.

Self-efficacy and authentic self-esteem. The exercise of personal agency through self-efficacy beliefs is a major focus of contemporary social-cognitive theory. According to Bandura (1989), people's self-efficacy beliefs influence their level of motivation and thus the amount and duration of effort they will expend when faced with obstacles. Bandura claims that a strong sense of self-efficacy will enable people to remain task-oriented in the face of failure. Perceived inefficacy to fulfill desired goals because one lacks ability or perseverance can result in depression directly, or by inhibiting engagement in interpersonal relationships that could buffer distress (Bandura 1988).

Parents' belief in their own ability to make a critical difference in their children's lives has been shown to enhance the quality of their caregiving. The remarkable achievement of native Japanese and Asian immigrant children in the United States is attributable in part to their parents' tremendous efforts, fueled by their Confucian-based belief that original human nature is uniform, and that phenotypic differences are due to childhood experiences constructed largely by parents and teachers to actively shape children's character and intellect (Lin and Fu 1990). To the extent that parents, correctly or incorrectly, believe that the locus of control for their children's outcomes lies largely in their hands, they are more likely to invest the needed effort to bring out the best in their children. Parents' denial of responsibility for negative outcomes can assuage their sense of failure and self-blame, but also discourage efforts to remediate the problem (Baumrind 1993). Parents' causal attributions that assign responsibility for child outcomes to genetic factors that parents cannot change has been found to undermine parents' belief in their own effectiveness. For example, in one study parents who attributed their child's dysfunctional behavior to the child's dispositional attributes rather than to their own practices were less likely to attempt to alter their child's negative behavior (Bugental, Blue, and Cruzcosa 1989). Low endorsement of self-attributions for caregiving success and failures was also associated in that study with negative parental affect and ineffective coercive behavior toward the child.

Discussing the institutional barriers to school achievement, Massey, Scott, and Dornbusch (1975: 10) concluded, "We have shown that oppression can arise out of warmth, friendliness and concern. Paternalism and a lack of challenging standards are creating a distorted system of evaluation in the schools." Students rewarded with social approval despite poor performance are not motivated to expend greater effort. False positive feedback about performance, or noncontingent praise is misleading so that short-term self-enhancement is offset by long-term disillusion with oneself, and with those who have provided the false feedback. As these investigators point out, the academic self-evaluation of African-American students, unlike that of Asian and white students, is often exaggerated relative to actual school achievement. In their study black students who were low in performance inflated their assessment of effort and achievement toward the average, and perceived teachers as warm towards them. But this warmth was manifested as low expectations and as praise for very little effort or achievement.

To the extent that self-efficacy beliefs motivate planning and sustained effort, such beliefs may provide a basis for authentic self-esteem by moderating performance. However, authentic self-esteem is based on proven mastery, not the reverse. Self-esteem may be regarded as authentic when it is manifested not merely by endorsement of self-enhancing statements on a self-report inventory, but by a sustained high level of aspiration on tasks that the respondent claims to be able to perform proficiently when that respondent expects his or her proficiency to be tested in the immediate future. The widely accepted practice of grade-inflation may reflect capitulation by educators to middle-class demands, with deleterious effects on under-privileged as well as middle-class children.

Dweck and Goetz (1978) found that teachers praised girls inordinately for their conduct rather than for their effort, and attributed girls' failure to lack of ability by contrast with the feedback they gave to boys, whose failure teachers attributed to lack of effort or to bad conduct rather than to (stable) ability. Dweck hypothesized that as a consequence of differential reinforcement, boys are likely to attribute teachers' negative feedback to teacher characteristics, and success to their own effort and ability, whereas girls are likely to attribute teachers' praise not to their own ability and effort, but rather to their niceness and compliance.

Weiner's (1974) work on achievement motivation and attribution theory describes the process by which a self-defeating cycle may be established in African-American children. Teachers often perceive black children as deficient in ability. Students perceived by their teachers as having low ability obtained *more* praise for less effort at every level of performance. These children's self-evaluation reflects the misleading feedback they are receiving, and their performance in turn is affected adversely by fraudulent feedback concerning the adequacy of their actual effort and performance. Their teachers' negative perception of these children's ability is reinforced and supported by their continued poor performance, and so the self-defeating cycle is perpetuated.

A pessimistic explanatory style has been linked to depression, physical illness, and failure (Peterson, Maier, and Seligman 1993). However, overly optimistic self-appraisals may be a mark of grandiosity and thus not stimulate persistent effort. Unwarranted optimism results in people overestimating their performance relative to their effort and to the performance of others, and thus in failing to see the point of working harder. Self-reported self-esteem is inauthentic when not based on active efforts to pursue a goal in the face of obstacles, and ultimately on successful attainment of desired goals. Self-efficacy beliefs are likely to be stable and motivating only when based on persons' efforts and their assumption of personal responsibility for future failure or success, rather than on misleading feedback that temporarily raises self-esteem.

Generativity and Meaning

Erik Erikson (1959) proposed that the two great tasks for the middle and later years are to achieve generativity and personal integrity. Full engagement in the interpersonal relationships and vocation of one's own life cycle ward off despair and give meaning to one's life and death. Michael Lerner (1994), the editor of *Tikkun,* a journal published bimonthly as a liberal Jewish critique of culture, politics, and society, has called for a "politics of meaning." In order to meet the personal need for meaning through connection to one another and a mission, Lerner urges his readers to make a moral commitment to the community. Amitai Etzioni, a leading sociologist, has spawned a new communitarianism of the professional middle class (1993). Etzioni and his followers argue that Americans have learned to expect rights and to reject responsibilities in accord with the emphasis of the civil libertarian of "me" over "we." In support of the common good, Etzioni exhorts us all to strike a balance between rights and responsibilities. These two movements are well-meaning and serious attempts to redress the moral malaise afflicting the United States today.

Unless accompanied by a politics of empowerment and material well-being, however, the obscene and ever-increasing extremes of wealth and poverty in this country are likely to sabotage any possibility of creating an ethically viable community. According to Aquinas, property is for persons, not for grasping and private domination. Money is not everything—provided that you have enough of it. Powerlessness, poverty, and prejudice erode peoples' sense of self-efficacy and their internalized regard for others unlike themselves. A just and compassionate community is the precondition for the development in the individual of a just and compassionate character and an autonomous, generous generativity. By distributing more equitably its resources, both material and social, a just and compassionate community incorporates in its vision of how life should be lived the values and voices of its underrepresented and disenfranchised members.

References

Allport, G. W. 1937. *Personality: A Psychological Interpretation.* New York: Holt.

Bakan, D. 1966. *The Duality of Existence: Isolation and Communion in Western Man.* Boston: Beacon Press.

Baldwin, A. L., C. Baldwin, and R. E. Cole. 1990. "Stress-Resistant Families and Stress-Resistant Children." In *Risk and Protective Factors in the Development of Psychopathology,* ed. J. Rolf, A. Masten, D. Cicchetti, K. Neuchtherlin, and S. Weintraub, 257–80. Cambridge: Cambridge University Press.

Bandura, A. 1988. "Self-Regulation of Motivation and Action through Goal Systems." In *Cognitive Perspectives on Emotion and Motivation,* ed. V. Hamilton, G. H. Bower, and N. H. Frijda, 37–61. Dordrecht, Netherlands: Kluwer Academic Publishers.

———. 1989. "Self-Efficacy: Toward a Unifying Theory of Behavior Change." *Psychological Review* 84: 191–215.

Baumrind, D. 1966. "Effects of Authoritative Parental Control on Child Behavior." *Child Development* 37(4): 887–907.

———. 1970. "Socialization and Instrumental Competence in Young Children." *Young Children* 26(2): 104–19.

———. 1971. "Current Patterns of Parental Authority." *Developmental Psychology Monograph,* Part 2, 4(1): 1–103.

———. 1972. "An Exploratory Study of Socialization Effects on Black Children: Some Black-White Comparisons." *Child Development* 43: 261–67.

———. 1973. "The Development of Instrumental Competence through Socialization." In *Minnesota Symposia on Child Psychology,* vol. 7, ed. A. Pick, 3–46. Minneapolis: University of Minnesota Press.

———. 1975. "Some Thoughts about Childrearing." In *Readings in the Development of Human Behavior,* ed. U. Bronfenbrenner, 396–409. New York: Dryden.

———. 1978. "Parental Disciplinary Patterns and Social Competence in Children." *Youth and Society* 9(3): 239–76.

———. 1980. "The Principle of Reciprocity: Development of Prosocial Behavior in Children." *Educational Perspectives* 19(4): 3–9.

———. 1982. "Are Androgynous Individuals More Effective Persons and Parents?" *Child Development* 53(1): 44–75.

————. 1983. "Rejoinder to Lewis' Reinterpretation of Parental Firm Control Effects: Are Authoritative Families Really Harmonious?" *Psychological Bulletin* 94(1): 132–42.

————. 1987. "A Developmental Perspective on Adolescent Risk-Taking Behavior in Contemporary America. In *Adolescent Social Behavior and Health,* ed. Charles E. Irwin, Jr., 93–126. New Directions for Child Development series, no. 37, San Francisco: Jossey-Bass.

————. 1989. "Rearing Competent Children." In *Child Development, Today and Tomorrow,* ed. W. Damon, 349–78. San Francisco: Jossey-Bass.

————. 1990. "Doing Good Well." In *Ethical Issues in Applied Developmental Psychology,* ed. C. B. Fisher and W. W. Tryon, 17–28. Norwood, NJ: Ablex.

————. 1991a. "Effective Parenting during the Early Adolescent Transition." In *Advances in Family Research,* vol. 2, ed. P. E. Cowan and E. M. Hetherington, 111–63. Hillsdale, NJ: Erlbaum.

————. 1991b. "Parenting Styles and Adolescent Development." In *The Encyclopedia on Adolescence,* ed. R. Lerner, A. C. Petersen, and J. Brooks-Gunn, 746–58. New York: Garland.

————. 1991c. "The Influence of Parenting Style on Adolescent Competence and Substance Abuse." *Journal of Early Adolescence* 11(1): 56–95.

————. 1993. "The Average Expectable Environment Is Not Good Enough: A Response to Scarr." *Child Development* 64: 1299–1307.

Baumrind, D., and A. Black. 1967. "Socialization Practices Associated with Dimensions of Competence in Preschool Boys and Girls." *Child Development* 38(2): 291–327.

Baumrind, D., and K. A. Moselle. 1985. "A Development Perspective on Adolescent Drug Abuse." *Advances in Alcohol and Substance Abuse* 4 (3/4): 41–67.

Benjamin, L. S. 1981. "A Psychosocial Competence Classification System." In *Social Competence,* ed. J. D. Wine and M. D. Smye, 189–231. New York: Guilford.

Block, J. 1995. "A Contrarian View of the Five-Factor Approach to Personality Description." *Psychological Bulletin* 117(2): 187–215.

Bok, S. 1979. *Lying: Moral Choice in Public and Private Life.* New York: Vintage Books.

Brehm, S. S., and J. W. Brehm. 1981. *Psychological Resistance: A Theory of Freedom and Control.* New York: Academic Press.

Bugental, D., J. Blue, and M. Cruzcosa. 1989. "Perceived Control over Caregiving Outcomes: Implications for Child Abuse." *Developmental Psychology* 25: 532–39.

Cessario, R. 1991. *The Moral Virtues and Theological Ethics.* Notre Dame, IN: University of Notre Dame Press.

Clausen, J. A. 1993. *American Lives: Looking Back at the Children of the Great Depression.* New York: The Free Press.

Colby, A., and W. Damon. 1987. "Social Influences and Moral Change." In *Moral Development through Social Interaction,* ed. W. M. Kurtines and J. L. Gewirtz, 5–19. New York: Wiley.

————. 1992. *Some Do Care: Contemporary Lives of Moral Commitment.* New York: The Free Press.

Coopersmith, S. 1967. *The Antecedents of Self-Esteem.* San Francisco: W. J. Freeman.

Costa, P. T., Jr., and R. R. McCrae. 1992. "The Five Factor Model of Personality and Its Relevance to Personality Disorders." *Journal of Personality Disorders* 6: 343–59.

Damon, W. 1988. *The Moral Child: Nurturing Children's Natural Moral Growth.* New York: The Free Press.

DeCharms, R. 1968. *Personal Causation: The Internal Affective Determinants of Behavior.* New York: Academic Press.

Deci, E. L. 1980. *The Psychology of Self-Determination.* Lexington, MA: Lexington Books.

Department of Human Health and Welfare. 1978. *The National Commission for the Protection of Human Subjects of Biomedical and Behavioral Research: The Belmont Report: Ethical Principles and Guidelines for the Protection of Human Subjects of Research.* DHEW Publication (OS) 78-0014. Washington, DC.

Dewey, J. 1916. *Democracy and Education.* New York: Macmillan.

Durkheim, E. 1961 [1925]. *Moral Education (Lectures at the Sorbonne 1902–3).* New York: The Free Press.

Dweck, C. S., and T. E. Goetz. 1978. "Attributions and Learned Helplessness." In *New Directions in Attribution Research,* vol. 2, ed. J. W. Harvey, W. Ickes, and R. F. Kidd, 157–79. Hillsdale, NJ: Erlbaum.

Erikson, E. H. 1959. "Identity and the Life Cycle." *Psychological Issues* 1 (Whole No. 1).

Etzioni, A. 1993. *The Spirit of Community: The Reinvention of American Society.* New York: Touchstone.

Ford, M. E. 1985. "The Concept of Competence: Themes and Variations. In *Competence Development,* ed. H. A. Marlowe and R. B. Weinberg, 3–49. Springfield, IL: Charles C. Thomas.

Frankena, W. K. 1963. *Ethics.* Englewood Cliffs, NJ: Prentice-Hall.

Furstenberg, F. 1976. *Unplanned Parenthood: The Social Consequences of Teenage Childbearing.* New York: The Free Press.

Geertz, C. 1984 [1974]. "From the Natives' Point of View: On the Nature of Anthropological Understanding." In *Culture Theory,* ed. R. Shweder and R. LeVine, 123–36. Cambridge: Cambridge University Press.

Gouldner, A. W. 1960. "The Norm of Reciprocity: A Preliminary Statement." *American Sociological Review* 25: 161–78.

Harrison, A., F. Serafica, and H. McAdoo. 1985. "Ethnic Families of Color." In *Review of Child Development Research,* vol. 7: *The Family,* ed. R. D. Parke, 329–71. Chicago: University of Chicago Press.

Harter, S. 1982. "The Perceived Competence Scale for Children." *Child Development* 53: 87–97.

Hsu, F. L. K. 1985. "The Self in Cross-Cultural Perspective." In *Culture and Self,* ed. A. J. Marsella, G. De Vos, and F. L. K. Hsu, 24–55. London: Tavistock.

Koestler, A. 1967. *Janus: A Summing Up.* New York: Random House.

Kohlberg, L. 1971. "From *Is* to *Ought:* How To Commit the Naturalistic Fallacy and Get Away with It in the Study of Moral Development." In *The Philosophy of Moral Development,* vol. 1, 101–89. San Francisco: Harper and Row.

Kohn, M. L. 1977. *Class and Conformity: A Study in Values.* 2d ed. Chicago: University of Chicago Press.

Kretschmer, E. 1925. *Physique and Character.* New York: Harcourt Brace.

Leary, T. 1957. *Interpersonal Diagnosis of Personality: A Functional Theory and Methodology for Personality Evaluation.* New York: Ronald Press.

Lerner, M. 1994. *Jewish Renewal.* New York: Corosset and Putnam.

Lin, C., and Fu, V. 1990. "A Comparison of Childrearing Practices among Chinese, Immigrant Chinese, and Caucasian-American Parents." *Child Development* 61: 439–43.

Lonner, W. J. 1980. "The Search for Psychological Universals." In *Handbook of Cross-Cultural Psychology,* ed. H. C. Triandis and W. W. Lambert, vol. 1, 143–204. Newton, MA: Allyn and Bacon.

Malerstein, A. J., and M. Ahern. 1982. *A Piagetian Model of Character Structure.* New York: Human Sciences Press.

Markus, H. R., and Kitayama, S. 1991. "Culture and the Self: Implications for Cognition, Emotion, and Motivation." *Psychological Review* 98(2): 224–53.

Marx, K. 1971 [1858]. *The Grundrisse,* ed. and trans. D. McLellan. New York: Harper & Row.

Massey, G. C., M. V. Scott, and S. M. Dornbusch. 1975. "Racism without Racists: Institutional Racism in Urban Schools." *The Black Scholar* 7(3): 2–11.

Ogbu, J. U. 1981. "Origins of Human Competence: A Cultural-Ecological Perspective." *Child Development* 52: 413–29.

Oliner, S., and P. Oliner. 1988. *The Altruistic Personality.* New York: The Free Press.

Parsons, T. 1951. *The Social System.* Glencoe, IL: The Free Press.

Peterson, C., S. F. Maier, and M. E. P. Seligman. 1993. *Learned Helplessness: A Theory for the Age of Personal Control.* New York: Oxford University Press.

Piaget, J. 1965 [1932]. *The Moral Judgment of the Child.* New York: The Free Press.

Pratt, M., P. Kerig, P. Cowan, and C. P. Cowan. 1988. "Mothers and Fathers Teaching 3-Year-Olds: Authoritative Parenting and Adult Scaffolding of Young Children's Learning." *Developmental Psychology* 24: 832–39.

Rawls, J. 1971. *A Theory of Justice.* Cambridge, MA: Harvard University, Belknap Press.

Robins, R. W., O. P. John, A. Caspi, T. E. Moffit, and M. Stouthamer-Loeber. 1996. "Resilient, Overcontrolled, and Undercontrolled Boys: Three Replicable Personality Types." *Journal of Personality and Social Psychology* 70(1): 157–71.

Rogoff, B., M. Gauvain, and W. Gardner. 1987. "Children's Adjustment of Plans to Cirumstances." In *Blueprints for Thinking: The Role of Planning in Cognitive Development,* ed. S. L. Friedman, E. K. Scholnick, and R. R. Cocking, 303–20. New York: Cambridge University Press.

Rotter, J. B. 1966. "Generalized Expectancies for Internal versus External Control of Reinforcement." *Psychological Monographs* 80 (Whole No. 609).

Rousseau, J. J. 1952 [1767]. *The Social Contract.* University of Chicago: Great Books, Encyclopaedia Britannica.

Schaefer, E. S. 1959. "A Circumplex Model for Maternal Behavior." *Journal of Abnormal and Social Psychology* 59: 226–35.

Selye, H. 1980. Epilogue. In *Selye's Guide to Stress Research,* vol. 1, ed. H. Selye. New York: Van Nostrand Reinhold.

Sheldon, W. 1942. *The Varieties of Temperament: A Psychology of Constitutional Differences.* New York: Harper.

Shweder, R. A., and E. J. Bourne. 1984. "Does the Concept of the Person Vary Cross-

Culturally?" In *Culture Theory,* ed. R. Shweder and R. LeVine, 158–99. Cambridge, MA: Cambridge University Press.

Silverstein, B., and R. Krate. 1975. *Children of the Dark Ghetto: A Developmental Psychology.* New York: Praeger.

Spence, J. T., and R. L. Helmreich. 1978. *Masculinity and Femininity: Their Psychological Dimensions, Correlates, and Antecedents.* Austin: University of Texas Press.

Spiro, M. E. 1933. "Is the Western Conception of the Self 'Peculiar' within the Context of the World Cultures?" *Ethos* 21: 107–53.

Stevens, J. H., Jr. 1984. "Black Grandmothers' and Black Adolescent Mothers' Knowledge about Parenting." *Developmental Psychology* 20(6): 1017–25.

Triandis, H. C. 1989. "The Self and Social Behavior in Differing Cultural Contexts." *Psychological Review* 96: 506–20.

Vygotsky, L. S. 1978. *Mind in Society.* Cambridge, MA: Harvard University Press.

Waddington, C. H. 1960. *The Ethical Animal.* Chicago: University of Chicago Press.

Weiner, B. 1974. "Attribution Theory, Achievement Motivation, and the Educational Process." In *Achievement Motivation and Attribution Theory,* ed. B. Weiner, 185–95. Morristown, NJ: General Learning Press.

———. 1979. "A Theory of Motivation for Some Classroom Experiences." *Journal of Educational Psychology* 71: 3–25.

Wiggins, J. S. 1979. "A Psychological Taxonomy of Trait-Descriptive Terms: The Interpersonal Domain." *Journal of Personality and Social Psychology* 37: 395–412.

Young, V. H. 1974. "A Black American Socialization Pattern." *American Ethnologist* 1: 405–13.

Zaretsky, E. 1976. *Capitalism, the Family, and Personal Life.* New York: Harper and Row.

PART ONE

Competence

CHAPTER TWO

Future Talk: The Role of the Family in the Development of Competence at Planning

MARY GAUVAIN AND
RUTH DURAN HUARD

In her Pulitzer Prize-winning book *No Ordinary Time,* which deals with Franklin and Eleanor Roosevelt during World War II, Doris Kearns Goodwin recounts a plan devised by the president to respond to Churchill's pleas for military aid even though Britain was on the verge of bankruptcy. After long contemplation, Roosevelt devised a plan called a lend-lease. When he was asked to explain how this plan worked, Roosevelt replied with an illustration:

> Suppose my neighbor's home catches on fire, and I have a length of garden hose four or five hundred feet away. If he can take my garden hose and connect it up with his hydrant, I may help to put out the fire. (194)

He then went on to explain that he could not ask his neighbor to pay $15 to cover the cost of the hose before he helped him, nor did he necessarily want $15 afterward. What he wanted back was the hose. If after the fire is out, the hose is undamaged, the neighbor can simply return it. If it is damaged by the fire, he can then replace it.

Where did this simple, yet unconventional plan come from? According to Frances Perkins, secretary of labor at the time, it was based on experiences Roosevelt had in his youth, as neighbors helped neighbors and reciprocity, mutual obligation, and trust formed the backbone of the community in which he lived and grew. This story tells several lessons. It, of course, tells about the ability of this former president to devise an ingenious and effective plan that, as history shows, emerged just in the nick of time. However, it also tells something about the process of planning itself, a process central to mature cognitive functioning. It suggests that competence at planning may be forged, in part, during the early years through the experiences that children have in and around the family and the community in which development occurs.

The research discussed in this chapter concentrates on the role of the family, especially parents, in facilitating the development of children's competence at planning from early childhood to early adolescence. It is guided by a theoretical view that suggests that children's thinking develops in practical contexts as other people guide the development and use of cognitive skill (Rogoff 1990, Vygotsky 1978). Much of the current developmental research examining social influences on cognitive development emphasizes the role of social interaction. This research builds on Vygotsky's (1978) notion of the *zone of proximal development,* concentrating on ways in which more experienced partners facilitate children's participation and learning in activities that are slightly beyond their current capabilities. The structure provided in communication serves as a scaffold for the learner, providing contact between old and new knowledge (Wood and Middleton 1975). In this way, the social world provides the child with cognitive opportunities—opportunities that originate in and are maintained through the contributions and goals of the participants—that encourage and support learning and growth. Extending this basic idea, the research reported here examines family influences on the development of planning. By introducing family experiences into the analysis of this cognitive developmental process, we hope to trace the interdependencies between social experience and the development of this skill, and thereby provide a more complete picture of the development of planning than when these contributions are treated separately.

In the next section we review research on children's planning in order to outline what is known about the developmental progression of these future-oriented skills. This is followed by a discussion of the role of social experiences in the development of these skills. Then our research on how experience in the family may affect the development of these skills will be presented.

The Development of Planning

A basic assumption of human development is that with age children will have increasing regulation of their own activities, a process that relies in important ways on the ability to plan. Competence at planning is essential to mature social and cognitive functioning. Plans are devised in order that certain actions may be accomplished in the future. With development children show increasing skill at planning actions in advance and in other metacognitive skills and strategies such as organizing task materials and remembering the steps of a plan that are required for effective planning (Friedman, Scholnick, and Cocking 1987). During early to middle childhood, children participate in increasingly complex individual and social activities, many of which rely on the ability to plan.

Research has shown that over the course of development children increase their competence at planning. There is evidence that children can plan as early as twelve months of age (Benson, Arehart, Jennings, Boley, and Kearns 1989; Rogoff, Mistry, Radziszewska, and Germond 1991; Willatts 1990). Beyond the first years, children's planfulness increases, with preschoolers capable of devising and executing simple plans in advance of action (Besevegis and Neimark 1987; Cocking and Copple 1987; Wellman, Fabricius, and Sophian 1985). By five years of age children have a fairly good conceptual understanding of what planning is and when it is needed (Gauvain 1989, Krietler and Krietler 1987, Pea 1982), they are capable of planning longer sequences of steps in advance (Klahr and Robinson 1981, Krietler and Krietler 1987), they are able to use knowledge of familiar events to plan flexibly (Hudson and Fivush 1991), and they consider more alternatives and correct their planning errors more readily during plan execution (Fabricius 1988). During the early to middle school years, children show increasing competence in devising elaborate and effective plans in advance of action on a broad range of cognitive activities (Brown and Campione 1984, Inhelder and Piaget 1964, Magkaev 1977, Szeminska 1965).

In general, the development of competence at planning is a protracted process, with children able to reach adult levels of performance on certain tasks very early. But on more complex tasks, adult-level performance is not reached until adolescence or later (Krietler and Krietler 1987, Parrila, Aysto, and Das 1994). Even among adults, skill at planning in advance of action can vary tremendously depending on task and experience (Goldin and Hayes-Roth 1980).

Explanations for increases in planning with age are twofold. First, with development children are better able to regulate and suspend voluntary action (Luria 1976, Vygotsky 1981), which permits greater opportunity for mental consideration of alternative procedures prior to action. This capability has clear benefits for the development of planfulness and may be related to the development of the forebrain at around five years of age (Pribram and Luria 1973). A second explanation stresses the role of practice in the development of planning competence. The underlying assumption is that with experience in planning, children come to understand the various components, benefits, and trade-offs of planning and, as a result, show increased incorporation of these skills in their activities.

Social Influences on the Development of Planning

What types of experiences do children have during the early years that may support and encourage the development and use of planning skills? Much of everyday planning, especially for young children, occurs in social settings as other people elicit and model planning-related behaviors for children. Such experiences may provide a formative base for the development of planning skills and research supports this claim (Goodnow 1987, Rogoff, Gauvain, and

Gardner 1987). Children learn about the process of planning as they coordinate plans with others and as they observe and interact with others who are more experienced planners (Gauvain 1992, Gauvain and Rogoff 1989, Gearhart 1979, Radziszewska and Rogoff 1988). Parents seem to play an especially important role in helping children develop planning skills by identifying culturally valued goals and helping children organize their actions to meet these goals. And children facilitate this process through their efforts to participate in and observe the skilled activities of others in the community (Rogoff 1990). For example, parents may help children fine tune their social planning skills during dinner conversations as they mull over the events of the day together and parents propose alternative solutions to the child for handling difficult moments he or she encountered that day.

An underlying assumption of our approach to the development of planning is the idea that the family is the predominant context in which children's short-term (i.e., parents' and children's roles in selecting and planning everyday activities) and long-term (i.e., basic approaches to identifying goals and planning actions to reach these goals) planning skills are fostered. In our research, we are interested in how parents help children identify activity goals and organize actions to meet these goals.

This interest directed our attention to the role of the family in providing opportunities for children to develop planning skills through interpersonal interactions that involve talking about and planning future activities. An initial question this raises is whether future-oriented concerns are commonplace in family discourse, and research suggests that it is so. Benson (1994) found that even parents of 9- to 36-month-old children believe that by establishing routines and talking about what will happen, they teach their children about the future. In accord with this belief, these parents reported that they often talk about the future to their children. A study by Lucarillo and Nelson (1987) of the conversations of mothers and their 2-year-olds is consistent with Benson's findings in that more than three-quarters of the observed conversations focused on future-oriented routines and events. Home observations of families with older children conducted by Ochs, Smith, and Taylor (1989) reveal a similar pattern. Much of the family interaction that was observed centered around planning-related discussions, which the authors refer to as *future planning narratives*. These narratives depict experiences that might take place at a future time, as in one of their observations of how a father responds to his children after dinner as the children chant "Haagen Dazs! Haagen Dazs! Haagen Dazs!"

> Father: "Okay, I'm not going to Haagen Dazs (raises hand to signal stop, sudden silence results). But I will take you to Pronto Market and let you have some of their ice cream if you want."

In this interaction the children display an active concern for a future event, and the father responds to this interest by constructing a plan of action. In other words, an event (finishing dinner) provoked an interest in what comes next by the children (dessert in the form of a specific type of ice cream), and the father responded with a plan of action (go to a certain market and when there get ice cream of a different sort). In this example, which is emblematic of many daily exchanges in family life, the act of planning is woven into the family process. Planning in these instances involves co-construction by the participants as they attempt to coordinate and direct future activities in ways that satisfy their mutual interests and needs. Ochs, Smith, and Taylor argue that such exchanges allow their creators to move their lives forward in time as they stretch present concerns into future events.

In our view, such exchanges also serve as opportunities for cognitive development as children and adults actively participate in the process of organizing or planning the future. Also noteworthy in terms of the development of planning is the fact that it is difficult to characterize these plans as solely the product of the child or the adult. Rather, these types of planning interactions involve contributions from all the participants as the planning problem is distributed across their various interests, goals, and skills. Unlike the planning process as it is often studied in psychological laboratories with children working alone on an assigned task that requires planning, the process of planning in the family context emerges from the social situation as individuals coordinate their needs and actions, and jointly attempt to direct their behavior toward future goals. Thus, the focus in describing the development of children's planning within contexts such as this is not the individual's competence at planning but on the participation of children and adults as the process of planning is initiated and evolves. The developmental question inherent in these planning interactions is, therefore, how does the child's role and responsibility for initiating and steering these planning discussions shift with the child's increasing age (Rogoff 1996)?

The active role of the child in these interactions is of particular interest. The child's contribution is expected to change with time as he or she becomes increasingly skilled at venturing into and shaping conversations about the future. The child's gradual and changing involvement in such interactions may contribute to the development of competence at planning. Hudson's (1991) research on the development of reminiscing supports this claim in a related area of study. In her observations of mother-toddler conversations about the past, she found that over an eight-month period the contributions by the child to these interactions increased as her skill at retrieving and talking about memories developed. Of course, increased skill of this sort would, not surprisingly, lead to more involvement on the child's part. However, Hudson argues that the child's participation in these interactions played a formative role in the development of these skills. This view is in keeping with our own: that participation by children in conversations about future activities with other family members, in particular parents, may play an important role in the development of planning competence. Furthermore, developing competence may be especially enhanced in domains like reminiscing and planning because such topics occur frequently in family interactions and they have much personal salience for family members.

Emphasis on participation as a central feature of cognitive development appears in the writings of several scholars, most notably Barbara Rogoff and Jean Lave. Rogoff (1990) describes the ways in which caregivers arrange and structure children's participation in activities so as to support and challenge the development of cognitive skill. By participating in culturally valued activities under the tutelage of more experienced cultural members, children appropriate the understanding and practices necessary for meeting the intellectual challenges of their community. In contrast to Rogoff who stresses mutual participation as a gateway to cognitive growth, Lave (Lave 1988, Lave and Wenger 1990) emphasizes the role of observation in exposing children, or less experienced cultural members, to more experienced members as they participate in valued cultural practices (also see Goodnow, Miller, and Kessel 1995). Lave calls this process legitimate peripheral participation and suggests that its role may be especially important in communities in which explicit adult-child instruction is less common than in our own. For Lave, the central point is that not all skills are learned by direct guidance and instruction. Rather, much of cultural learning occurs as children live alongside others who are participating in and thereby demonstrating valued cultural skills. A third, related process of social participation that is directly linked to the development of cognitive skill is apprenticeship (Lave 1988, Rogoff 1990). This process involves close and active coordination of an expert and a novice (or several novices) in the course of conducting an activity. Although some important distinctions exist between the notions of guided participation, legitimate peripheral participation, and apprenticeship, these views share a common thread in that they all emphasize the active role of adults in providing cognitive opportunities and of children in procuring or appropriating culturally valued skills as they participate together in the ordinary routines of everyday life.

Despite the frequent need to participate in planning-related interactions during everyday social activity, there are few studies of children's everyday lives that take as their focus the development of competence at planning. To help remedy this, we are currently engaged in research on children's everyday planning opportunities and practices (Gauvain and Duran 1993, Gauvain and Savage 1995). These projects examine the planning of children between the ages of six and twelve years from different cultural communities in the United States. However, due to the cross-sectional nature of the research, we are unable to study developmental processes such as whether opportunities to engage in planning-related activities at one point in time are related to planning-related competencies at a later point in time. Although such questions are essential to developmental study, they require longitudinal data. To our knowledge, no longitudinal data sets exist that address the development of planning directly. Thus, we became interested in whether any extant longitudinal data sets that focused more broadly on the development of competence in the family context might yield insights into this particular developmental process. The Family Socialization and Developmental Competence Project (FSP; Baumrind 1966, 1973, 1978, 1989, 1991) seemed to us to be a reasonable candidate for such investigation.

FSP is a longitudinal study, conducted by Diana Baumrind, that focuses on the development of children's social competence. The objective of Baumrind's research was to identify the family origins and maintenance of children's developing competencies and behaviors. Data were collected at three critical life stages: preschool (Time 1), primary school (Time 2), and adolescence (Time 3). Data collection began in 1968–69. Comprehensive information about parent and child behaviors was collected at each time period, including interviews of parents and children, assessments using standardized measures such as personality inventories and IQ tests, and naturalistic observation in the home. Given our interest in the role that parents play in the development and organization of complex cognitive skills like planning, these data offered a unique opportunity to study family processes that may support the development of these skills. In particular, we were interested in whether children's participation in planning-relevant discussions observed during the home observations changed over time. These observations provided a form of ethnographic data essential for investigating how social practices, specifically family interaction, may relate to opportunities for children to develop cognitive skills like planning.

We hypothesized that early in childhood, children's participation in these discussions would be minimal and would be limited to immediate events and concerns. However, we expected that even young children would often be privy to and participate in planning-relevant discussions as adults solicited information from them regarding a particular plan or discussed a plan in their presence. Beyond early childhood, we expected that children in the school years would be more actively involved in the family planning process and that they would show increasing participation in longer-range plans than they had shown in the earlier years. Finally, we expected that by early adolescence children would be active participants in planning interactions and that their planning-related concerns would be largely expressed through personal concerns and bids for independence.

**Planning-Related Interactions in Families in the
Family Socialization and Developmental Competence Project**

The Sample

A number of family types, such as two-parent and single-parent families, are
included in the FSP data set. This analysis focuses on a subset of these data,
namely families that had two parents in the home at the outset of the longitudinal study and that participated in the study at Times 1 (preschool), 2 (primary
school age), and 3 (mid-adolescence). This resulted in a sample of 76 families[1] being included in the analysis, with 31 of the target children female and
45 male. At Time 1, the average age for the target children in this sample was
four years ($M = 4$ yrs., 4 mos., $SD = 4$ mos.). At Time 2, the average age was
nine years ($M = 9$ yrs., 1 mo., $SD = 6$ mos.). At Time 3, the average age
was fifteen years ($M = 15$ yrs., 1 mo., $SD = 5$ mos.). All participants are Euro-
American.

Coding

Three aspects of the FSP data were used in the present analysis: child IQ, parenting style, and planning-related discussions recorded during the home observations. These data were collected at each of the three time periods studied.

Child IQ. The children's performance on standardized measures of intelligence was assessed by an experimenter at each data collection period. At
Times 1 and 2, child intelligence was measured using the Stanford-Binet Scale
of Intelligence. At Time 3 child intelligence was measured with the Wechsler
Intelligence Scale for Children-Revised (WISC-R).

Parenting style. Parenting style, rated according to Baumrind's typology of
parenting styles, was assessed at each of the three time periods. This rating,
which characterizes parenting along dimensions of demandingness, responsiveness, and restrictiveness, was conducted by Baumrind for her research on
parenting types and was shared with the authors for use in this analysis. Seven
parenting types were represented at each data collection period: authoritative,
democratic, nonauthoritarian-directive, authoritarian-directive, good enough,
permissive, and rejecting/neglecting.

Home observations. The planning-relevant discussions that formed the
main corpus of data were coded from the home-observational portion of the
FSP data set. Home observations were conducted twice at each data collection
period. (For a small number of families at Time 2 and Time 3 only one observation occurred due mainly to scheduling difficulties.) These observations
cover the time immediately preceding dinner, dinner time, after dinner, and
preparation for bed for the target child. They included descriptions of the activities and discussions of family members during this time. Field records were

made at the time of the home observations by a trained observer. Observers used an event recording system that involved taking notes, identified by the time at which they occurred, that described all family interactions and participants during the observation period.

For present coding purposes, these field notes were read in their entirety by Ruth Duran Huard. All family discussions that were related in any way to future-oriented activities were recorded in summary form from the original field notes. These summaries described the content of the discussions, the identity of the participants, and which participant was responsible for initiating the discussion. For instance, a discussion of a forthcoming family vacation would be recorded as follows: "Mother starts a discussion about the family's summer vacation. Mother, father, and child discuss summer vacation including details about when they will be leaving and how long they will be gone." The entire corpus of these individually described events, which are referred to as *future talk,* was then judged independently by Mary Gauvain as to whether they pertained to planning a future activity. Percent agreement for inclusion of the described events in the analysis was 100 percent.

In addition to identifying the participants and who initiated the future-oriented talk, we also identified these interactions along two dimensions: their temporal nature, that is, how far into the future the event was to occur; and their personal involvement, that is, whether the event pertained to an individual or a family issue. In terms of temporality, an event was identified as referring to either a short-term or a long-term goal. Future-oriented talk coded as short term concerned an event in the immediate future, that is, that same evening. Future-oriented talk coded as long term referred to an event farther into the future than the immediate evening. Although this is a crude division of time, we reasoned that one important developmental achievement in future talk may be children's increasing participation in interactions that stretch beyond the same day. Therefore, the code we devised emphasizes this distinction. In terms of personal involvement, each event was also coded in terms of whether it referred to an individual activity or pertained to a family activity (two or more members). Thus, each instance of future talk was identified as a long-term family event, a short-term family event, a long-term personal event, or a short-term personal event. An example of a long-term family event would be discussion of an upcoming family vacation. A short-term family event might be a father and a child planning to play a game together that evening. An example of a long-term personal event would be announcement of a child's musical concert the next weekend. A short-term personal event might be a reminder about the child's homework that evening. Reliabilities for these coded categories were conducted for all of the recorded events, and agreement was excellent, ranging from 97 to 99 percent.

Results

This section describes the results of the analysis of the home observation data. First, we examine the nature of future talk within each time period and how it changes over time, that is, as the target child develops. We then examine the distribution of participation in these planning-related interactions, again examining patterns at each time period as well as over time. We then investigated the connection between child initiation of future talk at each time period in relation to the parenting styles identified by Baumrind for this sample. Finally, we investigated whether earlier experiences in planning-related discussions predicted children's initiation of future-oriented talk at later times. Child IQ was considered in relation to the observed behaviors at various points in the analysis.

What Was Future Talk About?

Means for the proportion of future- or planning-related talk categorized as long-term family concerns, short-term family concerns, long-term personal concerns, and short-term personal concerns discussed during home observations are reported in Table 1. The nature of future-oriented talk that occurred during family interaction changed with development. Early on, most future talk focused on short-term family-related activities, such as what the family planned to do after dinner, and short-term personal actions, such as reminders about evening activities related to personal care. There was a decrease over the three time periods in the proportion of future talk focused on short-term family activities, $F (2,138) = 6.50$, $p < .002$ (using Repeated Measures Analysis of Variance), and short-term personal activities, $F (2,138) = 23.89$, $p < .001$. In both cases there was a linear decline ($F (1,69) = 9.48$, $p < .003$ for short-term family planning and $F (1,69) = 42.44$, $p < .001$ for short-term personal planning). Quadratic patterns were not significant. With development there was an increase in the rate at which members of the family discussed family activities that were to occur longer into the future, $F (2,138) = 14.77$, $p < .001$, as well as personal activities that were to occur longer into the future, $F (2,138) = 18.50$, $p < .001$. In both instances there was a linear trend ($F (1,69) = 27.53$, $p < .001$ for long-term family and $F (1,69) = 37.55$, $p < .001$ for short-term family), and a quadratic trend was not significant.

Comparison of event type within each time period supports the interpretation that over time family members devoted more future talk to long-term than short-term concerns. Of the six pairwise t-tests conducted at Time 1 comparing the proportion of the four event types, five were significantly different. In all cases the difference indicated that short-term planning concerns, both of a family and personal nature, dominated the family planning-relevant talk (see

Table 1 for the mean proportions of these variables and Table 2 for the t-values for Times 1, 2, and 3). The one comparison involving short-term family and short-term personal planning talk was also significant and indicated a higher proportion of future talk devoted to short-term personal than short-term family concerns. At Time 2 results also favor short-term concerns, however only three of the six comparisons are significantly different in this direction. Finally, at Time 3 there is a shift. The three significant results all point to a higher proportion of future talk devoted to long-term concerns. It appears that with development there is an increasing mixture of long-term and short-term concerns as the focus of family planning-related talk. In childhood, short-term planning dominates the future talk among family members. However, by adolescence long-term planning takes on a particularly salient role in family interactions.

Table 1

Mean Proportions (and Standard Deviations) of Four Types of Future Talk for Each Time Period

	Long-term family	Short-term family	Long-term personal	Short-term personal
Time 1	.11 (.1)	.26 (.2)	.15 (.1)	.47 (.3)
Time 2	.19 (.2)	.27 (.2)	.22 (.2)	.31 (.2)
Time 3	.28 (.2)	.16 (.2)	.37 (.2)	.21 (.2)

Table 2

t-tests Comparing Type of Future Talk at Each Time Period

	Long-term family	Short-term family	Long-term personal	Short-term personal
Time 1				
Long-term family		4.84***	1.89	9.17***
Short-term family			3.47***	4.68***
Long-term personal				7.90***
Short-term personal				
Time 2				
Long-term family		2.02*	.92	2.95**
Short-term family			1.11	1.05
Long-term personal				2.12*
Short-term personal				
Time 3				
Long-term family		2.74***	1.88	1.51
Short-term family			4.64***	1.19
Long-term personal				3.65***
Short-term personal				

$*p < .05$ $**p < .01$ $***p < .001$

Who Initiated Future Talk?

Longitudinal patterns were also evident in the patterns of initiation of future-oriented discussions observed among family members. (See Table 3 for the means of this variable.) Although mothers were the primary initiators of future talk at all time periods, their rate of initiation decreased over time, F (2,138) = 13.04, $p < .001$. This was a linear decrease, F (1,69) = 19.16, $p < .001$, and the quadratic pattern was not significant. The target children showed an increasing proportion of initiations of planning-relevant talk, F (2,138) = 17.11, $p < .001$. This trend was linear, F (1,69) = 23.75, $p < .001$; however, there was a marginal effect for a quadratic trend, F (1,69) = 3.58, $p < .06$. This suggests that the slope or incline between Time 2 and Time 3 is steeper than that between Time 1 and Time 2. Thus, children showed greater changes in initiating planning-related talk in the late school-age years than in the early school-age years. Neither fathers nor siblings changed in their rate of initiating planning-related talk over the three time periods (fathers: F (2,138) = .16; siblings: F (2,138) = 2.45). Both had fairly low rates of initiation relative to the mother and target child.

Comparison of the proportion of planning-relevant talk initiated by mothers, fathers, and the target child at each time period supports the view that as they develop children increase in their active participation in future-oriented talk. (The sibling data are limited in utility in this analysis due to a lack of specification in the coding scheme of the age, presence, and number of siblings, so they will not be included in these comparisons.) At Time 1, two of the three pairwise t-tests were significantly different. Mothers initiated more future talk than fathers, t (75) = 11.28, $p < .001$, and more future talk than the target children, t (75) = 9.51, $p < .001$. There was no difference in the proportion of initiation by fathers and target children, t (75) = .63.

This pattern maintained at Time 2 when the proportion of initiations of future talk by mother was greater than that of fathers, t (74) = 9.88, $p < .001$, and that of the target children, t (74) = 6.96, $p < .001$. Children produced a greater proportion of future talk at Time 2 than fathers, t (74) = 2.29, $p < .02$. At Time 3, mothers were still providing a greater proportion of future talk than fathers, t (69) = 5.51, $p < .001$, and children were contributing more than

Table 3
Mean Proportions (and Standard Deviations) of Future Talk Initiations
By Mothers, Fathers, Target Children, and Siblings

	Mother	Father	Target child	Sibling
Time 1	.59 (.2)	.15 (.2)	.16 (.2)	.10 (.1)
Time 2	.50 (.2)	.15 (.1)	.22 (.2)	.14 (.2)
Time 3	.40 (.3)	.14 (.2)	.33 (.2)	.13 (.1)

fathers, $t(69) = 5.52$, $p < .001$. There was no difference between the proportion of initiations by mothers and target children. Consideration of father absence due to separation or divorce does not eliminate these differences. When the ten single-parent families in which the father was not present for the observation are excluded, the same patterns appear, with mothers and children providing a greater proportion of the future talk than fathers, $t(59) = 4.69$, $p < .001$, and $t(59) = 4.93$, $p < .001$, respectively.

Child IQ was not related to the proportion of child initiation at any of the three time periods. Correlations ranged from $-.09$ to $.08$ at Time 1, from $-.18$ to $.07$ at Time 2, and from $-.08$ to $.18$ at Time 3.

These results are consistent with assumptions regarding increases in self-regulation and planning participation over the years of childhood. In the preschool years, children rarely initiated planning-related discussions. However, by age eight, they were more involved in initiating planning-related talk. And by mid-adolescence children were very involved in initiating planning-related interactions. These changes reflect general developmental patterns in involvement in and control over future-oriented experiences and are not related to intelligence as measured by IQ for children in the normal range. Thus, part of normal development involves increasing participation and support for children when they are in the company of family members as they discuss and organize future activities. The pattern of results for fathers is consistent with other research that shows that mothers are more involved than fathers in the details and arrangements of family life—exactly the type of information that is the focus in planning-related discussions in the home (Parke 1996).

Parenting Style and Child-Initiated Future Talk

To investigate the role of parenting style in fostering the development of planning competence, the proportion of future talk that children initiated at each of the three time periods was examined. This analysis was restricted to child-initiated contributions because we expected that both mothers and fathers of all the seven parenting styles would initiate similar rates of future-oriented talk since this is an important and necessary component of household interaction. However, we suspected that some parenting styles may be more facilitative than others of child-initiated future talk. In particular, we expected to see higher rates of child-initiated future talk in families with parenting styles that encouraged child independence and made high demands for mature involvement in activities, namely authoritative and democratic. (See Table 4 for the number of families at each data collection period according to parenting style.) Table 5 contains the proportion at each of the time periods for child-initiated future talk for each of the seven parenting styles observed. Because parenting style could change over the course of the longitudinal study, a series of pairwise

Table 4
Number of Families At Each Time Period by Parenting Style and
Parent Type

Parenting style	Time 1	Time 2	Time 3[a]
Authoritative	7	8	17
Democratic	10	11	13
Nonauthoritarian-directive	15	17	9
Authoritarian-directive	8	8	8
Good enough	16	14	9
Permissive	11	12	4
Rejecting/neglecting	9	6	15

a. One family refused to participate at Time 3.

Table 5
Mean Proportion (and Standard Deviation) of Children-Initiated Future Talk at
Each Time Period by Parenting Style

Parenting style	Time 1	Time 2	Time 3
Authoritative	.27 (.4)	.29 (.2)	.35 (.2)
Democratic	.16 (.2)	.24 (.2)	.36 (.2)
Nonauthoritarian-directive	.15 (.1)	.19 (.2)	.29 (.2)
Authoritarian-directive	.20 (.2)	.24 (.2)	.40 (.2)
Good enough	.11 (.1)	.24 (.2)	.30 (.2)
Permissive	.23 (.2)	.23 (.1)	.43 (.3)
Rejecting/neglecting	.11 (.2)	.06 (.1)	.29 (.2)

t-tests were conducted comparing each of these types at each time period for the rate of child-initiated future talk.

Of the twenty-one pairwise comparisons conducted at Time 1, the only difference was that children reared by parents rated as permissive initiated more future talk than children reared by parents rated as good enough, $t(25) = 2.26$, $p < .03$. At Time 2, five comparisons were significant. In all cases, these differences indicated that in households identified as having a rejecting/neglecting parenting style, children initiated a smaller proportion of future-oriented talk than children in families with authoritative, $t(12) = 2.54, p < .03$, democratic, $t(15) = 2.20, p < .04$, good enough, $t(18) = 2.13, p < .05$, permissive, $t(16) = 2.39, p < .03$, and authoritarian-directive, $t(12) = 2.22, p < .05$, parenting styles. There were no differences across parenting styles in the rate of child-initiated future talk at Time 3.

These patterns suggest that there are not many differences across parenting styles in the occurrence of child-initiated future talk at the three ages studied. However, it is important to note that the home observation data was limited in information as to the posture children adopted in these exchanges or regarding the tone of the interactions, which may have differed across parenting styles and over time. The results derived from our coding of the home observations do concord with Baumrind's typology in one regard: families with parents described as having a rejecting/neglecting style contained fewer instances of child-initiated future talk. Whether this lessened rate is due to constraints imposed by the parents, such as psychological distance, or disinterest on either the child's or parents' part is unclear. But such an observation is in line with the general conception of parenting in rejecting and neglecting households.

Relation of Earlier Participation in Future Talk and Child Initiations of Future Talk at Later Times

As a preliminary assessment we examined the correlations between planning-related talk, child initiation of this type of talk, and child IQ at the three time periods. Child IQ was stable across the three observation periods (correlations ranged from .48 to .73). However, child IQ was not related to the number of planning-related discussions observed (correlations ranged from −.04 to .16) nor to the number of planning-related discussions initiated by the child (correlations ranged from −.18 to .18). Therefore, child IQ was not included in the regression models tested.

The intercorrelations (see Table 6) between the frequency of planning-related discussions (future talk) and child initiations of this type of talk were used as the database for the regression analyses. These correlations are based on data for families of all the parenting types except for those labeled rejecting/

Table 6
Intercorrelations of Frequencies of Future Talk and Child Initiations of Future Talk at Times 1, 2, and 3 (N = 64)

	Time 1		Time 2		Time 3	
	Future talk	Child initiations	Future talk	Child initiations	Future talk	Child initiations
Time 1						
Future Talk						
Child initiations	.14					
Time 2						
Future talk	.27**	−.01				
Child initiations	.16	.13	.58***[a]			
Time 3						
Future talk	.25**	−.10	.34***	.12		
Child initiations	.29**	−.08	.29**	.23*	.73***[a]	

*p < .10   **p < .05   ***p < .01

a. These variables are based on related values with the frequency of plans initiated by the child at a given time period being a subset of the total frequency of future talk observed.

neglecting. Families with rejecting/neglecting parenting were shown in the prior analysis to have significantly lower rates of planning-related behaviors at Times 1 and 2 that are the primary focus in the following analysis. There were twelve families with parents identified as rejecting/neglecting, and thus the following analyses are based on the remaining sixty-four families.

Examination of the simple correlations indicates some relation in these same behaviors across time. The amount of future talk observed at Time 1 was related to the amount of future talk observed at Times 2 and 3, and the amount of future talk at Time 2 was related to the same behavior at Time 3. Child initiations of future talk were marginally related from Time 2 to Time 3; however, their initiations at Time 1 were not related to this behavior at either of the two later time periods.

Hierarchical regression analyses were used to test the extent to which the frequency of future talk observed in the family and child initiation of such talk are predicted by these same behaviors across the three time periods. Three sets of regressions were conducted. The first examined child initiations at Time 2 using future talk and child initiations at Time 1 as predictors. The second set examined child initiations at Time 3 using future talk and child initiations at Time 2 as predictors. The third set tested time-lagged influences by considering these planning-related behaviors at Times 1 and 2 as predictors of child initiations at Time 3. For each regression, the child initiations from the immediately preceding time period were entered first in order to control for the intercorrelations of these variables in subsequent steps in the model. Finally, for each regression, parenting style measured at Time 1 was entered after the planning variables to determine if this measure explained any additional variance beyond the observed planning behaviors in predicting the children's later planning performance.

Following recommendations by Hale (1977) for assessing contributions when several levels of a variable are involved, parenting style was entered by a series of planned contrasts. To conduct this analysis we divided the parenting styles into three groups, identified on an a priori basis, that are hypothesized to differ in the degree to which they may foster the development of skills like planning. Two styles, authoritative and democratic, are described along Baumrind's empirically derived dimensions as approaches to parenting that encourage high levels of independence and impose medium-high to high levels of demands for maturity on children. These two styles were grouped together and labeled inductive. We expected that this group, which included 16 families, would have the highest levels of planning-related behaviors across time. A second group, labeled noninductive, was composed of nonauthoritarian-directive, good enough, and permissive parenting styles. These styles differed from the inductive styles along the dimensions of maturity demands and responsiveness in the following ways. Nonauthoritarian directive parenting was less responsive than either of the two inductive styles but imposed similar maturity demands. Permissive parenting imposed fewer maturity demands but was similar in responsiveness to the inductive styles. Good enough parenting imposed fewer maturity demands and had less parental responsiveness than the inductive styles. Because these three types were mixed along these dimensions relative to the two inductive styles, and thereby collectively differ from the inductive styles while still not being rejecting/neglecting or authoritarian, they were grouped together for purposes of analysis. We expected that this group, composed of 41 families, would have moderate levels of planning-related behaviors over time. The final group was composed of seven families identified as authoritarian. We expected that this group would have the lowest levels of planning-related behaviors across time.

Planning in the family from preschool (Time 1) to the early school years (Time 2). Child initiations at Time 1 did not predict these same behaviors at Time 2, $R^2 = .018$, $F (1,62) = 1.12$. When future talk at Time 1 was entered, the amount of variance explained did not increase significantly, $R^2 = .039$, $\Delta R^2 F (1,61) = 1.34$. As a next step we entered the two parenting style contrasts, one at a time. The first contrast, comparing inductive and authoritarian styles, did not increase the amount of variance explained, $R^2 = .065$, $\Delta R^2 F (1,60) = 1.68$. Finally, when the second contrast involving inductive versus noninductive parenting styles was added, results were still not significant, $R^2 = .066$, $\Delta R^2 F (1,59) = .06$. In sum, neither planning-related performance nor parenting style measured at Time 1 predicted the children's initiation of future talk at Time 2.

Planning in the family from the early school years (Time 2) to early adolescence (Time 3). Child-initiated future talk at Time 2 was a marginally significant predictor of this same behavior at Time 3, $R^2 = .053$, $F (1,60) = 3.47$, $p < .07$. For the next step, inclusion of the frequency of future talk at Time 2 controlling for child initiations at Time 2, did not increase the prediction of child-initiated future talk at Time 3, $R^2 = .089$, $\Delta R^2 F (1,61) = 2.42$. Inclusion of parenting style, contrasting inductive and authoritarian styles, also did not add to the equation, $R^2 = .089$, $\Delta R^2 F (1,60) = .00$. The contrast comparing inductive and noninductive parenting styles was also not significant, $R^2 = .093$, $\Delta R^2 F (1,59) = .26$. Thus, planning-related behaviors and parenting style at Time 2 did not predict child initiations of future talk at Time 3.

Planning in the family from preschool (Time 1) and the early school years (Time 2) to early adolescence (Time 3). A final regression analysis examined a lagged effect to determine if certain planning-related experiences at Times 1 and 2 influenced child initiations of planning-related talk at Time 3. The first step, which examined the influence of future talk at Time 1 and child initiations of future talk at Time 2 on child initiations at Time 3, increased the prediction of the child initiations at Time 3 over and above what was predicted when frequency of child initiations at Time 2 alone was included. (See Table 7, which lists the regression coefficients (B), the standard error (SE B), the standardized regression coefficients (β) for each variable, the R^2 (and F-value) for each step, and the ΔR^2 (and F-value) for the equation. The ΔR^2 indicates how much of the additional variance in performance is accounted for when variables are added to the regression equation.) The parenting style contrast with inductive and authoritarian styles did not increase the explained variance in child initiations at Time 3. However, the equation with the contrast of inductive and noninductive parenting styles was significant and accounted for 21 percent of the variance in predicting child initiations of planning-related talk at Time 3. To examine this result in more detail we compared the intercept and slope of the planning variables for each of the three parenting-style groups. This indicated that these planning behaviors occurred at higher rates in families with noninductive parenting styles than in families with either inductive or authoritarian styles. A further, post hoc, contrast indicated that planning behaviors in families with an inductive parenting style tended to be higher than in families with an authoritarian parenting style, $R^2 = .193$, ΔR^2 F $(1,59) = 3.58$, $p < .10$.

To summarize, child initiations in the early school years (Time 2) were not well explained by planning-related behaviors of the family or the child when the child was a preschooler (Time 1). In predicting child initiations at adolescence, we see a connection between earlier planning-related behaviors and parenting styles and the child's later planning-related initiations. The best predictor of child initiations in adolescence occurred in the lagged-effects model, with inclusion of child initiations in the early school years and the amount of future talk and parenting style in the preschool years.

These patterns support the hypothesis that earlier participation in planning-related behaviors fosters increased participation in these behaviors over the years of childhood and into adolescence. They also indicate that beyond consideration of participation in planning-related behaviors, parenting style contributes significantly to the development of competence at planning. However, our hypothesis that inductive parenting styles would predict the highest rates of later child initiatives of planning-related talk was not supported. Noninductive parenting styles promoted more planning-related behaviors later on. Authoritarian parenting styles, as expected, were related to the lowest rates of planning-related behaviors by the children in adolescence.

In relation to the predictive power of parenting styles in this analysis, it is important to remember that the data used here are a subset of the data used by Baumrind to assign parents to the various parenting types in her research. Thus, these results, in part, confirm her assignment of parents to particular parenting styles. However, it is also the case that the aspects of the observational data used by Baumrind for her assignment and those used in the present research were different. Whereas Baumrind focused on disciplinary practices and affective

Table 7
Summary of Hierarchical Regression from Time 1 and Time 2 Variables Predicting Child Initiation of Future Talk at Time 3

Variable	B	SE B	β	R^2	F (df)	ΔR^2	F (df)
Step 1							
Child initiations	.21	.11	.23	.053	3.47 (1,62)	.053	3.47 (1,62)*
Step 2							
Child initiations	.17	.11	.19				
Future talk	.12	.06	.26	.120	4.18 (2,61)	.067	4.65 (1,61)**
Step 3							
Child initiations	.18	.11	.19				
Future talk	.12	.06	.26				
Inductive vs. authoritarian	.08	.31	.03	.121	2.76 (3,60)	.001	.07 (1,60)
Step 4							
Child initiations	.18	.11	.20				
Future talk	.11	.06	.23				
Inductive vs. authoritarian	.60	.36	.24				
Inductive vs. noninductive	−.60	.24	−.36	.208	3.86 (4,59)	.087	6.49 (1,59)***

*$p < .10$ **$p < .05$ ***$p < .01$

tone, we focused on the content of these discussions. In addition, our coding of the planning-related practices was based on open-ended field notes, not on previously coded materials. Thus, we feel that we have broadened the scope of what Baumrind considered in her analysis by suggesting that the parenting styles that she identified also are useful in understanding how family practices may contribute to the development of children's competence at planning.

Conclusion

This chapter has been concerned with the origins of cognitive competence for complex skills like planning. Certainly, much development in this domain is attributable to neural changes over the early years. However, these changes are coordinated with social experiences that children have as they grow, and these experiences help organize, support, and foster this aspect of mental development. We have concentrated on one component of early experience— the family process and how it may contribute to the development of planning skills. Although there has been much research on the influence of family experience on the development of intellectual competence, this research has tended to concentrate on what are considered to be more general intellectual characteristics such as child IQ. In this research, we have focused the lens a bit more by looking at behavioral practices related to a specific area of cognitive development and analyzed how children's participation in activities that rely on this type of cognitive competence changes over the course of development from preschool to adolescence. We have shown that the nature of children's participation in planning-related activities in the family does change over these years, that participation in these activities is not related to child IQ (at least for children in the normal range), and that there is some predictive association between earlier and later participation in these activities.

We were fortunate to be able to employ a data set that in its comprehensiveness lent itself extremely well to the questions raised here. Although there are limitations with any data set, especially one that is used for a purpose other than that which was originally intended, these data permitted some examination of the development of planning skills in the family setting. Some clear limitations of the data for present purposes did exist, such as the lack of experimental control. However, the richness of the data in conjunction with its longitudinal quality provides insights that are not easily tapped in research on cognitive development. We tried to apply a rigorous coding scheme that addressed some of the cognitive developmental questions inherent in the study of planning and in the analysis of cultural practices as contexts for development. We hope that our findings are interesting in their own right, as well as illustrative of how complex observational data may be used in a systematic way to advance understanding of cognitive development in social practice.

This research adopted a sociocultural approach to understanding the development of competence in one domain: planning skills. From this perspective the development of competence entails increasing skill at deploying cognitive resources and using them flexibly in the course of solving everyday problems to reach desired goals. Because most everyday problem solving is socially and cognitively complex, the development of competence has a protracted course as new situations introduce new problem domains to the child and the child, in turn, tries to integrate current understanding and skill with new demands.

How does one develop skills that are tailored to the circumstances that are likely to arise in the course of everyday life? Competence develops through participation with others in a cultural community where appropriate and valued goals and means to reach these goals are defined and passed across generations. Both development and culture consort in this process. Like development, culture is also structured (Gauvain 1995, Super and Harkness 1986), providing organized channels or processes through which participants gain access to valued goals and practices.

Three sociocultural processes seem central to the development of competence. First, direct social processes influence the development of competence via guided participation involving more and less experienced cultural members, peer collaboration, and social interaction involving younger and older children, such as peer tutoring (Rogoff 1990). Second, less direct, but still fundamentally social processes also influence the development of competence. Less experienced cultural members often observe more experienced members as they engage in valued community practices. In some instances, less experienced members may provide assistance to those more experienced. Such processes of legitimate peripheral participation (Lave and Wenger 1991) function in order to make children privy to valued cultural practices and thereby help them develop the skills necessary to engage in these practices. A third social process is less obviously social though its rudiments and consequences are clearly social (Gauvain 1995). This process concerns the provision of cultural tools, symbols, and artifacts as instruments for organizing the mind and its actions. These tools form the organizing link between cognitive skill and the particular form a skill takes in context. Taken together, these three cultural processes provide organized systems of support that help guide the development and display of human competence valued in the community in which development occurs.

So far we have considered mechanisms outside the person that may contribute to the development of competence. We also need to be concerned with internal contributions and changes if we hope to understand this important developmental process. In general, four cognitive developmental processes seem central to the development of competence at planning. With age children show increasing skill at identifying and considering relevant variables in a problem context. Children also show developmental gains in their skill at identifying realistic and valued goals. Their skill at sequencing actions to reach goals also increases. Finally, with development children are increasingly able to monitor their progress toward goals. All these skills pertain to increasing skill at goal-directedness and task orientation in the contexts in which competence at planning is manifested.

This study contributes to understanding the development of children's competence at planning in three respects. First, it broadens the scope of research on planning by focusing on how social practices in the family and the child's participation in these practices may contribute to the development of this type of cognitive competence. Second, by studying planning-related behaviors in the family context we have identified parenting practices that may contribute to the development of these skills. Finally, by drawing attention to everyday practices that may foster children's development in specific domains of intellectual functioning, we hope to contribute to current efforts to understand how everyday opportunities provided by the social community in which growth occurs are related to the development of cognitive competence.

Acknowledgments

This research was supported by a grant from the Character and Competence Research Program of the Henry A. Murray Research Center to Mary Gauvain. We are grateful for the support of Diana Baumrind throughout the project. We also thank Joseph Campos and the staff at the Institute for Human Development at the University of California, Berkeley, for their assistance in this research. We are especially grateful to Keith Widaman for his ideas on the analysis. Steve Reise also provided helpful comments on the research.

Note

1. Four families that were originally included in the FSP data according to our criteria were excluded from the analyses conducted here. Two were dropped because their home observational records were unavailable at the time. One was dropped because at Time 3 there were two fathers, a biological and a stepfather, included in the assessments. One was omitted accidentally from the case list used to identify the sample.

References

Baumrind, D. 1966. "Effects of Authoritative Parental Control on Child Behavior." *Child Development* 37: 887–907.
———. 1973. "The Development of Instrumental Competence Through Socialization." In *Minnesota Symposium on Child Psychology,* vol. 7, ed. A. Pick, 3–46. Minneapolis: University of Minnesota Press.

————. 1978. "Parental Disciplinary Patterns and Social Competence in Children." *Youth and Society* 9: 239–76.

————. 1989. "Rearing Competent Children." In *Child Development Today and Tomorrow,* ed. W. Damon, 349–78. San Francisco: Jossey-Bass.

————. 1991. "Effective Parenting During the Early Adolescent Transition." In *Advances in Family Research,* vol. 2, ed. P. E. Cowan and E. M. Hetherington, 111–63. Hillsdale, NJ: Erlbaum.

Benson, J. 1994. "The Origins of Future Orientation in the Everyday Lives of 9- to 36-month-old Infants." In *The Development of Future-Oriented Processes,* ed. M. M. Haith, J. B. Benson, R. J. Roberts, and B. B. Pennington, 375–407. Chicago: University of Chicago Press.

Benson, J. B., D. M. Arehart, T. Jennings, S. Boley, and L. Kearns. 1989. "Infant Crawling: Expectation, Action-Plans, and Goals." Paper presented at the Biennial Meeting of the Society for Research in Child Development, Kansas City, MO (April).

Besevegis, E., and E. Neimark. 1987. "Executive Control at an Early Age: Advance Planning in Solitary Play." Paper presented at the Biennial Meeting of the Society for Research in Child Development, Baltimore, MD (April).

Brown, A. L., and J. Campione. 1984. "Three Faces of Transfer: Implications for Early Competence, Individual Differences, and Instruction." In *Advances in Developmental Psychology,* vol. 3, ed. M. E. Lamb, A. L. Brown, and B. Rogoff, 143–92. Hillsdale, NJ: Erlbaum.

Cocking, R. R., and C. E. Copple. 1987. "Social Influences on Representational Awareness: Plans for Representing and Plans as Representation." In *Blueprints for Thinking: The Role of Planning in Cognitive Development,* ed. S. Friedman, E. Scholnick, and R. R. Cocking, 428–65. Cambridge: Cambridge University Press.

Fabricius, W. V. 1988. "The Development of Forward Search Planning in Preschoolers." *Child Development* 59: 1473–88.

Friedman, S. L., E. K. Scholnick, and R. R. Cocking. 1987. *Blueprints for Thinking: The Role of Planning in Cognitive Development.* Cambridge: Cambridge University Press.

Gauvain, M. 1989. "Children's Planning in Social Context: An Observational Study of Kindergartners' Planning in the Classroom." In *Social Interaction and the Development of Children's Understanding,* ed. L. T. Winegar, 95–117. Norwood, NJ: Ablex.

————. 1992. "Social Influences on the Development of Planning in Advance and During Action." *International Journal of Behavioral Development* 15: 377–98.

————. 1995. "Thinking in Niches: Sociocultural Influences on Cognitive Development." *Human Development* 38: 25–45.

Gauvain, M., and R. Duran. 1993. "What Do Children Do When They Have Nothing to Do?" Paper presented at the Biennial Meeting of the Society for Research in Child Development, New Orleans (April).

Gauvain, M., and S. Savage. 1995. "Everyday Opportunities for the Development of Planning Skills in Euro-American and Latino Children." Paper presented at the meeting of the American Psychological Society, New York City.

Gauvain, M., and B. Rogoff. 1989. "Collaborative Problem Solving and Children's Planning Skills." *Developmental Psychology* 25: 139–51 (August).

Gearhart, M. 1979. "Social Planning: Role Play in a Novel Situation." Paper presented at the Biennial Meeting of the Society for Research in Child Development, San Francisco (April).

Goldin, S. E., and B. Hayes-Roth. 1980. "Individual Differences in the Planning Process." Technical Report N-1488-ONR. Santa Monica, CA: The Rand Corporation.

Goodnow, J. J. 1987. "Social Aspects of Planning." In *Blueprints for Thinking: The Role of Planning in Psychological Development,* ed. S. L. Friedman, E. K. Scholnick, and R. R. Cocking, 179–201. Cambridge: Cambridge University Press.

Goodnow, J. J., P. J. Miller, and F. Kessel. 1995. *Cultural Practices as Contexts for Development: New Directions for Child Development,* no. 67. San Francisco: Jossey-Bass.

Goodwin, D. K. 1994. *No Ordinary Time: Franklin and Eleanor Roosevelt: The Home Front during World War II.* New York: Simon & Schuster.

Haith, M. M., J. B. Benson, R. J. Roberts, and B. F. Pennington. 1994. *The Development of Future-Oriented Processes.* Chicago: University of Chicago Press.

Hale, G. A. 1977. "On the use of ANOVA in developmental research." *Child Development* 48: 1101–06.

Hudson, J. A. 1991. "Learning to Reminisce: A Case Study." *Journal of Narrative and Life History* 1: 295–324.

Hudson, J. A., and R. Fivush. 1991. "Planning in the Preschool Years: The Emergence of Plans from General Event Knowledge." *Cognitive Development* 6: 393–415.

Inhelder, B., and J. Piaget. 1964. *The Early Growth of Logic in the Child.* New York: W. W. Norton.

Klahr, D., and M. Robinson. 1981. "Formal Assessment of Problem Solving and Planning Processes in Children." *Cognitive Psychology* 13: 113–48.

Krietler, S., and H. Krietler. 1987. "Conceptions and Processes of Planning: The Developmental Perspective." In *Blueprints for Thinking: The Role of Planning in Cognitive Development,* ed. S. Friedman, E. Scholnick, and R. R. Cocking, 205–72. Cambridge: Cambridge University Press.

Lave, J. 1988. *Cognition in Practice.* Cambridge: Cambridge University Press.

Lave, J., and E. Wenger. 1990. "Situated Learning: Legitimate Peripheral Participation." IRL Report 90-0013. Palo Alto, CA: Institute for Research on Learning.

Lucarillo, J., and K. Nelson. 1987. "Remembering and Planning Talk." *Discourse Processes* 10: 219–35.

Luria, A. R. 1976. *Cognitive Development: Its Cultural and Social Foundations.* Cambridge, MA: Harvard University Press.

Magkaev, V. 1977. "An Experimental Study of the Planning Function of Thinking in Young Children." In *Soviet Developmental Psychology: An Anthology,* ed. M. Cole, 606–20. White Plains, NY: Sharpe.

Ochs, E., R. Smith, and C. Taylor. 1989. "Dinner Narratives as Detective Stories." *Cultural Dynamics* 2: 238–57.

Parke, R. D. 1996. *Fatherhood.* Cambridge, MA: Harvard University Press.

Parrila, R. K., S. Aysto, and J. P. Das. 1994. "Development of Planning in Relation to Age, Attention, Simultaneous and Successive Processing." *Journal of Psychoeducational Assessment* 12: 212–27.

Pea, R. D. 1982. "What is Planning the Development of?" In *Children's Planning Strategies,* ed. D. Forbes and M. T. Greenberg, 5–27. San Francisco: Jossey-Bass.

Pribram, K. H., and A. R. Luria. 1973. *Psychophysiology of the Frontal Lobes.* New York: Academic Press.

Radziszewska, B., and B. Rogoff. 1988. "Influence of Adult and Peer Collaborators on Children's Planning Skills." *Developmental Psychology* 24: 840–48.

Rogoff, B. 1990. *Apprenticeship in Thinking.* New York: Oxford University Press.

———. 1996. "Developmental Transitions in Children's Participation in Sociocultural Activities." In *The Five to Seven Year Shift: The Age of Reason and Responsibility,* ed. A. J. Sameroff and M. M. Haith, 273–294. Chicago: University of Chicago Press.

Rogoff, B., M. Gauvain, and S. Ellis. 1992. "Development Viewed in its Cultural Context." In *Learning to Think,* ed. M. Woodhead, P. Light, and R. Carr, 292–339. London: Routledge.

Rogoff, B., M. Gauvain, and W. Gardner. 1987. "Children's Adjustment of Plans to Circumstances." In *Blueprints for Thinking: The Role of Planning in Cognitive Development,* ed. S. L. Friedman, E. K. Scholnick, and R. R. Cocking, 303–20. Cambridge: Cambridge University Press.

Rogoff, B., J. Mistry, B. Radziszewska, and J. Germond. 1991. "Infants' Instrumental Social Interaction with Adults." In *Social Referencing and the Social Construction of Reality in Infancy,* ed. S. Feinman, 323–48. New York: Plenum.

Super, C., and S. Harkness. 1986. "The Developmental Niche: A Conceptualization at the Interface of Child and Culture." *International Journal of Behavioral Development* 9: 545–69.

Szeminska, A. 1965. "The Evolution of Thought: Some Applications of Research Findings to Educational Practice." In European research in cognitive development, ed. P. H. Mussen, *Monographs of the Society for Research in Child Development* 30: 47–57.

Wellman, H., W. Fabricius, and C. Sophian. 1985. "The Early Development of Planning." In *Children's Searching: The Development of Search Skills and Spatial Representation,* ed. H. Wellman, 123–49. Hillsdale, NJ: Erlbaum.

Willatts, P. 1990. "Development of Problem-solving Strategies in Infancy." In *Children's Strategies: Contemporary Views of Cognitive Development,* ed. D. F. Bjorklund, 23–66. Hillsdale, NJ: Erlbaum.

Wood, D. J., and D. Middleton. 1975. "A Study of Assisted Problem-solving." *British Journal of Psychology* 66: 181–91.

Vygotsky, L. S. 1978. *Mind in Society.* Cambridge, MA: Harvard University Press.

———. 1981. "The Development of Higher Forms of Attention in Children." In *The Concept of Activity in Soviet Psychology,* ed. J. V. Wertsch, 189–240. Armonk, NY: Sharpe.

CHAPTER THREE

Competence in Sexual Decision-Making by African-American, Female Adolescents: The Role of Peer Relations and Future Plans

MARION K. UNDERWOOD

Adolescent females today must make a set of weighty decisions concerning sexual activity: whether to engage in sexual intercourse and with whom, how many sexual partners to have, whether to take contraceptive precautions so as not to bear a child, and whether to use condoms to avoid contracting sexually transmitted diseases (STDs), particularly the HIV virus. These choices bear serious consequences. Each year, approximately one million adolescents in the United States become pregnant before they are twenty. Numbers of adolescents who have contracted the HIV virus via sexual intercourse have increased alarmingly in recent years (Center for Disease Control 1992).

However, many young women survive adolescence without bearing a child or contracting an STD. Sexual decision-making constitutes an area of social, intellectual, and practical competence. This research explores competence in making decisions about sexuality for a sample of African-American adolescent females, a subset of participants in a large-scale, longitudinal investigation of the effectiveness of adolescent health care clinics (Adolescent Health Care Evaluation Study, Earls 1984). These secondary analyses focus on whether peer variables and future plans predict competence in making decisions about sexuality.

Prospective, longitudinal research on sexual decision-making in adolescence could provide valuable information for the design of programs to prevent serious, negative outcomes for adolescent females: unplanned pregnancies and contracting STDs. Bearing a child in adolescence has far-reaching negative consequences for girls. Adolescent mothers often must terminate their educations and constrain their own social and work opportunities (or the opportunities of those close to them, such as their mothers; Furstenberg, Brooks-Gunn, and Chase-Lansdale 1989). Most investigators agree that adolescent pregnancy is a negative outcome for teenage girls in our society, although there may be subcultural contexts in which this behavior may have adaptive value (Ralph, Lochman, and Thomas 1984). Adolescent motherhood results in serious educational, financial, and relationship problems for teenage girls (Furstenberg, Brooks-Gunn, and Chase-Lansdale 1989; Richardson 1996), and negatively affects girls' psychological functioning (Brown, Adams, and Kellam 1981). In addition, adolescent mothers are less competent and knowledgeable as parents (Furstenberg, Brooks-Gunn, and Chase-Lansdale 1989). The negative consequences for adolescent females from contracting sexually transmitted diseases, particularly the HIV virus, are so obvious and serious that they require little explanation.

Given that adolescent pregnancy is such a worrisome phenomenon, it is understandable that most previous investigators have focused on girls who become young mothers. However, this had led to much retrospective research that limits conclusions about causal processes, resulting in little information about what qualities predict avoiding negative outcomes. Recently, investigators have suggested that studying girls who avoid teenage pregnancy could inform prevention and intervention efforts (Burns Jones and Philliber 1983, McBride Murry 1995). Understanding which skills allow teenage girls to avoid these negative outcomes could help in designing prevention efforts in two ways: (1) this information might allow us to better identify groups of girls at highest risk, and (2) if we understood what skills help girls avoid pregnancy and STDs, we might be able to foster these abilities in intervention programs.

The secondary analyses reported here focus on African-American adolescent females for important reasons. Rates of sexual activity and adolescent pregnancy are higher among this population (Farber 1991, McBride Murry 1995). While investigators disagree as to whether this is due to socioeconomic factors or the fact that African-American adolescent females mature earlier (Rowe, Rodgers, and Meseck-Bushey, 1989; Rowe and Rodgers 1991), it seems important to examine possible protective factors for this group with a higher rate of risk. It is also important to note that this research focuses not only on negative outcomes, but on the development of competence. Scott-Jones (1993) has pointed out that although low-income samples have often been the focus of intervention efforts, research on normative developmental processes has rarely included samples of low-income or minority children and adolescents.

Although estimates of the proportion of adolescent females who are sexually active vary, earlier analyses of a subsample of the girls in the Adolescent Health Care Evaluation Study indicated that 69 percent of these 13- to 18-year-olds were sexually active (Stiffman et al. 1987). This figure likely underestimates the level of sexual activity in the total sample, because girls who were newly or recently pregnant and visiting clinics for pre- or postnatal care were excluded from these analyses. Given the high levels of sexual activity in this sample, surviving adolescence without an unplanned pregnancy or contracting an STD requires a variety of types of skills in self-management—for example, planning for and taking contraceptive precautions.

What Constitutes Competence in the Area of Sexual Decision-Making?

Although psychologists have had little difficulty defining psychopathology or problem behavior for youth, we have long struggled with the question of what competence means for adolescents. Previous investigators have conceptualized competence in diverse ways: as positive self-perceptions, lack of behavior problems, a set of cognitive abilities, and a personality trait. Some investigators use the term "competence" without ever clearly specifying what this means in operational terms (for example, Cassidy and Lynn 1991). Sternberg and Kolligan (1990) argued that competence includes many dimensions, but that self-perceptions of competence matter much more than competence defined in terms of behavior. Although East et al. (1992) never explicitly discussed how they define "psychosocial competence," the measure they used for this quality was the Harter Self-Perception Inventory (1983). Other investigators treat competence as synonymous with social competence, operationally defined as good grades in school and lack of behavior problems as reported by teachers and peers (Luthar 1991; Luthar and Zigler 1992; Luthar, Doernberger, and Zigler 1993). Mann, Harmoni, and Power (1989) proposed that competence in decision-making requires a specific set of cognitive skills. Clausen (1991, 1992) described competence as a cluster of personality traits labeled "adolescent planful competence," operationally defined as being high on three sets of traits: self-control, intellectual investment, and dependability.

Only a few investigators have defined adolescent competence in specific behavioral terms. For example, Beale Spencer et al. (1993) sought to investigate school-based competence among minority youth. They clearly specified that their definition of competence required behavioral products, which they operationally defined as high achievement test scores and academic self-esteem. However, academic self-esteem hardly seems to be a behavioral product related to competence, but more a measure of self-perceptions of competence. In their review of the prevention literature, Weissberg, Caplan, and Harwood (1991: 832) clearly stated that competence should be evident in behavior as well as self-perceptions, writing "Competence refers to the behavioral effectiveness of one's transactions with the environment, as well to one's sense of personal well-being in diverse aspects of life." This idea implies that clear, behavioral definitions of competence should be possible for particular domains.

The research described here explores competence in one particular domain, sexual decision-making, defined in terms of behavioral outcomes: avoiding pregnancy, using contraception consistently, and avoiding contracting STDs. Therefore, the type of competence explored here is that which leads to specific outcomes related to one area, making choices about sexuality. Whether predictors of these types of competence also predict competence in other domains is an empirical question and a matter for future research.

At the outset, it is important to recognize that in many ways, defining competence in sexual decision-making as avoiding negative outcomes is limited, perhaps even minimal. Some might argue that the only competent choice adolescents can make regarding sexual activity is to abstain from it entirely. Many might agree that competence in sexual decision-making includes choosing partners judiciously so that adolescent females can survive relationships with their emotional well-being and their self-worth intact. However, questions such as the extent to which adolescents ought to be engaging in sexual activity and which types of partners are suitable or best hinge on personal and religious values. Also, these variables were not assessed by the Adolescent Health Care Evaluation Study (Earls 1984). Therefore, for this investigation, competence in sexual decision-making will be operationally defined as surviving adolescence without becoming pregnant or contracting an STD. Future research should explore the more subtle aspects of competence in making decisions related to sexual activity.

What factors contribute to competence in the area of sexual decision-making? The research proposed here addresses whether positive peer relationships and future plans contribute to making competent decisions regarding sexuality.

Previous Research on Peer Relations, Aggressive/Delinquent Behavior, and Adolescent Pregnancy

Most earlier investigations of predictors of adolescent pregnancy, particularly for minority populations, have focused on family factors. Prior research has clearly demonstrated that many family variables are concurrently related to adolescent pregnancy, for example, low socioeconomic status and living in mother-headed households (see Furstenberg, Brooks-Gunn, and Chase-Lansdale 1989 for a review). However, one of the few prospective, longitudinal studies of adolescent motherhood showed that for a sample of African-American females, relationships with peers—as measured by sociometric status and peer-rated aggression in the fourth grade—significantly predicted childbearing in adolescence (Underwood, Kupersmidt, and Coie 1996). If peer relations in childhood predict childbearing in adolescence, it seems important to assess whether self-reported satisfaction with friendships in adolescence predicts competence in sexual decision-making later.

Previous research on peer relations provides several reasons to view adolescent females who are dissatisfied with their peer relationships as at heightened risk for teenage pregnancy. First of all, some of these girls may be socially rejected by peers. Children rejected by peers are more prone to a variety of types of acting-out behaviors, one of which might be early sexual activity. Rejected children in the second and fourth grades have been shown to exhibit more externalizing behavior problems than nonrejected children (French and Waas 1985). This pattern of acting-out behavior might continue into adolescence and might include early sexual activity.

The second reason one might expect girls with dissatisfactory peer relationships to be at a high risk for pregnancy in adolescence is that for rejected girls, having a child might represent an opportunity for companionship. Kupersmidt, Griesler, and Patterson (1995) found that rejected children have fewer companions across settings. Rejected children reported moderately less companionship with their best friends than nonrejected children (Patterson, Kupersmidt, and Griesler 1990). Therefore, not only do rejected children have fewer friends, but evidence suggests both that the friendships they do have are less satisfying and that they are aware of their own lack of companionship. These girls might see motherhood as an antidote to their loneliness and depression.

Adolescent females who behave aggressively with peers might also be at risk for adolescent pregnancy. In one of the few longitudinal studies that examined predictors of teenage parenthood, Cairns, Cairns, and Neckerman (1989) demonstrated that membership in an aggressive clique in seventh grade was related to dropping out of school, which was in turn related to adolescent childbearing. Two thirds of their adolescent mothers belonged to social groups considered to be "high risk" because of aggressiveness, poor academic performance, and low socioeconomic status. Cairns et al. (1988) found that aggressive girls have as many friends and were identified as members of social clusters equally often as nonaggressive girls. Also, Cairns et al. found that although aggressive girls may tend to be rejected by the social network as a whole, these girls tend to hang around with each other. Aggressive girls form cliques in which deviance and acting-out behavior are norms. Also, aggressive girls are at risk for a wide range of academic, social, and emotional problems (Parker and Asher 1987).

One theory about adolescent sexual activity (Jessor and Jessor 1977) is that it is one aspect of moderately deviant behavior. Some research suggests that adolescent sexual activity is related to both risk-taking behaviors such as smoking, drinking, and cheating in school (Rodgers and Rowe 1990) and more severe forms of deviance, such as aggression, stealing, and vandalism (Rowe, Rodgers, Meseck-Bushey, and St. John 1989). Zabin, Hardy, Smith, and Hirsh (1986) found adolescent sexual activity to be related to drug use. Based on longitudinal analyses of the National Youth Survey, Elliot and Morse (1989) concluded that sexual activity among youth was part of a complex of problem behavior, and that the most common temporal sequence is that drug use and delinquency precede the onset of sexual intercourse.

In one of the first longitudinal, follow-forward studies to assess the contribution of peer factors to adolescent childbearing, Underwood, Kupersmidt, and Coie (1996) examined the predictive relation among childhood sociometric status, aggression, and subsequent adolescent childbearing. Although analyses indicated significant differences in prevalence of births among peer sociometric status groups, the differences were not those hypothesized. Controversial girls (girls who received large numbers of like most *and* like least nominations from peers) were most likely to become adolescent mothers (50% in contrast to the base rate for the sample of 26%). Fifty percent of aggressive girls in the sample became adolescent mothers, in contrast to 25% of the nonaggressive girls. Survival and hazard analyses demonstrated that controversial and aggressive girls become pregnant earlier in adolescence than other girls.

In addition to suggesting that early controversial peer status places these girls at risk for adolescent childbearing, the findings also indicated that popularity may be a protective factor. Girls who were considered by peers to be especially socially competent and likable in the fourth grade very rarely became pregnant before age eighteen. Rutter (1987) has suggested several mechanisms by which interpersonal relationships may be protective factors: they modify exposure to potentially harmful activities and behaviors, they ameliorate the impact of negative events, and they enhance self-esteem and self-efficacy. Popular girls may have many avenues to social companionship available to them and are therefore less likely to become members of deviant peer groups in which antisocial and risk-taking behaviors are considered acceptable. Popular girls are less likely to be lonely and unhappy (Asher et al. 1990), and therefore less prone to viewing having a child as a way out of a bad situation, or as a source of status or companionship. Popular girls may also be more likely to have positive self-concepts (Patterson, Griesler, and Kupersmidt 1990) and clear ideas of future goals, which might make them less likely to engage in risk-taking behaviors such as early sexual activity that could jeopardize these plans. Finally, another more obvious and pragmatic type of explanation is that popular girls became pregnant less often because the same qualities that led them to be socially competent also enabled them to abstain from sexual activity or to engage in sexual activity only when they had planned for using contraceptive precautions.

An earlier analysis of a subsample of the Adolescent Health Care Evaluation Study indicated that adolescent females who had been pregnant did not differ from their never-pregnant peers in their satisfaction with their current relationships (Stiffman et al. 1987). However, a couple of methodological concerns suggest that the relationship between peer relations and pregnancy in this sample merits further exploration. First, because girls visiting clinics for pre- or post-natal care were excluded from the sample so as not to confound the findings for physical health, not all girls who were or had been pregnant were included in these analyses. Second, in analyzing data for "satisfaction with relationships," it appears that Stiffman et al. examined a combined index of satisfaction with peer and family relationships rather than exploring them separately.

Previous research has not addressed the relation between peer relations and contracting STDs. However, it seems reasonable to expect that girls who are satisfied with their relationships with friends and the larger peer group might be at lower risk for infection because they may be less likely to belong to groups that endorse high levels of sexual activity, less likely to engage in high levels of sexual activity because they are lonely and depressed, and more likely to have positive self-concepts and plans for the future that they would be unlikely to jeopardize by engaging in unprotected intercourse.

Another personal characteristic that may enhance competence in adolescent sexual decision-making is planfulness. Planfulness consists of thinking carefully about the long-term consequences of a particular choice or action, rather than thinking only of the immediate implications. For college-age samples, Frese, Stewart, and Hannover (1987) have demonstrated the reliability and validity of the construct of planfulness as measured by responses to hypothetical vignettes presented in questionnaires. Rutter, Quinton, and Hill (1991) have applied this construct of planfulness to real-life histories of youths reared in institutions. Rutter et al. operationalized planfulness as a composite variable of planning for work, planning for marriage, and planning for childbearing. For girls in this sample, planfulness served as an important mediating variable; young women who were high on planfulness had more positive psychosocial outcomes than those who were poor planners.

The Current Research

This prospective, longitudinal research explored whether self-reported positive peer relationships and future plans contribute to competence in sexual decision-making. The Earls data set allows exploration of three aspects of peer relationships: satisfaction with support provided by friends, aggressive behavior, and membership in a deviant peer group. For these analyses, planfulness consisted of consideration of long-term outcomes with respect to school and vocational plans. As stated earlier, competence in sexual decision-making was operationally defined as: avoidance of unplanned pregnancies, consistent use of contraceptives, and avoidance of sexually transmitted diseases.

This research focuses on three main questions. First, how do peer relationships contribute to adolescent health and sexual decision-making? Using the Earls data, several aspects of peer relationships were addressed: satisfaction with peer support, numbers of friends, frequency of interaction with friends, aggressive behavior with peers, and membership in a deviant peer group. Based on Hamburg's (1986) clinical observation that one subgroup of teenage girls who becomes pregnant views motherhood as a way of satisfying needs for intimacy and combating loneliness, satisfaction with peer relationships was expected to predict avoiding adolescent pregnancy. Given that Underwood, Kupersmidt, and Coie (1996) found that aggression significantly predicted adolescent childbearing, aggression was predicted to negatively predict avoiding adolescent pregnancy. Because aggression in childhood and adolescence has been demonstrated to be associated with a number of other risk-taking and impulsive behaviors, aggressiveness was expected to be a negative predictor of avoiding pregnancy, using contraception consistently, and not contracting an STD.

The second question addressed by this research is how do plans for the future relate to sexual decision-making? On the one hand, because taking contraceptive precautions before engaging in sexual intercourse is by definition a behavior that requires planfulness, ambitious future plans were predicted to be positively related to taking contraceptive precautions and negatively related to adolescent pregnancy. However, some researchers have suggested that adolescent childbearing may have adaptive value in some subcultural contexts (Ralph, Lochman, and Thomas 1984). Some adolescent females might consciously choose to bear a child during adolescence, perhaps because they witness that peers who have children do not suffer mentally, physically, or socially (Stiffman et al. 1987) and may even increase their level of independence and financial resources (McAnarny 1985). The third research question focuses on how peer relationships are related to academic and vocational plans.

Method
Participants

Participants for this investigation were 1,500 adolescent, African-American females, ages thirteen to nineteen, in the first two waves of the Adolescent Health Care Evaluation Study. Participants in the total sample for the first wave of data collection in 1984–85 numbered 2,788, and the second wave of data collection in 1985–86 included 2,415 from this original sample. The original sample was 76% female and 24% male. Because the focus of these analyses was sexual decision-making in females, only girls will be included here. The racial composition of the original sample was 71% African-American, 16% white, 12% Hispanic, and 1% other.

Beginning in November 1984, participants were recruited from ten health-care programs across the country: seven clinics at academic medical centers funded to provide primary health care for adolescents (Boston, MA; New Haven, CT; Indianapolis, IN; Chicago, IL; Jackson, MS; Dallas, TX; and Los Angeles, CA) and three clinics that served adolescents but did not offer specialized services for this age group (Buffalo, NY; St. Louis, MO; and New Orleans, LA). At each site, 150 to 360 adolescents were sampled, for a total of 3,102 selected to participate in the first wave. Of these, 2,788 completed interviews. Three hundred fourteen of these participants (10%) did not participate because they declined to be interviewed, were judged to be too ill, were outside of the age range, or could not be located. One year later in 1985–86, 2,415 of the sample originally interviewed (87%) were recontacted and interviewed again. Of these 2,415 participants interviewed at both Time 1 and Time 2, 1,500 were female and African American, and included in the analyses here.

Girls in the subsample for the analyses here ranged in age from thirteen to nineteen (at the time of the Wave 1 interview, 4.2% were thirteen, 9.7% were fourteen, 17.9% were fifteen, 22.1% were sixteen, 27.9% were seventeen, 18.1% were eighteen, and .1% were nineteen). At Wave 1, the mean age of participants was 16.15, $SD = 1.39$.

Procedures

At the time of the first data collection (Wave 1), participants were interviewed after visiting health-care clinics. The first interview included questions to assess: reasons for visiting the clinic, utilization of other health services, physical and mental health, family history, school adjustment, peer relations, social support, and stressful life events. The interview contained portions of the Diagnostic Interview for Children and Adolescents (DICA) to assess aggressive or antisocial traits, substance abuse, physical symptoms, and other psychological distress such as depression and anxiety. One year later (Wave 2), participants responded to a similar interview that included additional questions to measure changes in health and level of satisfaction with health care services.

Measures of Variables for These Analyses

The interview measures used in the first two waves of the Adolescent Health Care Evaluation Study contained items that addressed peer relationships, future plans, and sexual decision-making.

Quality of Peer Interactions

The following items assessed the quality of peer relationships. In Waves 1 and 2, participants were asked two questions to measure satisfaction with friendships: "How much of the time were you upset with any friends?" and "In the last month, how much of the time have you felt your friends might let you down if you needed them or wanted their sympathy or support?" Participants responded on a continuous scale (no friends coded as 0, almost all the time also coded as 0, good deal = 1, not much = 2, and almost never = 3). At Wave 2, participants were also asked "About how many days a week do you usually do things with friends?" and responded on a continuous scale (never = 1, 1 day a week = 2, 2–3 days a week = 3, 4–5 days a week = 4, and 6–7 days a week = 5). The Wave 2 interview also included the question "About how many *close* friends do you have?" and participants responded on a continuous scale (none = 0, 1 friend = 1, 2 or 3 friends = 2, 4 or 5 friends = 3, and 6 or more friends = 4).

Aggression. The following items in questionnaires for Waves 1 and 2 assessed aggressive behavior: "Have you even been in a physical fight?," "Have you ever hurt someone badly in a fight so that they had a black eye or a bloody nose or other injury?," "Have you ever threatened anyone with a knife?," "Have you ever been so angry that you tried to seriously kill someone?," and "Have you ever used a weapon in a fight?" For all of these questions, participants responded yes or no. Based on participants' responses to these and other related questions at Wave 1, interviewers coded the number of aggressive symptoms of conduct disorder, on a continuous scale of 0, 1, or 2. In addition, participants responded to a question that assessed aggressive or delinquent behaviors, "Have you ever been in trouble with a police or juvenile officer?," and if yes, "How many times?" Responses were coded on a continuous scale (never = 0, once = 1, twice = 2, three times = 3, four times = 4, and five times or more = 5).

Deviant behaviors among friends. For the Wave 1 interview, two items allowed some assessment of the deviance of the participants' peer groups: "How many of your friends have ever been in trouble with the police or a juvenile officer—none, a few, about half, or most or all?" and "How many of your friends use drugs or marijuana—none, a few, about half, or most or all?" For both of these questions, participants responded on a continuous scale: none = 1, a few = 2, about half = 3, most = 4, all = 5.

At the Wave 2 interview, participants were asked "How many of your friends are *not* in school or training and *don't* have a job?" Participants responded on a continuous scale: none = 1, a few = 2, about half = 3, most = 4, all = 5.

Future Plans

Two questions from the Wave 1 interview assessed participants' plans. Participants responded to the question "How far do you plan to go in school?" on a continuous response scale: quit before graduating = 1, high school diploma/ GED = 2, vocational/other training = 3, college = 4, graduate school = 5. Also at Wave 1, participants responded to the question, "What do you think you will be doing when you are 30?" on a continuous response scale: unskilled = 1, skilled blue collar = 2, white collar/clerical/sales = 3, managerial = 4, and professional = 5.

Although the interview employed here asked girls about their future aspirations for school and work, information was not available concerning other aspects of planfulness, such as the ability to form reasonable goals and the needed skills to achieve these. For more middle-class samples in which most youth would likely report plans for college and professional careers, one would hardly expect that simply having these plans would predict positive outcomes. However, the participants in this research were African-American girls, many of whom lived in poor, urban areas. For these young women, it may not be at all normative to have ambitious future plans. Therefore, the girls who reported ambitious future plans here must have done so for a reason. Perhaps they had cause to believe that these desires were realistic, because they had a strong positive sense of their own abilities including the capacity to think carefully about the future, because they were encouraged by authority figures in their environments, or because they had some realistic sense that they might have access to opportunities. For this investigation, future plans may have been a more appropriate index of the fuller construct of planfulness because girls who reported ambitious future plans were also likely to have some of the positive skills to be able to carry them out.

Sexual Decision-Making

The questionnaires from both waves of the project allowed careful assessment of choices about sexuality. For these analyses, three outcomes were examined: avoiding adolescent pregnancy, refraining from having sex without contraception, and not contracting a sexually transmitted disease.

Avoiding adolescent pregnancy. To examine avoiding pregnancy altogether as evidence of some competence in sexual decision making, a variable was created to indicate who had ever been pregnant and who had never become pregnant. In both interviews, participants were asked "Including live births, still births, miscarriages, and abortions, have you ever been pregnant?" Participants who responded "no" to this question at both Waves 1 and 2 were classified as never having been pregnant. Never-pregnant status was confirmed by participants' medical records.

Using contraception consistently. In both the Wave 1 and Wave 2 interviews, participants were asked detailed questions about contraceptive use: "Do you and your partner ever use birth control?" and "Do you and your partner use birth control most of the time, about half of the time, or seldom?" and "Why haven't you used birth control?" Because this research focused on competence in making decisions about sexuality, the dependent variable of interest here was whether a participant consistently used contraception or not. A variable was created to code whether or not participants reported having had sex without contraception at either Wave 1 or Wave 2.

Avoiding sexually transmitted diseases. The last outcome of interest related to competence in making sexual decisions was whether an adolescent female contracted a sexually transmitted disease or not. In both the Wave 1 and Wave 2 interviews, participants were asked "Have you ever had VD or a disease of the sex organs?" Follow-up questions were asked to determine whether participants had contracted gonorrhea, syphilis, herpes, pelvic inflammatory disease, chlamydia, or HIV.

Results

This section will begin with presentation of descriptive data for the predictor variables of interest (satisfaction with peer relationships, aggression and delinquency, deviant peer groups, plans for school, and plans for work) and outcome variables (avoiding pregnancy, using contraception consistently, and avoiding contracting sexually transmitted diseases). Then, the following sections will present results from the analyses of the predictive relations between peer and planning variables and sexual decision-making.

Qualities of Peer Relationships
Satisfaction with Relationships

In the Wave 1 interview, in response to the question about how often participants had been upset with friends in the past month, 6.4% reported that they had no friends or had been upset with friends almost all the time, 5.4% said a good deal of the time, 43.4% reported having been upset with friends not much of the time, and 44.9% said that they had been upset with friends almost never over the past month. When asked how often they thought their friends would disappoint them by not being available or supportive, 6.9% said almost all of the time, 5.8% said a good deal of the time, 28.8% said not much of the time, and 58.4% said almost never. These data indicate that overall, most participants reported a high degree of satisfaction with the quality of their peer relationships.

At the time of the second data collection, participants were asked additional questions about friendships. In response to the question about numbers of friends, 5.6% of participants said they had no close friends, 26.3% reported having 1 close friend, 45.3% said they had two or three close friends, 14% said they had three or four close friends, and 8.9% reported that they had six or more close friends. In answering the question about how many times a week participants did things with friends, 11.5% said never, 20.3% said one day a week, 41.7% reported that they do things with friends 2–3 days a week, 13.6% said 4–5 days a week, and 8.9% said that they usually do things with friends 6–7 days of the week.

Aggression and Delinquency

As part of the Wave 1 interview, participants responded to questions about several aggressive behaviors. When asked if they had ever been in a physical fight, 53.6% of participants said yes and 46.4% said no. Based on responses to this and other detailed questions about specific aggressive behaviors, interviewers coded the number of aggressive symptoms present at the first data collection: 93% were judged to have no symptoms of aggressive conduct disorder, 6.5% were rated as having one symptom, .3% had two symptoms, and .1% had three symptoms. Comparing the high frequency of any physical fighting to the low numbers of conduct-disorder symptoms suggests that the criteria for conduct symptoms required extreme, persistent behavior.

Also in the Wave 1 interview, participants responded to a question about whether they had ever had trouble with the police, and if so, how many times. Positive responses to this question could indicate aggressive behaviors, but also other illegal acts such as disturbing the peace or covert behaviors such as stealing. Most participants reported that they had had no trouble with police (91.2%), but 6% said they had had one episode of police trouble, 1.1% said they had had two episodes of police involvement, .6% said three times, .3% said four times, and .7% said five times.

Deviant Behavior among Friends

In response to the Wave 1 interview question about the number of friends who had had trouble with the police, 60.3% said none, 32.9% said a few, 4.5% said about half, 1.8% said most friends, and .4% said all their friends had been involved with the police. When asked how many friends used drugs, 37.3% said none, 36.6% said a few, 12.2% said about half, 9.1% said most, and 4.7% of participants reported that all of their friends used drugs.

As part of the Wave 2 interview, participants responded to a question about how many of their friends were *not* in school or a training program or were unemployed. Forty-three percent of participants said that all of their friends were in school or had jobs, 42.6% said that a few of their friends were not in school or working, 8.3% reported that about half of their friends were not in school or working, 4.4% said that most of their friends were not in school or working, and 1.7% said all of their friends were either not in school or were unemployed.

Relationships among Peer Relationship Variables

To examine whether some of the peer relations predictor variables were redundant, correlation coefficients among the peer variables were computed (see Table 1). While the large sample size resulted in many correlations of low magnitude achieving statistical significance, only two correlations appeared large enough to be meaningful. Ratings of how often friends would disappoint were strongly positively correlated with reports of how often participants had been upset with friends ($r = .54$, $p < .0001$). Given this strong relationship, these two variables were averaged for the purposes of further analyses into one index of satisfaction with peer relationships. Reported numbers of friends who used substances was highly, positively correlated with reported numbers of friends who had problems with the police ($r = .43$, $p < .0001$). Therefore, these two variables were averaged to form one index of deviant behaviors among friends.

Future Plans

In the Wave 1 interview, when asked about their school goals, none reported that they planned to quit before graduating, 19.8% reported that they planned to finish high school or get a GED, 11.5% said that they planned to complete vocational training, 57.9% said they planned to go to college, and 10.8% reported that they planned to go to graduate school. Participants also responded to a question about the type of work they expected to be doing at age thirty: 1.2% said they planned to be in unskilled occupations, 9.7% said skilled blue collar, 30.9% said white collar/clerical/sales, 40.9% said managerial, and 15.5% said professional.

Sexual Decision-Making

While results indicate that many of the girls in this sample became pregnant and failed to use contraception consistently, large proportions of the sample demonstrated competence in sexual decision-making as defined by these behavioral outcomes. Of the 1,409 girls who responded to all relevant questions, 730 (51.8%) reported that they had been pregnant at least one time and 679 (48.2%) had never been pregnant, as of the Wave 2 data collection. Of the

Table 1

Correlations Between Variables Measuring Qualities of Peer Relationships

	Upset with friends	Times friends disappoint	Number of friends	Frequency of interaction with friends	Problems with police	Aggressive conduct symptoms	Friends with problems with police	Friends who use drugs	Friends not in school or working
Upset with friends	—	.54*	.05	.02	-.10*	-.18*	-.15*	-.11*	-.05
Times friends disappoint		—	.09*	.04	-.12*	-.09*	-.11*	-.12*	-.07*
Number of friends			—	.21*	-.02	-.02	.01	-.05	.01
Frequency of interaction with friends				—	-.03	.01	.06*	.05	.04
Problems with police					—	.10*	.23*	.18*	.06*
Aggressive conduct symptoms						—	.19*	.19*	.04
Friends with problems with police							—	.43*	.14*
Friends who use drugs								—	.19*
Friends not in school or working									—

$*p < .05$

1,161 participants for whom the relevant data were available, 26.1% reported having failed to use contraception. Of the 1,018 participants for whom the relevant data were available, 19.8% reported having contracted a sexually transmitted disease at the Wave 2 data collection. None of the participants reported that they had the HIV virus.

How Do Peer Relationships Contribute to Sexual Decision-Making in Adolescent Females?

Independent variables for these analyses were continuous scores for satisfaction with peer relationships, aggressive behavior, and peer group deviance. Outcome variables were categorical: whether a girl ever became pregnant, had sex without contraception, or contracted a sexually transmitted disease. To explore whether peer variables predicted these categorical dependent variables, logistic regression analyses were employed. For all of the outcome variables pertaining to sexual activity, it seemed reasonable to expect that the likelihood of engaging in these behaviors increases with age. Therefore, age was entered into all regression models, along with the predictor variables, to examine whether qualities of peer relationships predicted variance in outcomes even beyond that explained by age. Given that the primary goal here was to examine predictive rather than concurrent associations, whenever possible given the content of the two interviews, the variables included in the regression models were those from Wave 1. However, interviews at Wave 2 addressed some additional issues of interest for these analyses (for example, numbers of friends). To examine the predictive power of these variables available only at Wave 2 and to avoid inflating the significance of the models that included too many variables and some that were highly correlated with each other, regression analyses for all dependent measures were first performed in two steps. First, a logistic regression was performed with the Wave 1 peer variables in addition to age; these models test whether qualities of peer relationships predict choices about sexuality one year later. Next, for each dependent measure, another separate logistic regression analysis was conducted including Wave 2 variables not available in Wave 1; these models test the strength of the relationship between concurrent peer relations and choices about sexuality. The results of the analyses examining Wave 1 and Wave 2 predictors are identical to results obtained when Wave 1 and Wave 2 variables were included in the same model. Therefore, the analyses presented here are for those models with Wave 1 and Wave 2 variables combined. Because the focus of these secondary analyses was on competence in sexual decision-making, the logistic regression models tested whether the peer variables predicted avoiding negative outcomes: pregnancy, contraceptive errors, and contracting a sexually transmitted disease.

Do Peer Variables Predict Avoiding Pregnancy Altogether
as of the Wave 2 Interview?

The logistic regression analysis indicated that the model was significant, χ^2 (9, N = 1,289) = 155.38, $p < .0001$. As seen in Table 2, there were significant effects for age, χ^2 (1, N = 1,289) = 100.01, $p < .0001$, and number of problems with the police, χ^2 (1, N = 1,289) = 6.43, $p < .05$. Both age and frequency of police problems both negatively predicted avoiding pregnancy altogether. Of the Wave 2 variables, there was a trend for number of friends, χ^2 (1, N = 1,289) = 3.58, $p = .06$, and a significant effect for frequency of interaction with friends, χ^2 (1, N = 1,289) = 18.21, $p < .0001$. Both number of friends and frequency of peer interaction positively predicted avoiding pregnancy altogether.

Do Peer Variables Predict Always Using Contraception?

Logistic regression analyses indicated that the model was significant, χ^2 (9, N = 1,119) = 44.42, $p < .0001$. As seen in Table 3, there were significant effects for age, χ^2 (1, N = 1,119) = 17.73, $p < .0001$, problems with the police, χ^2 (1, N = 1,119) = 6.80, $p < .01$, and a trend for number of friends engage in deviant behaviors, χ^2 (1, N = 1,119) = 3.72, $p = .05$. Age, problems

Table 2
Summary of Logistic Regression Analysis for Peer Variables Predicting Avoiding Pregnancy Altogether

Variable	df	Parameter estimate	Standard error	χ^2	p	Standard estimate
Age	1	−.47	.05	100.01	<.0001	−.36
Satisfaction with friends	1	.00	.09	.00	.96	.00
Problems with police	1	−.29	.12	6.43	<.05	−.10
Aggressive symptoms of conduct disorder	1	−.11	.21	.26	.61	−.02
Physical aggression	1	−.08	.12	.48	.49	−.02
Deviant peer group	1	−.12	.08	2.27	.13	−.05
Number of friends	1	.12	.06	3.58	.06	.06
Frequency of interaction with friends	1	.23	.05	18.21	<.0001	.15
Friends not in school or unemployed	1	−.06	.07	.76	.38	−.03

Table 3
Summary of Logistic Regression Analysis for Peer Variables Predicting Avoiding Contraceptive Errors

Variable	df	Parameter estimate	Standard error	χ^2	p	Standard estimate
Age	1	−.23	.05	17.73	<.0001	−.18
Satisfaction with friends	1	.01	.10	.01	.92	.00
Problems with police	1	−.28	.11	6.80	<.01	−.09
Aggressive symptoms of conduct disorder	1	−.17	.23	.57	.45	−.03
Physical aggression	1	−.14	.15	.96	.33	−.04
Deviant peer group	1	−.17	.09	3.72	.05	−.08
Number of friends	1	.06	.07	.67	.41	.03
Frequency of interaction with friends	1	.06	.07	.67	.41	−.03
Friends not in school or unemployed	1	−.08	.08	1.05	.31	−.04

with the police, and higher numbers of friends involved in deviant behaviors negatively predicted consistently using contraception.

Do Peer Variables Predict Avoiding Contracting Sexually Transmitted Diseases?

For avoiding the contraction of an STD, the logistic regression analysis indicated that the model was significant, χ^2 (9, N = 964) = 24.57, $p < .0001$. As shown in Table 4, there were trends for age, χ^2 (1, N = 964) = 3.23, $p = .07$ and satisfaction with friends, χ^2 (1, N = 964) = 2.98, $p = .08$, and a significant effect for numbers of friends engaged in deviant behaviors, χ^2 (1, N = 964) = 5.27, $p < .05$.

Do Academic and Vocational Plans Predict Competence Decisions about Sexuality?

To explore whether planfulness predicted choices related to sexuality, logistic regression analyses were performed with academic plans and work plans as predictor variables. Both questions about plans (school and work) were only included in the Wave 1 interview, so the following analyses examine the predictive power of academic and vocational plans at the time of the first data collection. Academic and vocational plans were continuous dimensions, where higher scores indicated plans for more schooling or more professional occupations, respectively.

Do Academic and Vocational Plans Predict Avoiding Pregnancy Altogether as of Wave 2?

For never having been pregnant as of Wave 2, the logistic regression analyses including planning variables as predictors indicated that the model was significant, χ^2 (3, N = 1,181) = 128.93, p < .0001. Table 5 shows that there were significant effects for all variables in the model: age, χ^2 (1, N = 1,181) = 78.03, p < .0001, school goals, χ^2 (1, N = 1,181) = 15.81, p < .0001, and

Table 4
Summary of Logistic Regression Analysis for Peer Variables Predicting Avoiding Contracting a Sexually Transmitted Disease

Variable	df	Parameter estimate	Standard error	χ^2	p	Standard estimate
Age	1	−.12	.07	3.23	.07	−.09
Satisfaction with friends	1	.20	.12	2.98	.08	.08
Problems with police	1	−.09	.11	.67	.41	−.03
Aggressive symptoms of conduct disorder	1	−.37	.25	2.27	.13	−.07
Physical aggression	1	−.15	.17	.74	.39	−.11
Deviant peer group	1	−.23	.10	5.27	<.05	−.11
Number of friends	1	−.08	.09	.81	.37	−.04
Frequency of interaction with friends	1	.12	.08	2.52	.11	.08
Friends not in school or unemployed	1	.14	.10	1.92	.17	.07

Table 5
Summary of Logistic Regression Analysis for Planning Variables Predicting Avoiding Pregnancy Altogether

Variable	df	Parameter estimate	Standard error	χ^2	p	Standard estimate
Age	1	−.42	.05	78.03	<.0001	−.32
Academic plans	1	.33	.08	15.81	<.0001	.16
Vocational plans	1	.20	.07	8.00	<.01	.11

vocational plans, χ^2 (1, N = 1,181) = 7.80, $p < .01$. As before, age was a negative predictor of having avoided pregnancy altogether. Plans for more advanced schooling and more professional occupations were significant predictors of not having ever become pregnant as of the Wave 2 interview.

Do Academic and Vocational Plans Predict Consistent Use of Contraception?

For always using contraception, the logistic regression analysis showed that the model was significant, χ^2 (3, N = 979) = 18.88, $p < .001$. As seen in Table 6, there was a significant effect for age, χ^2 (1, N = 979) = 14.12, $p < .001$, and a trend for school goals, χ^2 (1, N = 979) = 3.83, $p = .05$. As before, age negatively predicted using contraception consistently. There was a trend for plans for more advanced schooling to positively predict always taking contraceptive precautions.

Do Academic and Vocational Plans Predict Avoiding Contracting STDs of Wave 2?

With academic and vocation plans at Wave 1 as predictors, the logistic regression analysis indicated that the model was significant, χ^2 (3, N = 851) = 8.57, $p < .05$. As Table 7 indicates, there were significant effects for age, χ^2 (1, N = 851) = 3.86, $p < .05$ and school goals, χ^2 (1, N = 851) = 5.06, $p < .05$. Again, age negatively predicted avoiding STDs. Plans for more advanced schooling were a positive predictor of avoiding STDs. There was not a significant effect for vocational plans.

Table 6
Summary of Logistic Regression Analysis for Planning Variables Predicting Avoiding Contraceptive Errors

Variable	df	Parameter estimate	Standard error	χ^2	p	Standard estimate
Age	1	−.21	.06	14.12	<.001	−.16
Academic plans	1	.19	.09	3.84	.05	.09
Vocational plans	1	−.01	.08	.03	.87	−.01

Table 7
Summary of Logistic Regression Analysis for Planning Variables Predicting Avoiding Contracting a Sexually Transmitted Disease

Variable	df	Parameter estimate	Standard error	χ^2	p	Standard estimate
Age	1	−.14	.07	3.86	<.05	−.10
Academic plans	1	.24	.11	5.06	<.05	.12
Vocational plans	1	−.12	.10	1.72	.19	−.07

How are Peer Relationships Related to Academic and Vocational Plans?

To explore the concurrent relation between peer relationships and planfulness, correlational analyses were conducted. As Table 8 shows, while most of these correlations are significant due to the large size of the sample, none seem strong enough to indicate meaningful relationships between academic and vocational plans and self-reported qualities of peer relationships.

Discussion

For this sample of African-American adolescent females seen in health-care clinics, these secondary analyses provided modest support for the predictive relations between qualities of peer relationships, academic and vocational plans, and competence in sexual decision-making. Reporting problems with the police emerged as a strong, negative predictor for avoiding pregnancy and using contraception consistently. Frequency of interaction with friends contributed positively to avoiding pregnancy. Satisfaction with the quality of support provided by friends was not significantly related to avoiding pregnancy, but tended to positively predict avoiding contracting STDs. Deviant behavior among peers did not relate significantly to avoiding pregnancy, but was a negative predictor of using contraception consistently and avoiding STDs. For almost all outcomes, planning more years of school predicted competence in sexual decision-making. Plans for a more professional career positively predicted avoiding pregnancy.

These predictive relationships must be considered in light of the base rates of the relevant behaviors in this particular sample. In general, the overall level of satisfaction with support from friends was high. Some degree of aggressive behavior seemed fairly common for this group; just over half of participants reported that they had been involved in a physical fight in the year prior to the Wave 1 interview. While physical aggression was reported often, few had severe enough aggressive behavior to be coded as an aggressive symptom of conduct disorder. The great majority of participants reported no problems with the police. Participants' reports indicated moderate levels of peer group deviance for this sample: one third said they had friends who had problems with the police, two thirds of the sample reported that at least one good friend used drugs, and over half of participants reported that they had good friends who were not in school or not working.

Overall, among the variables related to interactions with peers, the strongest predictor of competence in sexual decision-making (in addition to age) was reported problems with the police. In addition to negatively predicting avoiding pregnancy, Underwood (1995) found that more problems with the police was significantly, positively related to higher numbers of pregnancies during adolescence and was also a negative predictor of using contraception consistently.

Table 8
Correlations Between Peer Relations and Planning Variables

	Upset with friends	Times friends disappoint	Number of friends	Frequency of inter- action with friends	Problems with police	Aggressive conduct symptoms	Friends with problems with police	Friends who use drugs	Friends not in school or working
Academic plans	.06*	.09*	.02	.05	−.06*	.04	−.07*	−.03	−.09*
Vocational plans	.07*	.03	.02	.07*	−.09*	.01	−.02	−.04	−.10*

*p < .05

Before interpreting these findings, it is important to note that problems with the police is, at best, an indirect measure of peer interactions. Problems with the police may be related to aggression among peers, or they may be related to covert antisocial behaviors committed alone or in groups. From the data available in the Adolescent Health Care Evaluation Study, it was not possible to determine the specific nature of the offenses that led to police involvement. Still, given the high rates of peer interaction reported by these participants and the significant correlation between having legal problems and having friends who use drugs, it seems reasonable to expect that at least a large proportion of police problems may have been related to activities with peers. Also, Giordana, Cernkovich, and Pugh (1986) found that delinquent girls did not differ from nondelinquent peers on several dimensions related to the intimacy of friendships, and concluded that girls who engage in delinquency are highly peer-oriented.

The consistent predictive relation between police problems and lack of competence in sexual decision-making found here supports earlier research that indicates that antisocial behavior and sexual promiscuity may be related (Rodgers and Rowe 1990, Rowe et al. 1989, and Zabin et al. 1986). Viewed in light of problem behavior theory (Jessor and Jessor 1977), adolescent sexual activity and problems with the police are both considered deviant behaviors, so this might be viewed simply as an instance of persistence forecasting, where antisocial behavior one year predicts antisocial behavior the next. However, the behaviors that lead an adolescent girl to have problems with the police and to become pregnant or contract an STD are actually quite different. Further research is needed to understand the process by which these variables influence each other.

Although problems with the police negatively predicted competence in sexual decision-making, it is important to note that self-reported physical fighting was not a strong predictor. This appears to contradict earlier research that indicated that physical aggression was related to adolescent childbearing (Cairns et al. 1989, Underwood, Kupersmidt, and Coie 1996). One reason for the different result obtained here may be that the measure of aggression relied on self-reports on a single interview item. In both earlier studies, peer ratings were the source of information about physical aggression and these may be more valid because they reflect information from multiple informants and are certainly less subject to distortion from trying to present oneself in a positive light.

For the outcome of avoiding pregnancy, other significant predictors from the Wave 2 interviews were self-reports of number of friends and frequency of interaction with friends. Although this information about high rates of involvement with friends in this study came from self-reports on a few interview items and may not be directly related to popularity as determined by sociometric ratings, this result fits with earlier suggestions that successful interactions with friends may protect girls from adolescent pregnancy. In a longitudinal study of the predictive relation between fourth-grade peer status and adolescent motherhood, Underwood, Kupersmidt, and Coie (1996) found that popular girls were less likely to become teenage mothers. Both of these results support Rutter's (1987) suggestions that youth who have successful interpersonal relationships may avoid negative outcomes because they have less exposure to harmful behaviors and activities and higher self-esteem and self-efficacy. However, another pragmatic and perhaps even more straightforward explanation for the relation between frequency of interaction with friends and avoiding pregnancy is that girls who reported low frequencies of doing things with friends may be spending a lot of time with boyfriends, perhaps increasing their chances of becoming pregnant.

Rutter (1987) also suggested that positive interpersonal relationships might protect young people from negative outcomes because they have more support when faced with stress. Interestingly, in this investigation, perceived level of support from friends was not a strong predictor of avoiding pregnancy. Perhaps support from friends is not central to the process by which peer relationships influence sexual choices; perhaps number of friends and frequency of interaction are more important. Alternatively, maybe the measures used in this investigation were not sufficiently sensitive to detect a relationship between perceived satisfaction with peer support and sexual choices. This latter interpretation is supported by the fact that most participants reported that they were rarely or never disappointed with support from friends.

Having friends who engaged in deviant behavior was not strongly related to avoiding adolescent pregnancy. This seems to contradict earlier research by Cairns et al. (1989) that showed that adolescents in deviant peer cliques were more likely to become young mothers. Here again, the discrepant findings may be due to different types and different sources of information. In the Cairns et al. study, membership in peer cliques was determined by asking everyone in the grade about who hangs around together. Deviance of the particular peer groups was determined based on peer ratings of aggression. In the Cairns study, both group membership and deviance (operationalized as aggression) were measured with data from multiple informants. In this investigation, girls were simply asked a few questions about whether their friends used drugs or had problems with the police. Also, another important difference here is that deviance was operationalized differently; in this study, deviance of peers was defined as having friends with police problems or friends who use substances. Having friends who engage in these illegal behaviors may have different consequences for adolescent motherhood than having friends who fight.

Although reports of deviant behavior among friends were not strongly related to avoiding pregnancy, they were significant, negative predictors of avoiding STDs and tended to negatively predict consistent use of contraception. This suggests that having friends with legal problems and who use drugs makes a girl less likely to use contraception consistently. If peers act as socialization agents for each other, perhaps having friends who may be prone to impulsive behaviors means that a girl is less likely to plan for and take contraceptive precautions and more likely to contract a sexually transmitted disease. Previous research suggests that peer attitudes may strongly influence adolescents' choices about contraception. For example, Shah and Zelnick (1981) found that most of the girls in their sample reported that their attitudes toward contraception were more similar to those of their friends than their parents, and girls whose contraceptive attitudes were more similar to those of friends rarely used contraception consistently. Billy, Rodgers, and Udry (1984) found that adolescent girls named best friends who reported similar levels of sexual experience. Rodgers and Rowe (1990) reported moderate and significant correlations between friends' reports of sexual experiences (for the African-American female subsample, $r = .35$). Kegeles, Adler, and Irwin (1988) found that adolescents' reported plans to use condoms were unrelated to whether they believed that condoms are effective in preventing pregnancy and STDs. Plans to use condoms were strongly related to perceived ease of use, and also to the extent to which participants believed that condoms were popular with peers. In a prospective, longitudinal study of health-risking sexual behavior among adolescent males, Capaldi and Yoerger (1995) demonstrated that deviant peer association predicted high-risk sexual behavior.

Another focus of this work was to examine how future plans for school and work relate to competence in sexual decision-making in adolescents. Planning more advanced schooling positively predicted competence in decision-making: avoiding pregnancy, using contraception consistently (trend), and not contracting an STD. Having more ambitious career goals was a positive predictor of avoiding pregnancy. These results confirm earlier research by Lauritsen (1994) that demonstrated that for girls, educational aspirations were associated with sexual activity. Lauritsen found that the strongest predictor of sexual activity for girls was educational frustration, expecting that attaining educational aspirations would be difficult or impossible. While the content of the data set used here did not allow exploration of the extent to which girls viewed their educational aspirations as realistic or possible, these findings are encouraging in that they suggest that for this sample of African-American, low-income girls, simply having lofty goals may be associated with competent choices related to sexuality.

Several explanations for these findings seems possible. Perhaps girls who have ambitious plans are more likely to avoid situations—such as becoming an adolescent mother—that will interfere with their goals. Maybe girls with high-level goals avoid pregnancy by abstaining from sex altogether, but this seems unlikely given the high rates of sexual activity in this sample. In light of the finding that more ambitious plans predict consistent use of contraception, it seems more likely that girls with goals make sure they use contraception if they are going to have sex.

Another possible explanation for the relationship between future plans and competence in sexual decision-making comes from previous research that indicates that girls who become pregnant have poor academic records (Miller 1985). Maybe these girls have cognitive limitations that interfere with both academic success and contraceptive planning. Sander, Watson, and Levine (1992) found that adolescents who used contraception consistently had higher IQ scores than girls who used contraception unreliably.

Gordon (1990) proposed that competence in sexual decision-making may be related to more advanced skills in formal-operational reasoning, including considering alternatives, perspective-taking, and considering probabilities. Perhaps more advanced formal-operational thinking explains the relation between higher academic goals and competence in sexual decision-making.

Somewhat surprisingly, the future plans variables were not strongly related to the measures that addressed qualities of peer interactions. For this sample, positive peer interactions seemed independent of girls' academic and vocational plans. Future research should address what factors influence the academic and professional goals of African-American adolescent females.

Overall, many of these results seem to support the tried and true adage that good things go together. For example, girls who stayed out of trouble with the police, reported interacting frequently with friends, and had ambitious future plans were more likely to survive adolescence without becoming pregnant. Results like this might suggest that competence is a broad construct, that competent youth have skills that will serve them well across domains. However, other findings indicated more specific relations between predictors and particular outcomes. For instance, having friends who engaged in deviant behavior did not predict avoiding pregnancy, but was negatively associated with using contraception consistently and avoiding STDs. Although precise understanding of the reasons underlying these findings awaits future research that focuses more closely on social processes among youth, these results suggest that examining whether variables predict particular competent outcomes seems worthwhile. If competence is domain-specific and even outcome-specific, the only way we will discover this is by testing for the possibility that different predictors are associated with particular outcomes. If competence is indeed a more broad set of skills that operates across positive outcomes or even across domains, patterns of results from future research examining specific relationships should also make this clear.

These findings must be considered in light of the following shortcomings. One limitation of this research was that the sample consisted of adolescent females who presented at health care clinics. While the fact that some of the programs were funded and some were not, and some were school-based and some were at hospitals increases the generalizability of these data, the concern remains that the most vulnerable group of female adolescents may not have had access to clinic programs at all and thus may not be represented in this sample.

Another potential shortcoming of this research is that it was a secondary analysis of data collected for purposes other than the questions posed here. The Earls data set is very comprehensive and includes responses to detailed questions to assess the variables of interest, particularly peer relations and sexual decision-making. However, it would have been interesting to examine questions that could not be addressed in this investigation because of lack of information. For example, many theorists and researchers (Anderson 1991, Stiffman et al. 1987) have proposed that adolescents may choose motherhood because many of their friends have already made this choice, thus it has become normalized, and also because girls witness their peers experiencing few negative consequences as a result of becoming mothers (Klerman 1993). Future research should examine whether having pregnant or mothering friends increases the likelihood of adolescent pregnancy.

Finally, another concern related to this research is that almost all of the measures were self-report, and therefore, we must question the extent to which subjects were willing or able to provide accurate information. For many of the peer variables, the accuracy issue is less serious, because this work focuses on perceived quality of peer relations. The data on sexual decision-making were collected by professional interviewers in private settings, which increased the likelihood that subjects would perceive that confidentiality was secure and therefore they would give more accurate responses, and also that they would feel more comfort in giving straightforward responses to interviewers they would not see in other contexts. Also, for adolescent sexual behavior in particular, self-report is really the only viable means of assessment, because observation is inappropriate and parents and peers are often not fully aware of the sexual activity of adolescents. Lauritsen and Swicegood (1995) reported empirical evidence that the majority of youth are consistent reporters of one variable related to sexuality: age of initiation of intercourse. Using modeling techniques, they also demonstrated that primary conclusions of research do not change when some unreliability in reporting is taken into account statistically.

The design of this investigation featured several methodological strengths that have been lacking in most previous research. Dissatisfaction with peer relations, aggression and delinquency, membership in deviant peer groups, and lack of planfulness were examined as predictors of sexual decision-making above and beyond the socioeconomic and family factors that have been demonstrated to correlate with adolescent pregnancy. Whereas most previous research on adolescent pregnancy has been retrospective or concurrent in design, this investigation was a prospective, longitudinal study of factors that are associated with competence in sexual decision-making, operationalized as avoiding pregnancy, using contraception consistently, and not contracting a sexually transmitted disease. Most importantly, this follow-forward investigation allowed exploration of protective factors that might enhance competent sexual decision-making, such as positive peer relationships and future plans.

All of these findings support the cogent suggestion that adolescents' choices about whether or not to engage in risk-taking behaviors related to sexuality should be considered in light of decision-making theory (Furby and Beyth-Marom 1992, Gardner and Herman 1990). Jacobs Quadrel, Fischoff, and Davis (1993) challenge the assumption that adolescents engage in risk-taking behavior because they feel invulnerable, and present empirical evidence that adolescents underestimate their own risk no more or no less than adults. Rather than viewing high rates of risky behaviors as evidence of irrationality or feelings of invulnerability, Furby and Beyth-Marom (1992) proposed that adolescents make choices depending on the social contingencies and also the options available to them. Perhaps girls who interact frequently with friends may avoid pregnancy because their peers support these efforts, or because they have other avenues for status or companionship. Girls with more ambitious plans may make competent sexual choices because they wish to protect attractive future options, which of course also requires that they view positive future goals as attainable.

These findings strongly support the argument that peer influences on adolescent behavior are not uniformly negative. Rather than suggesting that all types of friends put pressure on adolescent girls to have sex, these findings demonstrated that for this sample, girls who reported large numbers of friends were more likely to avoid pregnancy. Brown, Dolcini, and Leventhal (1995) proposed that a sophisticated understanding of how peer relations influence adolescent health behaviors will require a focus on the specific processes of social relationships.

Last, the results of this investigation suggest target groups for prevention efforts: girls who report police involvement, girls who interact with friends infrequently, and girls who do not have ambitious plans. In an ideal world of unlimited time and money for youth services, all adolescents could profit from programs to promote competent sexual decision-making. However, given limited resources, it seems desirable to target high-risk groups for more intensive prevention programs so that our efforts can be maximally effective.

What form should these prevention programs take? Weissberg, Caplan, and Howard (1991) argue convincingly that effective prevention programs will have a dual emphasis: building competence in individuals and creating environments that promote competence. Most previous efforts to prevent negative sexual outcomes have focused on trying to make individual adolescents more aware of the consequences of high-risk sexual behavior. However, these programs may have been misguided, given that empirical research does not support the assumption that adolescents view themselves any less or more vulnerable than adults. Future prevention efforts may need to foster other types of protective factors, and may need to focus on environments as well as individuals. The findings reported here suggest that prevention programs might profitably bolster positive peer affiliations, seek to change peers' as well as individuals' attitudes, encourage educational aspirations, and nurture hopes for future careers. These programs must be sensitive to adolescents' needs as well as their developing independence. As Jacobs Quadrel, Fischoff, and Davis (1993: 111) cautioned, "We do adolescents a disservice if we overestimate their decision-making competence (hence, deny them needed protections) or if we underestimate it (hence, deny them possible autonomy)."

Acknowledgements

The research described here is a secondary analysis of *The Adolescent Health Care Evaluation Study,* by Felton Earls. This research was partially supported by NIMH grant #MH52110.

References

Anderson, E. 1991. "Neighborhood Effects on Teenage Pregnancy." In *The Urban Underclass,* ed. C. Jencks and P. E. Peterson. Washington, D.C.: Brookings Institution.

Asher, S. R., J. T. Parkhurst, S. Hymel, and G. A. Williams. 1990. "Peer Rejection and Loneliness in Children." In *Peer Rejection in Childhood,* ed. S. R. Asher and J. D. Coie, 253–73. New York: Cambridge University Press.

Beale Spencer, M., S. P. Cole, D. DuPree, A. Glymph, and P. Pierre. 1993. "Self-efficacy among Urban African American Early Adolescents: Exploring Issues of Risk, Vulnerability, and Resilience." *Development and Psychopathology* 5: 719–39.

Billy, J. O. G., J. L. Rodgers, and J. R. Udry. 1984. "Adolescent Sexual Behavior and Friendship Choice." *Social Forces* 62(3): 653–78.

Brown, B. B., M. M. Dolcini, and A. Leventhal. 1995. "The Emergence of Peer Crowds: Friend or foe to adolescent health." Paper presented at the Biennial Meeting of the Society for Research in Child Development, Indianapolis, IN (March).

Brown, C. H., R. G. Adams, and S. G. Kellam. 1981. "A Longitudinal Study of Teenage Motherhood and Symptoms of Distress: The Woodlawn Community Epidemiological Project." In *Research in Community and Mental Health: A Research Annual,* ed. R. G. Simmons, 183–213. Greenwich, CT: JAI Press.

Burns Jones, J. and S. Philliber. 1983. "Sexually Active But Not Pregnant: A Comparison of Teens Who Risk and Teens Who Plan." *Journal of Youth and Adolescence* 12(3): 235–51.

Cairns, R. B., B. D. Cairns, and H. J. Neckerman. 1989. "Early School Dropout: Configurations and Determinants." *Child Development* 60: 1437–52.

Cairns, R. B., B. D. Cairns, H. J. Neckerman, S. D. Gest, and J. L. Gariepy. 1988.

"Social Networks and Aggressive Behavior: Peer Support or Peer Rejection?" *Developmental Psychology* 24(6): 815–23.

Capaldi, D. and K. Yoerger. 1995. "Prediction of Health Risking Sexual Behavior in At-risk Young Adults Males." Paper presented at the Biennial Meeting of the Society for Research in Child Development, Indianapolis, IN (March).

Cassidy, T. and R. Lynn. 1991. "Achievement Motivation, Educational Attainment, Cycles of Disadvantage and Social Competence: Some Longitudinal Data." *British Journal of Educational Psychology* 61: 1–12.

Center for Disease Control. 1992. *HIV/AIDS Surveillance Report* (October).

Clausen, J. S. 1991a. "Adolescent Competence and the Shaping of the Life Course." *American Journal of Sociology* 96, 4: 805–42.

———. 1991b. "Adolescent Competence and the Life Course, or Why One Social Psychologist Needed a Concept of Personality." *Social Psychology Quarterly* 54(4): 4–14.

Earls, F. 1984. *Adolescent Health Care Evaluation Study.* Longitudinal data set housed by the Henry A. Murray Research Center for the Study of Lives through Time, Radcliffe College, Cambridge, MA.

East, P. L., R. M. Lerner, J. V. Lerner, R. T. Soni, C. M. Ohannessian, and L. P. Jacobson. 1992. "Early Adolescent-Peer Group Fit, Peer Relations, and Psychosocial Competence: A Short-Term Longitudinal Study." *Journal of Early Adolescence* 12(2): 132–52.

Elliot, D. S. and B. J. Morse. 1989. "Delinquency and Drug Use as Risk Factors in Teenage Sexual Activity." *Youth and Society* 21(1): 32–60.

Farber, N. 1991. "The Process of Pregnancy Resolution Among Adolescent Mothers." *Adolescence* 26 (103): 697–716.

French, D. C. and G. A. Waas. 1985. "Behavior Problems of Peer-Neglected and Peer-Rejected Elementary-Age Children: Parent and Teacher Perspectives." *Child Development* 56: 246–52.

Frese, M., J. Steward, and B. Hannover. 1987. "Goal Orientation and Planfulness: Action Styles as Personality Concepts." *Journal of Personality and Social Psychology* 52(6): 1182–94.

Furby, L. and R. Beyth-Marom. 1992. "Risk-Taking in Adolescence: A Decision-Making Perspective." *Developmental Review* 12: 1–44.

Furstenberg, F. F, J. Brooks-Gunn, and L. Chase-Lansdale. 1989. "Adolescent Sexual Behavior." *American Psychologist* 44(2): 249–57.

Gardner, W. and J. Herman. 1990. "Adolescents' AIDS Risk-Taking: A Rational Choice Perspective." *New Directions in Child Development* 50: 17–34.

Giordano, P. C., S. A. Cernkovich, and M. D. Pugh. 1986. "Friendship and Delinquency." *American Journal of Sociology* 91: 1170–1201.

Gordon, D. E. 1990. "Formal-Operational Thinking: The Role of Cognitive-Developmental Processes in Adolescent Decision-Making about Pregnancy and Contraception." *American Journal of Orthopsychiatry* 60(3): 346–56.

Hamburg, B. A. 1986. "Subsets of Adolescent Mothers: Developmental, Biomedical, and Psychosocial Issues." In *School Age Pregnancy and Parenthood: Biosocial Dimensions,* ed. J. B. Lancaster and B. A. Hamburg, 115–45. New York: DeGruyter.

Harter, S. "Supplementary Description of the Self-Perception Profile for Children: Revision of the Perceived Competence Scale for Children." Manuscript.

Jacobs Quadrel, J., B. Fischoff, and W. Davis. 1993. "Adolescent (In)vulnerability." *American Psychologist* 48(2): 102–16.

Jessor, R. and S. L. Jessor. 1977. *Problem Behavior and Psychosocial Development.* New York: Academic Press.

Kegeles, S. M., N. E. Adler, and C. E. Irwin, Jr. 1988. "Adolescents and Condoms: Associations of Beliefs with Intentions to Use." Paper presented at the Annual Convention of the American Psychological Association, Atlanta, GA (August).

Klerman, L. V. 1993. "Adolescent Pregnancy and Parenting: Controversies of the Past and Lessons for the Future." *Journal of Adolescent Health* 14: 553–61.

Kupersmidt, J. B and J. D. Coie. 1990. "Preadolescent Peer Status, Aggression, and School-Adjustment as Predictors of Externalizing Problems in Adolescence." *Child Development* 61: 1350–62.

Kupersmidt, J. B, P. C. Griesler, and C. J. Patterson. 1995. "Sociometric Status, Aggression, and Affiliation Patterns of Peers." Manuscript.

Lauritsen, J. L. 1994. "Explaining Race and Gender Differences in Adolescent Sexual Behavior." *Social Forces* 72(3): 859–84.

Lauritsen, J. L. and C. G. Swicegood. 1995. "The Consistency of Self-Report Initiation of Sexual Activity: Longitudinal Findings from the National Youth Survey." Manuscript.

Luthar, S. S. 1991. "Vulnerability and Resilience: A Study of High-Risk Adolescents." *Child Development* 62: 600–616.

Luthar, S. S., C. H. Doernberger, and E. Zigler. 1993. "Resilience in Not a Unidimensional Construct: Insights from a Prospective Study of Inner-City Adolescents." *Development and Psychopathology* 5: 703–17.

Luthar, S. S., and E. Zigler. 1992. "Intelligence and Social Competence among High-Risk Adolescents." *Development and Psychopathology* 4: 287–99.

Mann, L., R. Harmoni, and C. Power. 1989. "Adolescent Decision-Making: The Development of Competence." *Journal of Adolescence* 12: 265–78.

McAnarny, E. R. 1985. "Adolescent Pregnancy and Childbearing: New Data, new Challenges." *Pediatrics* 75: 973–74.

McBride Murry, V. 1995. "Variation in Adolescent Pregnancy Status: A National Tri-Ethnic Study." In *Resiliency in Ethnic Minority Families,* vol. 2: *African-American Families,* ed. H. I. McCubbin, E. A. Thompson, A. I. Thompson, and J. A. Futrell, 179–205. University of Wisconsin: Center for Excellence in Family Studies.

Miller, B. C. 1985. "Adolescent Pregnancy and Chidbearing in Utah and the United States." *Utah Science* 46: 32–35.

Moore, K. A., S. L. Hofferth, S. B. Caldwell, and L. J. Waite. 1979. *Teenage Motherhood: Social and Economic Consequence.* Doc. 1146-7. Washington, D.C.: Urban Institute.

Morrison, D. M. 1985. "Adolescent Contraceptive Behavior: A Review." *Psychological Bulletin* 98(3): 538–68.

Parker, J. G. and S. R. Asher. 1987. "Peer Relations and later Personal Adjustment: Are Low Accepted Children at Risk?" *Psychological Bulletin* 102(3): 357–89.

Patterson, C. J., J. B. Kupersmidt, and P. C. Griesler. 1990. "Children's Perceptions of Self and of Relationships with Others as a Function of Sociometric Status." *Child Development* 61: 1335–49.

Ralph, N., J. E. Lochman, and T. Thomas. 1984. "Psychosocial Characteristics of Pregnant and Nulliparous Adolescents." *Adolescence* 19: 283–94.

Richardson, R. A. 1996. "Competence in the Transition to Adulthood: Exploring the Influence of Adolescent Motherhood for Low-Income, Urban, African-American Women." Manuscript.

Rodgers, J. L. and D. C. Rowe. 1990. "Adolescent Sexual Activity and Mildly Deviant Behavior." *Journal of Family Issues* 11: 274–93.

Rowe, D. C. and J. L. Rodgers. 1991. "An 'Epidemic' Model of Adolescent Sexual Intercourse: Applications to National Youth Survey Data." *Journal of Biosocial Sciences* 23: 211–19.

Rowe, D. C., J. L. Rodgers, and S. Meseck-Bushey. 1989. "An 'Epidemic' Model of Sexual Intercourse Prevalences for Black and White Adolescents." *Social Biology* 36: 127–45.

Rowe, D. C., J. L. Rodgers, S. Meseck-Bushey, and C. St. John. 1989. "Sexual Behavior and Deviance: A Sibling Study of Their Relationship." *Developmental Psychology* 25: 61–69.

Rutter, M. 1987. "Psychosocial Resilience and Protective Mechanisms." *American Journal of Orthopsychiatry* 57(3): 316–31.

Rutter, M., D. Quinton, and J. Hill. 1990. "Adult Outcome of Institution-Reared Children: Males and Females Compared." In *Straight and Devious Pathways from Childhood to Adulthood,* ed. L. Robins and M. Rutter, 135–57. New York: Cambridge University Press.

Sander, A. D., T. E. Watson, and M. D. Levine. 1992. "A Study of the Cognitive Aspects of Sexual Decision-Making in Adolescent Females." *Developmental and Behavioral Pediatrics* 13 (3): 202–07.

Scott-Jones, D. 1993. "Ethical Issues in Reporting and Referring in Research with Minority and Low-Income Samples." Paper presented at the Biennial Meeting of the Society for Research in Child Development, New Orleans, LA (April).

Shah, F. and M. Zelnick. 1981. "Parent and Peer Influence on Sexual Behavior, Contraceptive Use, and Pregnancy Experience of Young Women." *Journal of Marriage and the Family* 339–48.

Sternberg, R. J., and J. Kolligan, Jr. 1990. *Competence Considered.* New Haven, NJ: Yale University Press.

Stiffman, A. R., F. Earls, L. N. Robins, K. G. Jung, and R. Kulbok. 1987. "Adolescent Sexual Activity and Pregnancy: Socioenvironmental Problems, Physical Health, and Mental Health." *Journal of Youth and Adolescence* 16(5): 497–509.

Underwood, M. K. 1995. "The Contribution of Peer Relations and Planfulness to Competence in Sexual Decision Making by Female Adolescents." Manuscript.

Underwood, M. K., J. B. Kupersmidt, and J. D. Coie. 1996. "Peer sociometric status and aggression as predictors of adolescent childbearing." *Journal of Research on Adolescence* 6(2): 201–23.

Weissberg, R. P., M. Caplan, and R. L. Harwood. 1991. "Promoting Competent Young People in Competence-Enhancing Environments: A Systems-Based Perspective on Primary Prevention." *Journal of Consulting and Clinical Psychology* 59(6): 830–41.

Zabin, L. S., J. B. Hardy, E. A. Smith, and M. B. Hirsh. 1986. "Substance Use and Its Relation to Sexual Activity among Inner-City Adolescents." *Journal of Adolescent Health Care* 7: 320–31.

CHAPTER FOUR

The Long-Term Reach of Adolescent Competence: Socioeconomic Achievement in the Lives of Disadvantaged Men

JOHN H. LAUB AND
ROBERT J. SAMPSON

This chapter examines the relationship between adolescent competence and socioeconomic achievement in the lives of 1,000 disadvantaged men. Our work on this topic stems from a long-term research project using archival data from Sheldon and Eleanor Gluecks' classic longitudinal study of 500 delinquents and 500 nondelinquents initiated in 1940 (see Sampson and Laub 1993, Laub and Sampson 1993). The 1,000 male subjects in the Gluecks' study grew up in disadvantaged neighborhoods in Boston during the period of the Great Depression and World War II. These men came to adulthood during the late 1940s, 1950s, and 1960s—a time of expanding economic opportunity in the United States. Moreover, 500 of these men were serious and persistent offenders in their youth. Thus, the Glueck data archive provides a unique opportunity to study a large group of persistent adolescent delinquents and their nondelinquent counterparts from a disadvantaged urban setting. A key question is: How is it that men from impoverished backgrounds manage to attain successful adult outcomes? Moreover, among serious juvenile delinquents, are there factors in adolescence that are associated with successful outcomes in adulthood?

To date, the relationship between adolescent competence and socioeconomic achievement in adulthood among those who grow up in disadvantaged settings has not been well explored in the existing research. Inspired by the work of John Clausen (1991, 1993), we examine in this chapter the long-term reach of adolescent competence on later socioeconomic achievement among economically disadvantaged youth, and, in the case of the 500 delinquents, officially stigmatized men. Questions about competence abound. What does it mean to be competent in adolescence? Why should adolescent competence matter, especially over the long term? Among juvenile delinquents, do those who are more competent have different life-course outcomes than those with less competence? In other words, is adolescent competence an indication of resiliency, that is, some quality in an individual that enables one to face difficulties and overcome them (Werner and Smith 1992)? Or is adolescent competence a protective factor that modifies risk factors and increases the probability of favorable outcomes over the life course?

Although there are many unanswered questions, our main objective in this chapter is to see whether adolescent competence is related to later outcomes in adulthood. The theoretical framework we are using comes from Clausen, who argues that adolescent competence interacts with and modifies opportunities or obstacles that are encountered in the course of adult development (see Clausen 1993). More specifically, Clausen speculates that adolescent competence should lead to thinking through career and marital choices and inhibiting tendencies to make unwise choices. Competence is especially important in the transition to adulthood because the choices that one makes will be, to some degree, thought through. Competent adolescents will begin to contemplate these questions early on in the life course and start to plan for them. Overall, those high in competence will obtain more education, have lower rates of divorce, have more orderly careers, achieve higher occupational status, experience life crises less often, and show less personality change over the adult years. In this context, competence is regarded as a multi-faceted set of cognitive, affective, and behavioral functions that enable the attainment of personally and socially desired outcomes in a wide variety of social contexts (Baumrind 1989).[1] What is not clear is whether or not this theoretical framework applies to a disadvantaged and antisocial population of adolescents.

The chapter is organized as follows. In the next section, a brief review of the relevant literature is provided. Then, we describe the Gluecks' longitudinal data and the key measures used in our study. In the section that follows, we outline our analytical strategy and present major findings as derived from quantitative analyses of the Gluecks' data. Because we are interested in integrating quantitative and qualitative data analyses, we also present some life-history data that illustrate the importance of adolescent competence over the life course. In the final section, we discuss the conclusions and implications of our research.

Literature Review

While there is a fairly large body of literature on the development of competence among adolescents (see, for example, Baumrind 1978; Mann, Harmoni, and Power 1989; Gullotta, Adams, and Montemayor 1990), there is very little literature that assesses its long-term impact with respect to adult development. Although not the focus of this chapter, it appears that adolescent competence is related to a variety of variables including parental socioeconomic status, IQ, parental socialization practices (e.g., the values parents hold for their children, the standards they set, intellectual stimulation, consistency of discipline, and supportiveness and availability), personal attributes (e.g., race, ethnicity, physique, attractiveness), household composition, parental divorce, and economic depression (see Clausen 1993 for a review). Although we do not examine the antecedents of competence in this chapter, in our analyses below we control for some of the key variables that are strongly implicated in the development of adolescent competence (for example, IQ).

Few longitudinal studies have examined competence in adulthood. For example, in her study using data from the Cambridge-Somerville study, McCord (1991) defined competence as positive social adjustment and achievement in adulthood. Specifically, adjustment was assessed by the presence or absence of evidence that a man was alcoholic, criminal, manic-depressive, schizophrenic, or had died prior to age thirty-five. Achievement was defined by occupational status (e.g., whether a man had attained a white-collar occupation). McCord found that while the social status of the family had little influence on outcomes, family interaction and maternal/paternal competence were related to adult competence. That is, both forms of competence (achievement and adjustment) were fostered by good family interaction in childhood.

One problem in the literature concerns the definition of competence. Oftentimes studies define competence as part of the variable of interest (e.g., academic and occupational achievement). Or, competence is defined as the converse of antisocial, disruptive behavior. For example, Zigler, Taussig, and Black (1992) write that "not engaging in criminal acts is one indicator of competence." Given potentially serious problems of confounded relationships, there is a need to define competence in a way that avoids a tautology.

The main body of literature that is directly relevant to the topic at hand is the work of John Clausen (1991, 1993). As noted above, Clausen has conceptualized adolescent planful competence as a cluster of attributes that are likely to have a substantial bearing on successful role performance beyond adolescence. He defined planful competence as including the following: the ability to assess one's options and to have thought seriously about what possibilities exist; a fairly clear idea of who one is, especially knowledge of one's intellectual abilities, social skills, and emotional responses to others as well as recognition of weaknesses that need to be overcome, and the interests and strengths that need developing; the ability to make accurate assessments of the aims and actions of others in order to interact responsibly with them; the ability to make and keep commitments; sufficient self-confidence to pursue objectives in the face of obstacles; self-esteem, ego resilience and control, and intellectual ability.

Using data from the Berkeley Guidance Study, the Berkeley Growth Study, and the Adolescent (Oakland) Growth Study, Clausen found that for men competence assessed in high school predicted educational attainment, occupational attainment, and personality resemblance. Clausen did note that competence as defined above had more coherence for males than females. Reflecting the historical context of his study cohort, Clausen found that planfully competent women married men who attained high occupational status (see Clausen 1993 for more details).

Werner and Smith (1992) examined high-risk children growing up in Hawaii and found that resiliency in adolescence predicted successful adult outcomes with respect to education, employment, and family. Thus, similar to Clausen, Werner and Smith uncovered continuity in life course trajectories; namely, competent or resilient adolescents are more likely than incompetent adolescents to become competent adults.[2]

The Gluecks' *Unraveling Juvenile Delinquency* Data

The Gluecks' prospective study of the formation and development of criminal careers was initiated in 1940 and involved a sample of 500 delinquents and 500 nondelinquents. The delinquent sample contained persistent delinquents recently committed to one of two correctional schools—the Lyman School for Boys in Westboro, Massachusetts, and the Industrial School for Boys in Shirley, Massachusetts. The nondelinquent sample, or what they called a "control-group" (Glueck and Glueck 1950: 14), was drawn from the public schools in the city of Boston. Nondelinquency status was determined by criminal record checks as well as through a series of interviews with key informants (e.g., parents and teachers). The Gluecks' sampling procedure was designed to maximize differences in delinquency—an objective that by all accounts succeeded (see Glueck and Glueck 1950: 27–29). For example, approximately 30% of the delinquent group had a juvenile court conviction at age ten or younger, and the average number of convictions for all delinquent boys was 3.5 (Glueck and Glueck 1950: 293).

A unique aspect of the *UJD* study was the matching design whereby the 500 officially defined delinquents and 500 nondelinquents were matched case-by-case on age, race/ethnicity, intelligence, and neighborhood socioeconomic status (SES). The delinquents averaged 14 years, 8 months, and the nondelinquents 14 years, 6 months when the study began. Regarding ethnicity, 25% of both groups were of English background, 25% Italian, 20% Irish, less than 10% old American, Slavic, or French, and the remaining were Near Eastern, Spanish, Scandinavian, German, or Jewish. And, as measured by the Wechsler-Bellevue Test, the delinquents had an average IQ of 92 and nondelinquents 94. The matching on neighborhood ensured that both delinquents and nondelinquents grew up in "underprivileged neighborhoods"—slums and tenement areas—of central Boston. Given the similarity in neighborhood conditions the areas were in essence matched on delinquency rate along with poverty. Overall, then, the 1,000 male subjects in the *UJD* study were matched on key criminological variables thought to influence both delinquent behavior and official reactions by the police and courts. That 500 of the boys were persistent delinquents and 500 avoided delinquency in childhood and adolescence thus cannot be attributed to residence in urban slum areas, age differences, ethnicity, or IQ.

The original sample was followed up at two different points in time—at age twenty-five and again at age thirty-two (see Glueck and Glueck 1968). Over a 25-year period from 1940 to 1965, the Gluecks collected a wealth of multifaceted information on the delinquents and controls in childhood (retrospectively), adolescence (concurrently), and adulthood (prospectively) using a combination of official records, observations, and interviews with both the subjects and key informants (e.g., parents, spouses, neighbors, and employers). Extensive data are available for analysis relating to family life, education, employment history, military experiences, recreational activities, and criminal histories at three interview waves. More important, data are available for 438 of the original 500 delinquents (88%) and 442 of the original 500 nondelinquents (88%) at all three interview waves. When adjusted for mortality, the follow-up success rate is approximately 92%—relatively high by current standards (see, for example, Wolfgang, Thornberry, and Figlio 1987). The low attrition rate is testimony to the Gluecks' rigorous research strategy, but also to lower residential mobility and inter-state migration rates in the 1940s and 1950s compared to today. It should be noted, though, that the follow-up of criminal histories and official records covered 37 states, the most common involving California, New York, New Hampshire, Florida, and Illinois (Glueck and Glueck 1968: xix).

Key Measures

According to Clausen, competence entails "knowledge, abilities, and controls" (1991: 808). Clausen's index of "planful competence" contains three components of personality—self-confidence versus victimization, intellectual investment, and dependability. Although we could not replicate Clausen's measure with the Gluecks' data, we tried to construct a measure of adolescent competence that was consistent with his theoretical idea that competence is both "a measure of maturity that provides a 'head start' and a measure of attributes associated with effective functioning throughout the adolescent and adult years" (Clausen 1991: 834).

We constructed our measure of adolescent competence from several sources in the Gluecks' data. In this regard, our measure of competence is not tied to any specific domain. For example, from the psychiatric interview, we used five variables:

1. Whether the boy had academic or vocational ambitions: those who expressed a desire for further schooling or to learn a specialized trade were scored a one;

2. The boy's planfulness in the use of money: those who had "a natural tendency to save or use money for necessities or with some regard for the future" were scored a one;
3. The boy's attitude towards school: those who accepted and liked school were scored a one;
4 and 5. In determining the personality traits of the boy during the psychiatric interview, those who were categorized as intellectual ("impulse to face things as they are, to investigate and plan") and conscientious ("inclined to follow a code of conduct which has been accepted after due consideration") were scored a one in each category;
6. From the social investigation, the boy's grades in school were obtained from the interview with his teacher: those who performed well on grades in school were scored a one.

In short, our measure of adolescent competence is a summary composite of these six variables and ranges from 0 to 6.[3] In Table 1 we present the frequency distribution of adolescent competence for both the delinquent and nondelinquent groups. The data reveal that the measure of adolescent competence captures the differences between these two groups as one would expect given the Gluecks' design. Moreover, our measure of adolescent competence is negatively related to "unofficial" delinquency (defined below) within each group ($-.24$ and $-.31$ for both delinquents and controls, respectively). This suggests that our measure of adolescent competence is related to, but not defined by, crime. Perhaps even more important, the correlation between competence and measured intelligence is .42, suggesting that the measure is related to IQ in the direction predicted yet it appears to have discriminant validity.

As one outcome measure of socioeconomic achievement, we examine educational attainment at age twenty-five. In this regard, the design and historical context of the Gluecks' study are paramount: like many men of this era, more than 80% did not graduate from high school, and only 65 of the 1,000 went to

Table 1
Frequency Distribution for Adolescent Competence Measure by Delinquent and Nondelinquent Group

	Delinquents		Nondelinquents	
	Frequency	Percent	Frequency	Percent
.00	141	31.0	38	8.1
1.00	153	33.6	68	14.6
2.00	102	22.4	99	21.2
3.00	36	7.9	119	25.5
4.00	15	3.3	87	18.6
5.00	8	1.8	39	8.4
6.00	0	0	17	3.6
Total	455	100.0	467	100.0

college. Given this restricted range, it is unlikely that educational attainment alone can explain exits from poverty. Nevertheless, we incorporate education as both an outcome and an intervening process, measured by a seven-point scale ranging from less than a sixth grade education (11% of the overall sample) to post–high school education (7%).

Follow-up information at age thirty-two on occupational attainment, economic status, wages, and job stability was collected by the Gluecks on both delinquents and controls. The measure of occupational attainment originally included eight categories, ranging from unskilled workers (e.g., laborers, janitors) to professionals (e.g., teachers, lawyers). However, less than five percent of the delinquents achieved professional or even semi-professional status. In fact, 75% of the delinquents cluster in the bottom two categories—unskilled and semi-skilled jobs. Because of this highly skewed distribution, the eight occupational groups were recoded into an ordered indicator of occupational status consisting of three categories: unskilled, semi-skilled, and skilled/professional. As expected, occupational outcomes for the control-group reflected a higher status: over half of the men achieved skilled or professional/managerial jobs.

Economic status is a three-category measure of the economic condition of the men at age thirty-two, ranging from dependence on welfare (continuous receipt of outside aid) to financial independence with savings and investments. We also coded average weekly income at age thirty-two, ranging from under $60 to over $200.

To capture differences in attachment to work, job stability is measured by a standardized index that combines three interrelated variables—employed at age thirty-two, length of time employed on present or most recent job (ranging from less than 3 months to 48 months or more), and work habits at ages twenty-five to thirty-two. Individuals were classified as having poor work habits if they were unreliable in the work setting or if they failed to give any effort to the job; fair work habits were characterized by a generally good job performance except for periodic absences from work or periods of unemployment; good work habits referred to reliable performance on the job as noted by the employer as well as instances in which the subject was considered an asset to the organization. Cronbach's alpha reliability is .78 for job stability at age thirty-two.[4]

For ease of presentation, we constructed a summary scale of socioeconomic achievement at age thirty-two. The SES scale was formed by summing standardized indicators of occupational attainment, economic status, job stability, and wages (Cronbach's alpha = .83 for the delinquents and .79 for the nondelinquent controls).[5]

We were fortunate to gain access to information from a follow-up study of the control group at age forty-seven originally collected as part of the Study of Adult Development (see Vaillant 1983). Using information from the age forty-seven assessment on housing (e.g., value, size of home), detailed occupation, and educational attainment (Vaillant 1983: 324), the Hollingshead and Redlich (1958) social-class scale was constructed for each of the control-group subjects. Considering the historical context, the Hollingshead scale is directly relevant to assessing SES outcomes among the Glueck men.

Our models of adult socioeconomic achievement also include central variables from the status attainment tradition: father's occupation, parent's education, and family economic status. Given the historical context and study design, the SES background was low—less than a third of the parents attended high school, and most fathers were concentrated in low-status jobs. The latter is represented by a three-category indicator of father's occupation ranging from unskilled (e.g., laborer, janitor, elevator operator) to skilled or semi-skilled (e.g., plumber, electrician, public service) to professional/managerial (e.g., shopkeeper, lawyer). Education is a dichotomous variable where a one indicates that the subject's parent(s) attended high school (30%). To tap variations in family economic status, we created a standardized (z-score) index comprising the average weekly income of the family (per person) and the family's financial independence. The latter measures whether the family was living in comfortable circumstances (having enough savings to cover four months of financial stress), marginal circumstances (little or no savings but only occasional dependence on outside aid), or financially dependent (continuous receipt of outside aid for support). A high score on the resulting index means that the boy's family enjoyed relatively high per-capita income in addition to financial savings.

To account for individual differences not captured by the delinquent/control group design, we examine three measures of prior antisocial behavior: (1) the average annual frequency of official arrests up to age seventeen while not incarcerated; (2) a composite "unofficial" scale ranging from 1 to 26 of self-, parent-, and teacher-reports of delinquent behavior (e.g, stealing, vandalism) and other misconduct (e.g, truancy, running away) not necessarily known to the police (see Sampson and Laub 1993: 51); and (3) a dichotomous indicator of whether the subject engaged in violent and habitual temper tantrums while growing up (39% of delinquents; 7% of controls). The latter teacher- and parent-reported measure refers to tantrums that were "the predominant mode of response" by the child to difficult situations growing up (Glueck and Glueck 1950: 152), corresponding to the indicator used by Caspi (1987). Finally, we consider individual differences in intelligence as measured by the Wechsler-Bellevue IQ test (mean score = 93; range = 53 to 130).

Research Strategy and Key Findings

In order to fully examine the effects of adolescent competence on later adult outcomes we analyze data for both delinquents and controls. As mentioned above, the Gluecks' research design maximized differences in childhood antisocial behavior yielding two qualitatively distinct samples that are treated separately in the analyses below (see also Sampson and Laub 1993: 148; Vaillant 1983: 278). The examination of these two similar yet different samples will provide a powerful test of the long-term reach of adolescent competence.

We begin our analyses by examining the relationship between adolescent competence and educational attainment among the delinquent and nondelinquent controls. Since it is well known that family background and measured intelligence are important predictors of educational attainment (see, for example, Sewell, Hauser, and Wolfe 1980), we include these key variables in our multivariate models in order to assess the independent effects of adolescent competence. Following Clausen (1991, 1993), we expect that adolescent competence will be positively related to educational attainment among both delinquents and controls.

The data in Table 2 (Model 1) show that adolescent competence is significantly related to educational attainment at age twenty-five among the delin-

Table 2
Estimated Coefficients for Regression of Educational Attainment on Family Background Characteristics, IQ, Childhood Antisocial Behavior, and Adolescent Competence, Delinquent Group

| | Educational attainment at age 25 | |
	Model 1	Model 2
IQ score	.04**	.04**
	(8.93)	(8.98)
Parent's SES	.02	.01
	(.47)	(.17)
Father's occupation	.15	.10
	(1.57)	(1.03)
Parent's education	.18	.25
	(1.44)	(1.92)
Juvenile arrests	—	−.14
		(−.63)
Unofficial delinquency	—	−.04**
		(−2.81)
Tantrums	—	−.06
		(−.50)
Adolescent competence	.33**	.28**
	(6.33)	(5.04)
Constant	−1.74**	−1.06*
	(−3.92)	(−2.16)
Adj. R^2	.36	.36
N of Cases	383	369

Note: Numbers in parentheses are t-statistics.
  *$p < .05$ **$p < .01$ (two-tailed tests)

quent group (B = .29), despite controlling for measured intelligence (B = .41) and several family background variables. Interestingly, for this delinquent sample, none of the family background factors are significantly related to later educational attainment. Consistent with Clausen, we find that adolescent competence emerges as an important influence on later educational attainment among this group of disadvantaged youth who were institutionalized and officially stigmatized for their delinquent behavior.

Recognizing the largely unappreciated reality of continuity in deviant behavior across divergent life-course settings (Sampson and Laub 1993, chapter 6), in Model 2 we control for antisocial behavior during childhood and adolescence using three key measures (see Table 2). Again, we find that measured intelligence and adolescent competence both have independent effects on educational attainment (B = .42 and .24, respectively). Unofficial delinquency is the only other variable significantly related to educational attainment (B = −.12).

Table 3 examines the same two models for the nondelinquent controls. In Model 1, measured intelligence, parent's SES, and adolescent competence are significantly related to later educational attainment. Intelligence has the largest influence (B = .40), followed by adolescent competence (B = .26), and parent's SES (B = .18). Model 2 takes into account antisocial behavior, and overall the results hold. Similar to the delinquent group, unofficial delinquency is significantly related to educational attainment among the controls (B = −.16).

In short, it appears that adolescent competence is related to later educational attainment, despite controlling for measured intelligence, key family background variables, and antisocial behavior during childhood and adolescence. Moreover, the results are virtually identical for both delinquents and nondelinquent controls. Thus, for this sample of disadvantaged and delinquent men, adolescent competence appears to be an important factor in accounting for later educational attainment.

Next, we turn to an examination of the relationship between adolescent competence and adult socioeconomic outcomes using our summary scale of SES at age thirty-two. Because prior research has established that family background, measured intelligence, and educational attainment predict later status attainment (see, for example, Featherman 1980; Sewell, Hauser, and Wolf 1980), we include these variables in our analyses. Following Clausen (1991, 1993), we expect that adolescent competence will be positively related to higher socioeconomic achievement among the delinquent and nondelinquent controls.

The data in Table 4 (Model 1) show that measured intelligence, father's occupation, and adolescent competence are significantly related to socioeconomic achievement at age thirty-two among the delinquent group. In fact, adolescent competence has the largest influence of these three variables (B = .20). Note

Table 3

Estimated Coefficients for Regression of Educational Attainment on Family Background Characteristics, IQ, Childhood Antisocial Behavior, and Adolescent Competence, Control Group

| | Educational attainment at age 25 | |
	Model 1	Model 2
IQ score	.05**	.05**
	(9.07)	(9.37)
Parent's SES	.18**	.15**
	(4.39)	(3.59)
Father's occupation	.03	.02
	(.29)	(.16)
Parent's education	.04	.03
	(.26)	(.22)
Juvenile arrests	—	−.28
		(−1.84)
Unofficial delinquency	—	−.11**
		(−3.89)
Tantrums	—	−.32
		(−1.30)
Adolescent competence	.27**	.20**
	(5.79)	(4.19)
Constant	−1.15*	−.61
	(−2.14)	(−1.14)
Adj. R^2	.34	.38
N of Cases	407	407

Note: Numbers in parentheses are t-statistics.
  $*p < .05$ $**p < .01$ (two-tailed tests)

though the R^2 is much lower in Table 4 compared with the R^2 in Table 2. Model 2 displayed in Table 4 includes educational attainment at age twenty-five as a predictor of SES at age thirty-two. Interestingly, although adolescent competence and father's occupation remain significant (B = .15 for both measures), educational attainment seems to mediate the effect of measured intelligence. As it turns out, the largest predictor of socioeconomic achievement at age thirty-two is educational attainment at age twenty-five (B = .18).

Table 5 presents the same multivariate models for socioeconomic achievement at age thirty-two among the nondelinquent controls. Three variables emerge as significantly related to the summary SES scale: measured intelligence, parent's SES, and adolescent competence (B = .29, .14, and .13, respectively). Importantly, when educational attainment is included for the controls (see Model 2), adolescent competence becomes insignificant. It appears then that educational attainment mediates the effect of adolescent competence

Table 4

Estimated Coefficients for Regression of Summary SES Scale on Family Background Characteristics, IQ, Educational Attainment, and Adolescent Competence, Delinquent Group

	Summary SES Scale at age 32	
	Model 1	Model 2
IQ score	.01**	.00
	(2.60)	(1.28)
Parent's SES	.04	.04
	(1.67)	(1.63)
Father's occupation	.23**	.21**
	(3.00)	(2.68)
Parent's education	.05	.02
	(.52)	(.24)
Educational attainment	—	.11**
		(−2.58)
Adolescent competence	.14**	.10*
	(3.44)	(2.39)
Constant	−1.45**	−1.25**
	(−4.12)	(−3.49)
Adj. R^2	.13	.14
N of Cases	305	305

Note: Numbers in parentheses are *t*-statistics.
　　$*p < .05$　　$**p < .01$ (two-tailed tests)

for the controls. As for the delinquent group, the strongest predictor of socioeconomic achievement at age thirty-two among the controls is educational attainment at age twenty-five (B = .27).

Overall, adolescent competence is related to socioeconomic outcomes in adulthood independent of IQ and family background. However, when educational attainment is taken into account, the consequences of adolescent competence varies. For the delinquents, adolescent competence still maintains a significant relationship to later socioeconomic outcomes. For the nondelinquent controls, educational attainment mediates the effect of adolescent competence on later socioeconomic outcomes. Regardless of these differential processes, our analyses demonstrate that adolescent competence is an important concept in accounting for later socioeconomic achievement among economically disadvantaged youth generally, and, in the case of the 500 delinquents, officially stigmatized youth.

In Table 6, we examine the effects of adolescent competence on socioeconomic achievement at age forty-seven for the control-group subjects. Unfortunately, a comparable measure for the delinquent group subjects is not available. Nevertheless, because of the long-term nature of these follow-up

Table 5
Estimated Coefficients for Regression of Summary SES Scale on
Family Background Characteristics, IQ, Educational Attainment,
and Adolescent Competence, Control Group

	Summary SES Scale at age 32	
	Model 1	Model 2
IQ score	.02**	.01**
	(5.58)	(3.15)
Parent's SES	.07**	.05
	(2.90)	(1.93)
Father's occupation	−.00	.00
	(−.02)	(.00)
Parent's education	−.14	−.14
	(−1.74)	(−1.82)
Educational attainment	—	.13**
		(4.54)
Adolescent competence	.06*	.03
	(2.41)	(1.19)
Constant	−1.93**	−1.73**
	(−6.04)	(−5.51)
Adj. R^2	.14	.18
N of Cases	374	371

Note: Numbers in parentheses are t-statistics.
$*p < .05$ $**p < .01$ (two-tailed tests)

data, we decided to present these results here. The data show that measured intelligence, parent's SES, and adolescent competence are significantly related to Hollingshead SES at age forty-seven (B = .26, .17, and .19, respectively). Thus, our main variable of interest, adolescent competence, has a strong influence on adult outcomes more than thirty years after adolescence.

However, for the control-group subjects, when educational attainment is included in the analysis (Model 2), the effects of adolescent competence and measured intelligence appear to be mediated. The only significant predictors of Hollingshead SES at age forty-seven are parent's SES (B = .10) and educational attainment (B = .44). Thus, for the control-group subjects, the long-term effects of adolescent competence are indirect and seem to work through educational attainment, which is, in turn, related to a variety of socioeconomic outcomes as captured by our summary measure.

Life-History Data

In this section, we present four qualitative life histories drawn from the delinquent group subjects. We use these life histories to illustrate the relationship

Table 6
Estimated Coefficients for Regression of Hollingshead SES on
Family Background Characteristics, IQ, Educational Attainment,
and Adolescent Competence, Control Group

	Hollingshead SES at age 47	
	Model 1	Model 2
IQ score	.02**	.01
	(5.08)	(1.54)
Parent's SES	.09**	.05*
	(3.61)	(2.26)
Father's occupation	.01	−.00
	(.15)	(−.08)
Parent's education	−.04	−.06
	(−.44)	(−.78)
Educational attainment	—	.21**
		(−8.08)
Adolescent competence	.10**	.04
	(3.61)	(1.61)
Constant	−.46	−.09
	(−1.40)	(−.29)
Adj. R^2	.17	.30
N of Cases	371	368

Note: Numbers in parentheses are *t*-statistics.
   *$p < .05$ **$p < .01$ (two-tailed tests)

between competence in adolescence and adult outcomes with respect to work, marriage, social deviance, and crime. Our goal is to integrate these life-history data with the quantitative analyses presented above. In particular, we hope to use the life-history data to explicate the mechanisms by which competence in adolescence (or the lack thereof) assists (or hinders) the Glueck men in meeting the opportunities and challenges encountered in the transition to adulthood (see Clausen 1991: 805).

The first two life histories we present were selected because they varied in our quantitative classification of stability. We specifically focus on both ends of stability: (1) a delinquent subject (Tom) who had low competence in adolescence and low job stability as an adult; and (2) a delinquent subject (Ray) who had high competence in adolescence and high job stability as an adult. These data allow us to examine the sources of continuity on both ends of the competence dimension.

Continuity in Lives

Tom was one of the delinquent subjects selected for the *UJD* study. By his own admission, he began stealing at the age of nine. Tom maintained that he was influenced by other boys in his neighborhood. He fell into a group that was stealing small items from neighborhood stores. A report in his case folder from a local social-service agency stated that "Tom was referred for conduct disturbance, and he is sexually precocious, steals, fights, sets fires, plays truant from school, engages in temper tantrums, and is defiant, and unmanageable at home."

This description was confirmed in an interview with Tom's father who told the Gluecks' interviewer: "When we moved to this neighborhood at the time of my second marriage, that was the pay-off. The boy got in with bad companions, older than himself, soon he joined a gang—a tough one—and soon he began stealing." The boy's father went on to say that he felt that Tom was led into stealing by older boys who used him because he was younger.

According to the narratives, Tom received practically no supervision or training from his parents. He lived in an disorganized family situation that was exacerbated by considerable residential mobility. At the age of six, Tom would run away frequently, often staying away for days at a time. During this time, he was also frequently truant from school. Tom's parents gave him 75 cents a day to buy his meals in a restaurant. Overall, his level of parental supervision was lax. Typically, both of his parents were out nights. His biological parents separated for a short period, while his mother went to live with relatives. Both parents accused the other of having affairs.

Tom lived with his father and stepmother in a rather large lodging house. According to Tom, his father drank constantly and was erratic in his discipline style. The narrative data in the social investigation interview indicated that Tom was subjected to frequent whippings by both his father and stepmother. Other than these whippings the parents paid little attention to his behavior. There was little affection between Tom and his parents.

Based on quantitative information from the Wave 1 interview, we categorized Tom as having low competence in adolescence as defined above. As evidenced above, Tom had many of the family characteristics that lead to low adolescence competence (see Clausen 1993). In Tom's case, low adolescent competence manifested itself in adulthood. As an adult, Tom lacked direction. The Gluecks' interviewer remarked that Tom was "immature for his age." As revealed below, Tom seemed unable to accept responsibilities across various domains of life. Moreover, his adult life was characterized by a lack of planning and foresight—the qualities of low adolescent competence as suggested by Clausen. For example, at the Wave 2 interview (age twenty-five), it was reported that Tom served in the U.S. Army for 69 months during age seventeen to twenty-five period. He entered the Army in 1943 and was discharged in 1945. He re-enlisted and was discharged three years later. He enlisted for a third time and was discharged two years later. During his last stint, he had received a "dishonorable discharge" for going AWOL. According service records, Tom went AWOL when his request to stay in the U.S. was denied.

Tom met his wife while he was in the Army and stationed in Puerto Rico. They married after a six-month courtship. The narrative data contained evidence that the couple experienced "strained relations." Tom was unable to accept the responsibilities of marriage and family life. For example, Tom did not discuss with his wife his intention of re-enlisting in the Army. Moreover, he did not correspond with his wife and family while he was in the Army. He also deserted his wife when financial pressures mounted. The couple had no savings and, according to interviewer notes, Tom was "always borrowing money."

Before he went into the Army, Tom had worked irregularly as a farmhand and laborer. According to interviewer notes, he often pretended to have work when he didn't even have a job. His wife claimed he was "just plain lazy." Throughout the age seventeen to age twenty-five period, Tom made no effort to improve his occupational status.

At the Wave 3 interview (age thirty-two), Tom was still married, but it was reported that he frequently deserted his wife. According to the narrative information, the couple had "poor conjugal relations." Their child had been placed in foster care because he was "unruly." Both parents were impatient and cruel with the child as well as neglectful. Tom had no stable pattern of employment whatsoever. In fact, it was reported that he had 60 jobs over a two-year period. He would quit a job on a whim or a spur of temper. His sister described him as "unreliable and irresponsible." Tom had developed alcoholic trends and it was reported that he "drank to excess." His official criminal offense history revealed one arrest as an adult for vagrancy.

Now consider the life history of Ray, another delinquent subject in the *UJD* study. Ray started stealing when he was eleven or twelve, "because most of the boys in the neighborhood did it." In fact, Ray's older brother was involved in delinquency and Ray's father thought that Ray unwisely followed his brother's example. During adolescence, Ray was arrested for stubbornness, burglary, auto theft, and larceny.

According to the narratives, Ray's mother died when he was born and he was raised by his father and a series of housekeepers. Ray's father was described as a "harsh disciplinarian" who was very strict and unrelenting. Ray would occasionally run away from home to escape from his "harsh and exacting" father. During this time, he was also frequently truant from school. There was little affection between Ray and his father.

Although Ray expressed a "casual attitude toward school" during adolescence, he received B's and C's in school and did not repeat any grades. His teachers reported that "he was not a classroom problem." Ray's ambition was to secure a skilled job. Ray left school at age 15 and 9 months, after he completed the ninth grade. Based on our measure of adolescent competence, Ray was classified in the high range among the delinquent subjects.

At the Wave 2 interview, Ray was living with his wife and child in a working-class neighborhood in Boston. He was almost twenty-three at the time of his marriage while his wife was nineteen. The couple dated for over a year before they married. According to narrative data in his interview, Ray appeared to take his family responsibilities very seriously "claiming that he has to work almost 68 hours a week in order to provide for his family." As for employment, Ray worked regularly since he married. He was afraid to change jobs because he did not want to lose any income. At the age twenty-five interview, he was working as a truck driver and a fruit and vegetable clerk, a job he had held for the last 24 months.

At the Wave 3 interview, Ray was still living with his wife and now two children in the Boston area. The couple appeared to get along quite well. The Gluecks' interviewer wrote that Ray's "wife seems to have had a good effect on the subject. . . . Subject appears to take wife's confidence in him and uses it as a springboard for ambitious future plans." Ray's wife was a high-school graduate while he dropped out in the ninth grade. According to interviewer notes, Ray's wife was continually planning for his advancement.

At age thirty-two, Ray was working as a truck repairman, a job he held for the last three years. During the interview, Ray stated that "he likes the type of work he is doing now and will do his best to make good on it." Although he purchased his house in Boston, he was saving money so that he could build his own house in New Hampshire. Ray wanted to leave Boston in order to provide a better environment for his kids. Ray took his role as father and husband seriously. He had ambitious plans to make life better for his family.

Change in Lives

In this section, we turn to the issue of change. Although not addressed in our quantitative analyses, a key question is: How do adolescents with low competence turn their lives around? How do they become successful in adulthood? Conversely, it is important to ask: Why do some competent adolescents have poor adult outcomes? What events change their life-course trajectory? The life-history data presented here provide clues to begin to answer these complex questions.

First, we examine the life history of Joey, a delinquent subject who had high competence in adolescence as defined above and low job stability as an adult. We then present the life history of Mario, a delinquent subject who scored low on our competence measure in adolescence and yet achieved high job stability as an adult. This latter case is of interest because it sheds light on the processes involved in overcoming childhood disadvantage (see Vaillant 1993, chapter 12).

Joey was selected for the *UJD* study as a delinquent. His first arrest (a larceny) occurred at age eleven and he was arrested three times prior to his first incarceration experience. According to information in the Wave 1 interview, Joey received good grades in school and he wanted to obtain a semi-skilled or skilled job. His teacher related that he was "quick to learn." After interviewing the boy, the psychiatrist reported that Joey was "conscientious." According to our quantitative scale of competence, Joey scored in the upper range for adolescent competence. Based on this measure we would have expected that Joey was on his way to a successful transition to adulthood.

At the Wave 2 interview (age twenty-five), Joey was "at sea" working for the U.S. Merchant Service. He had worked as a seaman since he was seventeen, the age he was released from reform school. Joey's mother stated that he worked quite regularly and, in fact, one year he was home only three weeks in the whole year. According to the narratives, Joey intended to make a career of the Merchant Service. Joey was a member of the Seafarers International Union. He appeared to be "unhappy at any shore job," i.e., work not involving maritime activities. His criminal record between the ages of seventeen and twenty-five included 4 arrests, but no jail time. One offense was for purse snatching. Joey stated that he was drinking prior to committing that crime. It was also reported that he "drank to excess" every weekend. During this period, Joey remained single.

At the Wave 3 interview, Joey was again "at sea" working for the Merchant Marine. He was still single at age thirty-two. His problem with drinking had continued and he was characterized as an "alcoholic" in the case files. According to the narratives, Joey worked only when he needed money and his poor work habits were due to his drinking and his desire "not to work regularly." Joey remained an able-bodied seaman, but he did not advance in his position since the age twenty-five interview. According to Joey's sister, he had been in trouble with several shipping lines because of his drinking and insubordination. Joey was "logged" by numerous shipping companies, which meant he would not be hired to work on that particular shipping line again.

As further evidence of Joey's difficulties as an adult, he was arrested several times for being drunk both in the United States and Europe. According to his sister, "When ashore he drinks and does not eat; when at sea, he eats and does not drink." She went on to describe her brother as an alcoholic who was vicious and abusive when drunk. The narrative stated that Joey had assaulted both his mother and sister in the past. It was also reported that he intentionally did not take his prescribed medicine for an ear ailment in order to "loaf and collect benefits from union under the status of unfit for duty." It was reported by multiple sources that Joey began drinking to excess when he entered the U.S. Merchant Service at the age of seventeen.

The life history of Mario provides evidence of a different kind of change over the life-course trajectory. Mario became involved with delinquency at the age of ten (e.g., hopping on street cars and stealing small articles). Although he came from a close-knit family, Mario was not well supervised as a young teenager. In his interview at age fourteen, Mario told the Gluecks' interviewer how he frequently stayed out late at night and came in after his parents were in bed, so they never knew what time he came home. Mario's parents fluctuated between "lax" and "erratic" in disciplining him.

Mario also reported at the Wave 1 interview that he wanted to "stop school now." He was in ninth grade at the time of the interview. During his schooling, he had repeated two grades in school and his teacher stated that he had "reached his intellectual ceiling in 8th grade" (despite a verbal IQ score of 93). Although Mario received average grades in all subjects, he had no interest whatsoever in high school. He eventually dropped out of school at the age of sixteen. Overall, Mario's level of adolescent competence was scored as low on our scale.

At the Wave 2 interview, Mario was living with his mother and siblings in a neighborhood in Boston. His father had died when he was almost twenty-two. Mario had served 37 months in the U.S. Marine Corp (January 1943 to February 1946) and received an "honorable discharge." Most of this time he spent in the Pacific theater participating in two major battles. After the war, Mario received two medals including a good conduct medal. Although he remained single during this period, he received strong family support during his transition from military to civilian life. In the narratives, there was evidence of strong attachments to his mother and siblings. Mario had worked as a painter— a skill he acquired when he was incarcerated at the Lyman School—but he was "in-between jobs" at the time of the interview. Mario also received financial support (Readjustment Compensation) from the Veteran's Administration.

At the Wave 3 interview, it was reported that Mario had married and had two children. At the time of his marriage, Mario was twenty-five and his wife was nineteen. Unlike Mario, his wife was a high-school graduate. From the narratives, there was evidence of strong marital attachment and the couple were described as "devoted to improving the lives of their sons." The Gluecks' interviewer described the subject as "well-adjusted" with "drive, ambition, and good common sense."

Mario was employed full-time as a plumber and gas fitter. In addition, he did private plumbing at night. Mario learned this trade in an "on the job training program" sponsored by the Veterans Administration. He attended this program for two years with the support of the G.I. Bill. Mario decided to take advantage of the G.I. Bill shortly after his marriage. In the narratives, it was reported that he was a steady, reliable worker and he did not experience any unemployment during the age twenty-five to thirty-two period. Moreover, at the age thirty-two interview, Mario was saving money so that he could start his own plumbing business. Mario was not involved in any criminal activity as an adult, nor did he drink alcohol or use drugs.

As the life histories of Tom, Ray, Joey, and Mario illustrate, selecting cases that reflect continuity and change over the life course reveal how adolescent competence influences later adult development. Moreover, these life histories stimulate important questions for further analyses. On the positive side, Ray's life shows how adolescent competence can help an individual to decide what is important, to have the determination to reach goals, and to make commitments to self and others (see Clausen 1993: 169). As reflective of adolescent competence, Ray has exhibited a substantial level of maturity across the life course. In contrast, Tom's life shows how low competence leads to a lack of direction over the life course and an immature outlook. Moreover, in Tom's life major transitions such as a change in marital status or moving from the military to civilian life are fraught with difficulty. Tom does not handle these life transitions well, and subsequently, he does not successfully manage any of his adult roles as worker, provider, husband, and father in a responsible manner.

Examining the "off diagonal" cases is an important way of stimulating questions for future research. For example, what is the relationship between adolescent competence and alcohol abuse, both as an adolescent and as an adult? The life history of Joey suggests the onset of serious drinking in a unique setting like the Merchant Marines can overwhelm the potential of high competence in adolescence. This is consistent with Vaillant's research on alcoholism, which establishes that alcoholism is a life event that can throw a person off track. While alcoholism may be related to personality traits, it is also the case that it can cause dramatic transformations over the life span (see Vaillant 1983).

On the other hand, certain features of military service may help some men overcome the negative effects of low competence in adolescence. As exhibited in the life history of Mario, the military, especially post-military benefits like G.I. Bill, seemed to provide a means for learning a trade—a form of competence that was not realized in adolescence (see also Sampson and Laub 1996; Werner and Smith 1992: 114–116; and Elder 1986). In this case, competence in the work setting coupled with a successful marriage facilitated adult achievement, and ultimately, escape from poverty. However, it is important to recognize that military experiences are not homogeneous, but need to be placed in a larger context of time and place in one's life course. For example, Tom's third stint in the Army lead to a dishonorable discharge. In fact, Tom's life history supports the idea that low competence in adolescence can spill over to a variety of settings in adulthood including the military (see also Gottfredson and Hirschi 1990: 164–65).

The qualitative life-history narratives also suggest that factors besides adolescent competence are important in fostering strong ties to work and marriage in adulthood. It is interesting that Mario, who scored low on competence and high on job stability, had a strong attachment to his mother as an adult. Perhaps positive parental relationships in adulthood along with important attributes of marital partners can facilitate successful adult development. For example, Ray's life history reveals that not only do wives play an influential role with respect to emotional support and companionship, but also that wives can assist their husbands in planning for the future.

Conclusions and Implications

Consistent with the research of Clausen (1991, 1993), we find that adolescent competence emerges as an important influence on later socioeconomic outcomes, despite controlling for measured intelligence, key family background variables, and antisocial behavior during childhood and adolescence. What is particularly noteworthy about these findings is that they are derived from a sample of disadvantaged youth, half of which were institutionalized and officially stigmatized for their delinquent behavior. Many of our results are virtually identical for both delinquents and nondelinquent controls.

One exception occurred when educational attainment was taken into account. For the delinquents, adolescent competence maintained a significant relationship to later socioeconomic outcomes. For the nondelinquent controls, educational attainment mediates the effect of adolescent competence on later socioeconomic outcomes. Thus, for nondelinquents the long-term effect of adolescent competence is indirect. Regardless of these differential processes, our analyses demonstrate that adolescent competence is an important concept in accounting for later socioeconomic achievement among economically disadvantaged youth generally, and, in the case of the 500 delinquents, officially stigmatized youth.

Our findings have important implications for both research and practice relating to adolescents. Our results suggest that adolescent competence is a major factor in understanding socioeconomic achievement in adulthood among disadvantaged youth in the period from 1940 to 1960. Indeed, adolescent competence as defined here appears as important as more traditional variables in the status-attainment literature like parental occupation/education and intelligence. More research needs to be directed to the question of *why* adolescent competence is such a salient concept. It is not clear from our analyses what the precise mechanisms are by which adolescent competence emerges as an important factor across the life course. For instance, does adolescent competence provide delinquent youth with the capacity to take advantage of opportunities that emerge in adulthood with respect to marriage, work, and the military? In contrast, for nondelinquent youth, does adolescent competence lead to success in school which in turn facilitates socioeconomic success in adulthood? A more fundamental question concerns the extent to which adolescent competence is bound by historical context and specific to particular race and sex groupings (in our case, white males). More research is needed on the meaning of competence for adolescent women and minorities growing up in current social, economic, and political circumstances. Nevertheless, our research has important implications for practice. To the extent that one can generalize from historical data such as those used here, our findings support intervention strategies that promote competence through the training of social skills early on in the life course in order to promote successful development and avoid juvenile delinquency and antisocial behavior (see, e.g., Coie, Underwood, and Lochman 1991; Tremblay et al. 1991; and Zigler, Taussig, and Black 1992). Moreover, our findings are also supportive of efforts to enhance competence among juvenile delinquents in order to assist them in adapting to later social experiences in a healthy and successful manner.

In short, our findings point to competence as a key concept for future research and practice relating to adólescent development and its consequences. More research is clearly needed on how adolescent competence facilitates successful adult development. At the same time, more attention should be given to interventions that develop or strengthen adolescent competence among disadvantaged youth, especially those who are involved in crime and antisocial behavior. If nothing else, our study demonstrates that adolescent competence is related to adult outcomes over the long term. Given the long-term reach of adolescent competence, more research should be devoted to understanding why this is the case.

Acknowledgments

This chapter was prepared for the Character and Competence Research Program. The data are derived from the Sheldon and Eleanor Glueck archives of the Harvard Law School Library, currently on long-term loan to the Henry A. Murray Research Center of Radcliffe College. This research was generously supported by the Russell Sage Foundation (Grant #998.958) and the Character and Competence Research Program at Radcliffe College. We thank George Vaillant for his assistance in allowing us to code a key outcome measure. Research assistance by Jinney Smith and Sandra Gauvreau is also gratefully acknowledged. A version of this chapter was presented at the Biennial Meeting of the Society for Research on Adolescence, March 9, 1996. We thank Anne Colby, Jackie James, and Dan Hart for their helpful comments on this chapter and their suggestions throughout this project.

Notes

1. Whether one refers to these notions as indicative of competence or resilience may well depend on disciplinary perspectives. As defined below, competence is a broad concept covering a range of skills, attitudes, and behaviors. Resilience conveys the notion of elasticity, i.e., the ability to stretch but not break. Since our work is building upon the work of John Clausen, we will use the term competence throughout this chapter.

2. In a study of personality types employing factor analysis of Q-sort data, Robins et al. (1996) identified a cluster of children for whom the label "resilient" is appro-

priate. Using cross-sectional data, they found resilient children were more likely to be intelligent, successful in school, unlikely to be delinquent, and relatively free of psychopathology.

3. Our measure of adolescent competence is similar to the dimension labeled "conscientiousness" in factor analyses of personality inventories (see, for example, McCrae and Costa 1990). The factor conscientiousness includes traits such as conscientious, hardworking, well organized, punctual, ambitious, and persevering (McCrae and Costa 1990: 3). Research has shown that this trait is highly correlated with educational achievement in adolescence (Digman 1989) and longevity over the life span (Friedman et al. 1995).

4. Suggesting an initial balance of convergent and discriminant validity, socioeconomic achievement outcomes were significantly correlated in a moderate to strong positive direction. For example, occupational status is correlated .55 with wages, .43 with economic status, and .49 with job stability among delinquents. The corresponding correlations for the control group are .54, .47 and .39 (all coefficients significant at $p < .05$).

5. Because preliminary analysis showed that missing data on the individual SES indicators were randomly distributed with respect to key independent variables, a conditional imputation procedure was used to preserve cases in calculating the summary scale. The imputation incorporated predicted values of missing SES measures from the set of observed SES measures.

References

Baumrind, D. 1978. "Parental Disciplinary Patterns and Social Competence in Children." *Youth and Society* 9: 239–76.
————. 1989. "The Permanence of Change and the Impermanence of Stability." *Human Development* 32: 187–95.
Caspi, A. 1987. "Personality in the Life Course." *Journal of Personality and Social Psychology* 53: 1203–13.
Clausen, J. A. 1991. "Adolescent Competence and the Shaping of the Life Course." *American Journal of Sociology* 96: 805–42.
————. 1993. *American Lives: Looking Back at the Children of the Great Depression.* New York: The Free Press.
Coie, J. D., M. Underwood, and J. E. Lochman. 1991. "Programmatic Intervention with Aggressive Children in the School Setting." In *The Development and Treatment of Childhood Aggression,* ed. D. J. Pepler and K. H. Rubin, 389–410. Hillsdale, NJ: Erlbaum.
Digman, J. M. 1989. "Five Robust Trait Dimensions: Development, Stability, and Utility." *Journal of Personality* 57: 195–214.
Elder, G. H., Jr. 1986. "Military Times and Turning Points in Men's Lives." *Developmental Psychology* 22: 233–45.
Featherman, D. L. 1980. "Schooling and Occupational Careers: Constancy and Change in Worldly Success." In *Constancy and Change in Human Development,* ed. O. G. Brim, Jr. and J. Kagan, 675–738. Cambridge, MA: Harvard University Press.
Friedman, H. S., J. S. Tucker, J. E. Schwartz, C. Tomlinson-Keasey, L. R. Martin,

D. L. Wingard, and M. H. Criqui. 1995. "Psychosocial and Behavioral Predictors of Longevity: The Aging and Death of 'Termites' " *American Psychologist* 50: 69–78.

Glueck, S. and E. Glueck. 1950. *Unraveling Juvenile Delinquency.* New York: Commonwealth Fund.

———. 1968. *Delinquents and Nondelinquents in Perspective.* Cambridge: Harvard University Press.

Gottfredson, M., and T. Hirschi. 1990. *A General Theory of Crime.* Stanford, CA: Stanford University Press.

Gullotta, T. P., G. R. Adams, and R. Montemayor, eds. 1990. *Developing Social Competency in Adolescence.* Newbury Park, CA: Sage.

Hollingshead, A. B., and F. C. Redlich. 1958. *Social Class and Mental Illness.* New York: Wiley.

Laub, J. H., and R. J. Sampson. 1993. "Turning Points in the Life Course: Why Change Matters to the Study of Crime." *Criminology* 31: 301–25.

Mann, L., R. Harmoni, and C. Power. 1989. "Adolescent Decision-Making: The Development of Competence." *Journal of Adolescence* 12: 265–78.

McCord, J. 1991. "Competence in Long-term Perspective." *Psychiatry* 54: 227–37.

McCrae, R. R., and P. T. Costa, Jr. 1990. *Personality in Adulthood.* New York: Guilford Press.

Robins, R. W., O. P. John, A. Caspi, T. E. Moffitt, and M. Stouthamer-Loeber. 1996. "Resilient, Overcontrolled, and Undercontrolled Boys: Three Replicable Personality Types." *Journal of Personality and Social Psychology* 70: 157–71.

Sampson, R. J., and J. H. Laub. 1993. *Crime in the Making: Pathways and Turning Points through Life.* Cambridge, MA: Harvard University Press.

———. 1996. "Socioeconomic Achievement in the Life Course of Disadvantaged Men: Military Service as a Turning Point, circa 1940–1965." *American Sociological Review* 61: 347–67.

Sewell, W. H., R. M. Hauser, and W. C. Wolf. 1980. "Sex, Schooling, and Occupational Status." *American Journal of Sociology* 86: 551–83.

Tremblay, R. E., J. McCord, H. Boileau, P. Charlebois, C. Gagnon, M. LeBlanc, and S. Larivee. 1991. "Can Disruptive Boys Be Helped to Become Competent? *Psychiatry* 54: 148–60.

Vaillant, G. E. 1983. *The Natural History of Alcoholism.* Cambridge: Harvard University Press.

———. 1993. *The Wisdom of the Ego.* Cambridge: Harvard University Press.

Werner, E. E., and R. S. Smith. 1992. *Overcoming the Odds: High Risk Children From Birth to Adulthood.* Ithaca, NY: Cornell University Press.

Wolfgang, M. E., T. P. Thornberry, and R. M. Figlio, 1987. *From Boy to Man, From Delinquency to Crime.* Chicago: University of Chicago Press.

Zigler, E., C. Taussig, and K. Black. 1992. "Early Childhood Intervention: A Promising Preventative for Juvenile Delinquency." *American Psychologist* 47: 997–1006.

CHAPTER FIVE

An Expert-Novice Approach To Assessing Implicit Models of the Self

JILL BOND CAIRE, PATRICIA PLINER,
AND SARAH C. STOKER

In optimal adult development, character and competence are inextricably related. Character, in the context of this research program, "refers to dimensions such as positive values, social responsibility, and moral commitment" (Henry A. Murray Research Center 1993). Yet, competence is also implied. Without it individuals would be unable to realize their values. Similarly, competence—the ability to function proficiently in a particular domain—without character denotes individuals with limited or destructive personal characteristics and values. Optimal functioning, then, requires not only that individuals be able to identify worthwhile goals, capacities, and interests, but that they also learn to cultivate them constructively.

Such a complex task of recognition and development requires well-defined useful models—ways of representing, prioritizing, and evaluating information—of one's goals, capacities, and potentials. Indeed, scientists take for granted the need for well-defined, coherent models to understand and utilize other complex systems. Is developing a well-defined, coherent model of their own equally complex system as important if individuals are going to be able to understand and utilize their own resources?

The purpose of this research project was to adapt an innovative, highly successful cognitive science approach to studying implicit mental models and their effect on functioning to the self: Specifically, how do implicit mental models of the self affect general functioning, including behavioral adaptation and psychological well-being? A significant body of investigations into the nature of expertise—the factors contributing to proficient functioning—suggests that strong relations exist between the quality of knowledge structures (mental models) and proficiency (Chi, Glaser, and Farr 1988; Gentner and Stevens 1983; Newell and Simon 1972; Simon 1992). Thus far, cognitive scientists have limited these studies to domains such as chess, school subjects, or physics, in which normative knowledge exists that is relatively easy to detail explicitly (Gentner and Stevens 1983). However, it is also important to know if similar relationships exist between individuals' implicit mental models of who they are and how they function more generally. It may be that individuals who readily solve personal problems, function optimally, and are, in effect, "experts" at living, have mental models of the self that differ from those of less functional individuals in the same ways as the models of chess, physics, and dinosaur experts differ from those of less proficient performers.

The idea that models of the self affect functioning is not new. Craik's (1943) hypothesis that people form mental models that affect their thinking and behavior included models of the self. Kelly's (1955) theory of personal constructs explicitly assigned to individuals the role of scientists whose behavior was determined by their models of the world, including the self. Self-schemas, "cognitive generalizations about the self . . . that organize and guide the processing of self-related information" (Markus 1977: 77) have also become a focus of research in social psychology (e.g., Cantor, Mischel, and Schwartz 1982; Rogers, Kuiper, and Kirker 1977; Derry and Kuiper 1981; Higgins 1987).

However, there are important differences between self-schemas and the mental models posited by cognitive psychologists (e.g., Johnson-Laird 1983). Personality/social psychology approaches typically do not evaluate self-schemas in terms of quality of information or usefulness. That is, personality/social psychologists do not characterize individual self-schemas as better or worse, useful or detrimental.

Further, Hazel Markus (1990) has noted that the principal weakness of current self-schema research in both clinical and social/personality fields has been its emphasis on content to the neglect of structure, especially of the overall self-system. In expert-novice studies, structural properties most clearly differentiate between the mental models of experts and novices in other domains. The models of experts not only possess more useful information; they are organized in a way that makes knowledge more accessible, functional, and efficient. Experts' knowledge is extensively cross-referenced, exhibiting a richer network of connections. Thus, without an understanding of the structure of models of the self, it is difficult to evaluate them and their effects on functioning.

Certainly, the neglect of structure by personality/social and clinical psychologists is not an absolute one, and, indeed, structural aspects of conceptual self-systems do appear to be related to adaptive and maladaptive functioning. Linville's (1982) research demonstrated that less complex self-structures are related to greater affective lability and depression. Further, in clinical psychology, Horowitz and Zilberg (1983: 286) noted that individuals with "advanced ego development" always exhibit a superordinate self-organization, "a larger structure that patterns interconnections between various self concepts." Conversely, poorly integrated conceptions of the self virtually define the predominant personality disorders (e.g., borderline and narcissistic) diagnosed today (American Psychiatric Association 1994).

Applying the expert-novice construct to mental models of the self can expand our methods for studying the self and increase our understanding of general functioning. First, the expert-novice construct has generated a number of well-developed methods for representing and evaluating both the content and structure of mental models. Second, the emphasis on functionality (how do people who function expertly in a given domain represent information differently than those who function poorly) has led to some remarkably successful applications in areas as diverse as remedial reading (Palincsar and Brown 1984), college physics (Gentner and Gentner 1983), and writing (Hayes and Flower 1986). For example, Palincsar and Brown (1984) used "think aloud" techniques to specify the implicit models of expert elementary school readers (i.e., specify their goals, assumptions, and representations). When Palincsar and Brown explicitly taught these models to remedial readers, they were able to increase the majority of the children's reading skills three to four grade-levels with only ten hours of instruction.

If, as is the case with models in other domains, better quality models of the self (who one is) are associated with better general functioning, it may be that we will be able to specify the types of models of the self that enhance general functioning. If we can specify better quality models of the self and the steps needed to create them, we may be able to teach individuals how to develop better models of themselves and thereby improve their capacity to function well in life.

Mental Model and Expert-Novice Research

Mental model (e.g., Gentner and Stevens 1983) and expert-novice studies (e.g., Bédard and Chi 1992) both developed from Newell and Simon's (1972) early investigations into the processes contributing to intelligent behavior. To ensure that they could identify differences, Newell and Simon began with a simple strategy. They selected especially skilled individuals (experts) and beginners (novices) in chess, gave them typical chess problems to solve, and asked them to "think aloud" while they solved them. Newell and Simon found that content and special capacities could not account for all the variability they observed. Many of the differences were better explained by how experts and novices differentially represent, organize, and use information. For example, they found that chess masters did not possess greater powers of memory as previously had been hypothesized. Chess masters remembered no more positions than novices when chess pieces were placed randomly on the board. During play, chess masters remember more positions because they have learned to "chunk" information more efficiently.

Newell and Simon's investigations guided a whole generation of research into implicit mental models and their relationship to functioning. As mentioned previously, what distinguishes mental model and expert-novice research is their focus on both content and structure of complex representations that affect functioning in particular domains. These approaches also emphasize participant-generated verbal productions and select participants based on levels of functioning (e.g., the inclusion and comparison of very high- and low-ability performers in particular domains).

Although primitive, simple, and complex concepts are all types of mental models (Johnson-Laird 1983), expert-novice studies suggest that simple concepts (e.g., single sets of assumptions) insufficiently represent the cognitive factors that affect functioning in complex domains (Gentner and Stevens 1983). To understand the relationship between implicit mental models and functioning, it is necessary to represent structure as well as content: That is, how goals, domain knowledge (content), and assumptions about that knowledge relate to, support, or contradict one another.

Expert-novice and mental model investigators (e.g., Gentner and Stevens 1983, Johnson-Laird 1983, Norman 1983) also tend to share certain assumptions about models. First, they view models as tools or heuristics that allow one to solve problems. Thus, they emphasize the utility of models and evaluate them according to their effectiveness in enhancing functioning. Second, most conceive of models as constructions, not direct reflections of "reality." That is, models do not have to be "true" to be useful (Johnson-Laird 1983). Further, models may provide an advantage over the direct perception of "reality" in the sense that they allow one to reduce domain information to only that which is relevant to particular goals (Ashby 1970, Norman 1983). Third, these investigators assume that implicit mental models are not precise, elegant formal models. Implicit mental models are fuzzy, generally containing partial descriptions and areas of uncertainty (Norman 1983). Finally, although mental models are implicit (you cannot simply ask someone what their model is), expert-novice and mental model researchers assume that, under the right conditions, these implicit models can be elicited.

Thus, mental models are not simple representations of content knowledge about a domain. Although domain knowledge is important, the quality and structure of the models—that is, how useful and accessible the information is—are seen as more critical in determining proficiency in a domain.

Extensive research suggests that the mental models of skilled and unskilled performers differ similarly across a variety of domains, from chess champions to preschoolers with a passion for dinosaur lore (Gobbo and Chi 1986). In the following, "expert" is equivalent to proficient performer. "Novice" loosely refers to less proficient performers, though they may not be novices in the strict sense (e.g., remedial readers). In general, experts' models are more carefully defined, exhibit fewer inconsistencies, and are organized so that problem-solving information is salient. Thus, experts not only possess a greater amount of domain knowledge, but also their knowledge is organized so that it is more accessible, functional, and efficient than less effective performers. That is, the expert performer possesses more quality information and knows which information to use when. In contrast, poorer performers' models are more imprecise (full of partial descriptions and inconsistencies), unstable (details are easily forgotten or confused with similar situations and devices), and they maintain unwanted or unneeded behaviors (Norman 1983).

Summarizing twenty years of findings, Bédard and Chi (1992) noted that experts' models are better because they pay far more attention to defining their models and to the strategies they employ. First, expert performers spend more time representing problems, defining goals and constraints, and planning. Less effective performers typically try to solve problems directly. Second, experts tend to classify problems on the basis of the assumptions needed to solve problems (meaning), whereas poor performers tend to sort problems on the basis of surface features. Experts in physics, for example, know that springiness is a higher-order concept that allows them to predict more often how materials will act when dropped than rigidity, a surface feature. Third, experts' knowledge is extensively cross-referenced, exhibiting a richer network of connections than that of poor performers. Preschoolers with expertise about dinosaurs organize information about carnivorous dinosaurs together thematically and superordinately, for example, that meat-eaters tend to exhibit similar characteristics, such as smaller body size and larger heads. Poorer performers may be able to identify particular dinosaurs, such as tyrannosaurs, as carnivores, but their information is discrete. They lack the general, cross-referenced assumptions necessary to identify most carnivorous dinosaurs (Gobbo and Chi 1986). Finally, both expert performers and "expert" learners—individuals who learn more quickly and effectively than most—exhibit metacognitive orientations. They tend to notice and be bothered by information deficits and contradictions. Poorer performers are less consistent about the criteria they use for making judgments and are less concerned by their inconsistencies (Gobbo and Chi 1986). The most effective performers and learners also consistently evaluate their representations and problem-solving strategies for utility (Bransford et al. 1982). For example, when Arthur Ashe faced Jimmy Connors at Wimbledon, Ashe predicted that he would lose if he played his preferred game of hitting far into the backcourt, where Connors excelled. To win, Ashe realized he would have to keep Connors where he was less effective, close to the net. Commenting later that although it is one thing to make a plan and another to execute it, Ashe was able to enact his plan and win the Wimbledon title.

Implicit Mental Models of the Self

Do individuals who function exceptionally well in personal domains exhibit characteristics similar to those of experts in other domains? Are their goals, assumptions, and self-representations (self-descriptors) as well explicated and useful? Is relevant information organized so that it is readily available? Are their goals, assumptions, and self-descriptors well integrated? Finally, do highly functioning individuals display metacognitive strategies? That is, do they think about their goals and assumptions in terms of usefulness?

To answer these questions, we adapted an expert-novice approach to assess individuals' implicit mental models of themselves in personal narratives. We assumed that we could derive an adequate representation of individuals' implicit models by collecting information about their goals (what they need, want, and value), assumptions (beliefs), and self-descriptors. We also assumed that these models could be rated on an expert-novice continuum. That is, as in more obviously cognitively oriented domains, the most psychologically competent individuals would have "expert" implicit models of themselves: Their goals would be carefully considered, their assumptions and self-descriptors would be consistent and serviceable toward accomplishing those goals, and they would use more metacognitive strategies.

We predicted that goodness of model and level of functioning would be positively correlated. That is, individuals with poorly defined models—whose information about themselves is insufficient, inaccurate, or organized in ways that make it difficult to evaluate as measured by poorly explicated, conflicting, or maladaptive goals, assumptions, and self-descriptors—would exhibit poorest functioning in personal domains. Individuals with better defined, organized, and more useful goals, assumptions, and self-descriptors that contain few or minor conflicts would exhibit mid-range functioning. Finally, individuals with the best defined (i.e., expert) models—whose goals, assumptions, and self-descriptors are very well explicated, consistent, and adaptive, integrate subordinate organizations of experience, and exhibit metacognition—would exhibit the highest functioning.

Method
Subjects

Transcripts from Whitbourne and Dannefer's study, "Identity Development in Adult Women and Men, 1980–1982," reported in Whitbourne (1986), were reanalyzed using expert-novice (E-N) criteria as described below. Whitbourne's sample of 47 men and 47 women were randomly selected from the telephone directory of a moderately sized city and its surroundings in upstate New York and matched for demographic characteristics (Whitbourne 1986). The sample was equally divided by sex and ranged in age from twenty-four to

Table 1
Demographic Characteristics by Sex and Age

Sex	Age	N	Education (Yrs.)	Occupation	Income (in $)	Years Married
Male	24–32	14	14.64 (1.95)	5.50 (2.06)	13–16,999	4.44 (2.5)
	33–42	13	14.62 (2.31)	5.92 (2.43)	20–24,999	7.67 (4.35)
	43–51	10	12.80 (2.64)	5.50 (1.75)	17–19,999	20.88 (4.48)
	52–61	10	14.50 (3.91)	6.20 (2.09)	20–24,999	27.29 (9.71)
Total		47				
Female	24–32	12	13.58 (2.13)	5.57 (2.13)	17–19,999	5.10 (2.63)
	33–42	12	14.17 (1.68)	5.57 (1.18)	20–24,999	13.20 (4.79)
	43–51	12	12.92 (2.10)	5.75 (1.71)	25–34,999	27.88 (3.79)
	52–61	11	13.45 (2.39)	5.86 (1.13)	25–34,999	31.11 (3.70)
Total		47				

Source: Whitbourne (1986), p. 248. Reprinted with permission.

sixty years. There were thirty women who were employed part- or full-time outside the home and seventeen full-time homemakers. The sample was divided according to the Hollingshead Four Factor Index of Social Status and included twenty-three nonprofessionals (e.g., skilled laborers, clerical, and sales) and twenty-four professionals (technical and above). See Table 1 for the demographic characteristics.

The original narratives ranged in length from 20 to 50 pages. Before the interview, participants filled in a pie chart of "The Most Important Areas of My Life" and completed a "Life Drawing" (Whitbourne and Dannefer 1986). During the interview, participants were asked about the most important areas of their lives as they had indicated in their pie charts (almost always family and work), their values, and their views about their age and gender. Finally, they were asked to relate their life histories. In the present study, we reanalyzed 92 of the transcribed narratives (with 1 missing and 1 containing insufficient data), a group that was comprised of 46 females and 46 males.

Measurements
Implicit Models of Self Assessment

The Implicit Models of Self Assessment (IMSA) consists of three levels with the data for each successive level being derived from the previous level.

Level 1 Assessment: Raters collected all statements and supporting evidence, in the individuals' own words, about goals (e.g., needs, wants, and values: "What I want now is to help my daughter get through college"), assumptions (e.g., beliefs: "You have to do things yourself if you want them done"), and self-descriptors (e.g., "I'm fat . . . funny . . . the sort of person who

---

Goal Assessment 1

Goal __1__: Create a better life for myself and my children

- Made goals, left drug dealer: "I didn't want to be what I learned to be or what I was forced into being. I wanted to be a mother."

- Used to steal, now has a job. "I conned, I stole, I used drugs so my kids could have the best of everything." "Then I realized what drugs really were, people are dying from them." "I'm going to get a job and get off the streets first. I'm not going to jail for no drugs."

- Sets a goal, then when she achieves it, sets a newer, higher goal. "I keep moving in the process to find just totally what I want to do."

- Fought through the union for a nontraditional (for women) job in the steel industry, "There's a lot of sex discrimination. They'll give the men the easier jobs that comes with the pay." "I won the case on that job. It took me about a year."

- Bought a house in the suburbs.

- Now fighting for promotion: "I'm entitled to that job. I would like to feel more comfortable."

- Teaches children the value of planning. "I teach my son, life be what's you wants it to be when you plan."

Mentions G __10__ times.   Supports G __15__ times.   Contradicts G __0__ times.

Goal __2__: Rely on myself and God

- Supported herself since she was 15 years old.

- "I will never be less than independent." "I don't like being weak at all."

- "I know I can do it. When it comes to fixing things, you know, I can just go ahead."

- When her doctor told her she didn't have to go back to work because of her heart condition, said she wanted to work.

Mentions __10__ times.   Supports __15__ times.   Contradicts __0__ times.

Note. Examples taken from Case 4, a black female who is discussed more fully in the Discussion Section.

FIGURE 1

can't let anything go") relating to the two predominant domains, relationships and work. As can be seen in Figure 1, raters noted frequency, emphasis, and support for each of the above categories and, when given, included three examples of supportive statements from the narratives.

Level 2 Assessment: Raters selected two or three predominant goals, assumptions, and self-descriptors in each of the two primary domains from the Level 1 Assessment. Raters determined the predominant goals, assumptions, and self-descriptors by adding the number of times each was mentioned to the amount of supporting evidence given throughout the narratives. Raters also included goals, assumptions, or self-descriptors for the few cases in which these were mentioned infrequently, but appeared to affect participants' feelings and behavior significantly. For example, if a participant mentioned, "I am basically no good," even if only once, raters would include this self-descriptor in the Level 2 Assessment if there was evidence that it affected the participant's feelings or behavior (e.g., never tried to apply to college or ask for a date). As Figure 2 shows, the raters then evaluated these principal goals, assumptions, and self-descriptors on ten-point scales assessing quality (utility) of information (maladaptive to functional and poorly elaborated to well explicated) and structure: (1) narrative coherence (relevance, match between statements and examples, and support of global statements); and (2) structural coherence (fixed to flexible, ordering, superordinance, and metacognition).

E-N Assessment: Finally, the raters assessed the models on an expert-novice

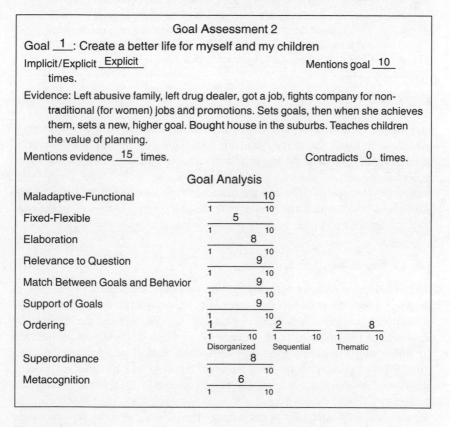

FIGURE 2

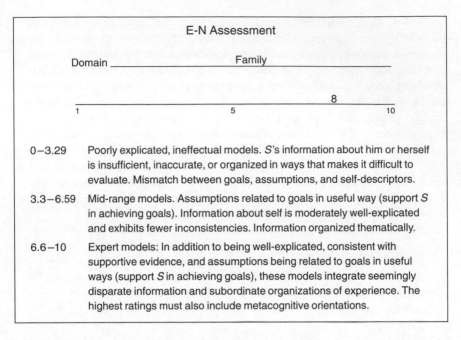

FIGURE 3

continuum as detailed in the predictions section for each of the two primary domains. To make the final assessment (see Figure 3), raters drew from both Assessment 2 individual ratings and from consistency across the different categories. For example, a primary goal ("I do not want to be alone") and a primary self-descriptor ("I'm not the sociable type") may not be maladaptive when considered separately. However, if the two conflict as they do in the previous example, the final E-N score will be lowered.

Global Assessment of Functioning

The Whitbourne data set contained no independent measures of functioning, so it was necessary to derive a measure of functioning from the same materials from which we derived the expert-novice ratings. We selected the Global Assessment of Functioning (GAF) because it provides a single overall measure of functioning, is widely used and studied in clinical populations, and has demonstrated good reliability and validity. The GAF is a modified version of the Global Assessment Scale (GAS) (Endicott et al. 1976) that was based on Luborsky's (1962) Health Sickness Rating Scale (HSRS). The GAF correlates with measures of adequacy of personality functioning, severity of symptoms,

quality of interpersonal relationships, prediction of improvement in psychotherapy, and treatment outcome (Endicott et al. 1976). The GAF was first included in *DSM III-R* (American Psychiatric Association 1987) and is currently
in the *DSM-IV* (American Psychiatric Association 1994) as Axis V, the principal measure of overall functioning in psychiatric diagnoses.

The GAF assesses psychological, social, and occupational functioning along
a hypothetical 100-point continuum of mental illness to health. Arranged in
blocks of ten, ratings range from 1 to 10, indicating "Persistent danger of severely hurting self or others (e.g., recurrent violence) OR persistent inability to
maintain minimal personal hygiene OR serious suicidal act with clear expectation of death," to 91 through 100, indicating "Superior functioning in a wide
range of activities, life's problems never seem to get out of hand, is sought out
by others because of his or her many positive qualities. No symptoms."

Procedure

Training in IMSA occurred over a six-week period with the two raters (JC and
SS) meeting weekly to rate and discuss seven randomly selected narratives.
To assess initial reliability, we separately analyzed another randomly selected
set of ten narratives. Since reliability was acceptable, we then divided the remaining sample. Ongoing reliability checks were made by randomly selecting
14 narratives (seven of Rater 1's and seven of Rater 2's) from this sample to be
analyzed by the other rater. The final intraclass correlation coefficients based
on two judges were .89 for the Relationship Domain and .94 for the Work
Domain.

Two additional raters who were blind to the study were trained to use the
GAF using a manual developed at San Francisco General Hospital where the
GAF is used routinely for chart review and research purposes. These two raters
each read all the narratives and assessed them according to the GAF scale. The
intraclass correlation coefficient for the two judges each rating all the narratives
was .92.

Results

The most important results are the substantial relations between the IMSAs and
the GAF in both domains. Because we had assumed that individuals could have
well-defined models in one domain of personal functioning and not in another,
we assessed implicit models of the self separately in the two primary domains
of personal functioning. However, the IMSAs in each domain were highly correlated ($r = .82$), suggesting that these dimensions are not independent. As
shown in Table 2, the Pearson product-moment correlation between the IMSA

E-N ratings with the two combined scores from domains of relationship and work (all the correlations reported are between the final E-N ratings and the other variables) and the GAF was r (87) = .46, p = .000. Separately, the correlations between the E-N ratings in the Relationship and Work Domains and the GAF were, respectively, r (91) = .47, p = .000 and r (88) = .43, p = .000. Alpha levels of .05 were used for all statistical tests.

There were no statistically significant correlations between sex, education, occupation, or income and the IMSAs. One demographic variable, education, was weakly correlated to the GAF (r (92) = .23, p = .03).

Table 3 shows the means and standard deviations for the IMSAs and the GAF. Table 4 shows the frequency distributions for the IMSA and the GAF ratings. There were no significant gender differences in IMSA or GAF ratings in either domain. As expected in a matched sample, males and females differed in only one demographic variable, occupation, which reflects the large number of women (14%) who did not work outside the home.

Table 2
Intercorrelations between IMSAs, GAF, and Demographic Data

Variable	GAF	EDU	INC	AGE	EN-WORK
E-N Combined	.46**	.08	.04	−.03	—
P Value	.0000	.44	.72	.76	
N	87	86	84	86	
E-N Relationship	.47**	.04	.14	.02	.82**
P Value	.0000	.73	.21	.87	.0000
N	91	90	88	90	91
E-N Work	.43**	.14	−.05	.11	—
P Value	.0000	.19	.67	.30	
N	88	87	85	87	
GAF	—	.23*	.05	.02	—
P Value		.03	.67	.82	
N		92	90	93	

*p < .05   **p < .001

Table 3
Means and Standard Deviations of IMSAs and GAF

	N	M	SD
E-N Relationship	91	4.57	2.01
E-N Work	88	4.23	1.91
E-N Combined	87	4.41	1.88
GAF	93	74.45	10.92

Table 4
Frequency Distributions of IMSAs and GAF

	Low (0–3.29)	Medium (3.3–6.59)	High (6.6–10)
E-N Assessment GAF	<70	70–79.5	>79.5
E-N Relationship	35% (32)	43% (39)	22% (20)
E-N Work	41% (36)	45% (40)	14% (12)
E-N Combined	39% (34)	47% (41)	14% (12)
GAF	31% (29)	35% (32)	34% (23)

Discussion

As hypothesized, the quality of mental models—that is, how well explicated and organized they are—appears to be as powerful a predictor of general functioning as specific functioning in domains assumed to be more dependent on higher-level cognition. Before completely accepting this conclusion, however, the major weakness of the study has to be addressed. Because the Whitbourne data set had no independent measures of functioning, it was necessary to derive the measure of functioning (the GAF) from the same materials from which we derived the expert-novice ratings. Do the substantial correlations mean that the IMSA and the GAF are simply a result of coding the same material in two ways?

Although IMSA and the GAF are both measures of functioning, they measure different types of functioning. IMSA measures a type of cognitive functioning—the quality of implicit mental models of self—hypothesized to *affect* behavioral adaptation and psychological well-being. The GAF is a measure that is designed to *represent* functioning. Further, IMSA, as previously seen in Figures 1–3, is a detailed measure designed to collect specific information about goals, assumptions, and self-descriptors systematically, using participants' own words, and to analyze this information in a highly prescribed way. The GAF is a loosely constructed global measure designed to appraise overall level of functioning. Scores are derived from general behavior and the presence or absence of psychological symptoms.

Because both sets of raters saw the same data, we cannot be absolutely certain that the GAF raters did not use some of the same information as IMSA raters. However, we attempted to decrease that possibility by selecting separate raters for the GAF who were blind to the purposes of the study. Further, although some information from the narratives might be utilized by both GAF and IMSA raters, it would have been used very differently. For example, the statement "I am an active alcoholic" would have been used as a representation of symptomatic behavior by the GAF raters. IMSA raters would have identified the statement as a self-descriptor and, if it met criteria as a principal self-descriptor, would have evaluated it in terms of utility, structure, and relationship to principal goals.

It is also important to differentiate model quality from that of intelligence; that is, we are not arguing that smarter people are better adjusted. Indeed, in the cognitive psychology literature a number of studies have demonstrated that the quality of an individual's mental model of a domain is not related to intelligence. Although Ceci and Liker (1986) did not evaluate the utility of models for predicting post-time odds, they found that complexity of the model was not related to WAIS IQ scores in a group of avid, nonprofessional racetrack handicappers. We had no independent measure of intelligence in the present study, however, we did find that education did not predict model quality. In future research, we intend to obtain measures of intelligence, expecting that they will be uncorrelated with quality of the model.

A final question concerns how to report results. Although the two domains of family and work were highly correlated ($r = .82$), we reported the correlations separately as well as together. We may ultimately need to drop this distinction. However, because of the lack of objective measures of functioning in the original data set, we cannot determine whether implicit mental models in both domains will be equally good predictors of other measures of functioning. Further, at present we cannot reliably predict whether these two domains will be as highly correlated in other samples.

Advantages of the IMSA

First, a measure based on a mental model construct offers several advantages over schema theory. In clinical psychology, a commonly accepted definition of schemas "holds that schemata consist of organized elements of past reactions and experiences that form a relatively cohesive and persistent body of knowledge capable of guiding subsequent perception and appraisals" (Segal 1988: 147). However, schema theory has been criticized for inadequately representing the complexity of human behavior. Human thinking and behavior often appear more disorganized and erratic than scripted or schematized (Gergen 1971, Neisser 1976). IMSA's capacity to represent structure (how goals, domain knowledge, and assumptions relate to, support, or contradict one another) in addition to content allows it to better represent the range of models—from well explicated, well organized, and useful to maladaptive, ambiguous, and disorganized—and, thus, to predict erratic and disorganized functioning as well.

Second, IMSA powerfully predicts the GAF and may prove to be an even better predictor of better measures of functioning. The case studies detailed below suggest that if we use the participants' behavior as a criterion of functioning, IMSA seems to be a more useful representation of overall functioning than the GAF. It may even be, given the recent development of the IMSA and the very general nature of the GAF, that the relationship between mental models and functioning in personal domains is inadequately represented. Only further studies that include objective measures of functioning can determine the extent of the relationship.

A third advantage resulting from IMSA's capacity to represent model quality, is its greater ability to identify individuals at the extremes compared with other methods of assessing adult development. The Harvard Grant Study of Adult Development, for example, defined high functioning in terms of a composite score based on income, family stability, enduring friendships, low to moderate alcohol intake, job satisfaction, and a willingness to take vacations (Vaillant 1977). However, Vaillant questioned how well these criteria for maturity actually represented the whole range of higher-level functioning. He noted that the criteria did not adequately represent two different extremes: Individuals who do meet the criteria, but exhibit other reprehensible behavior, or those who do not meet the criteria, but exhibit other extraordinary qualities or behavior.

For example, Vaillant observed that Stanley Kowalski, a brutal, insensitive character from Tennessee William's play *A Streetcar Named Desire,* would be a model of maturity in the study schema of mental health: Stanley was regularly employed, loved his wife, looked forward to having a child, drank moderately, and sustained his friendships (played cards with the same men for years). Yet, in this play, Stanley also cruelly exposed the prior sexual activities of his wife's sister, Blanche, to a man who was interested in her, and then raped Blanche while his wife was in the hospital having their baby.

The study criteria also failed to identify the proficient functioning of one of the most creative men in the Grant Study. Poe, the study participant's pseudonym, was placed at the "bottom fifth of mental health" (Vaillant 1977: 353) because he had a low income, three failed marriages, and long periods of personal turmoil before he recognized and accepted his homosexuality. Yet:

> Poe was one of the very few writers in the Study who had persevered, and for thirty years he disciplined himself to write every day. Since his works were not published, he supported himself through a series of explicitly "moral" jobs: teaching English at inner-city schools, writing advertising copy for the Sierra Club, and always sharpening the talent that at forty-five finally began to bear fruit. In middle life, his unpublished novels had evolved into published poems, often in small West Coast literary reviews, and occasionally in the *New Yorker* and the *Atlantic.* (353)

IMSA would have better predicted both Stanley's reprehensible behavior and Poe's progressively adaptive functioning. Stanley's implicit model of self is poorly defined and conflicted. As portrayed by Williams and Vaillant, Stanley acts according to his "nature." However, Stanley's two primary goals are deeply conflicted. One implicit goal, to act in accord with any sexual and aggressive drives ("nature"), is maladaptive and powerfully conflicts with his goal of sustaining his marriage. Further, Stanley exhibits no metacognition. He does not recognize that he did anything wrong, that his wife is suffering from the psychological destruction of her sister, or that his wife's feelings may change toward him as a consequence of his cruelty. Lacking metacognition, Stanley is unlikely to learn anything from his mistakes.

By representing Poe's evolving high-level model, IMSA would have better accounted for Poe's evolving high-level functioning. By continually examining and organizing his experience under the aegis of his personal goals (metacognition), Poe ultimately achieved a coherence that enabled him to function even more effectively than participants who adopted and achieved traditional goals.

The following four cases illustrate more fully the advantages of IMSA that we have been discussing: How it provides a rich representation of the models and predicts the functioning of a whole range of individuals, especially those at the extremes, who do not fit standard categories.

Case Studies

To identify the following case studies, we adapted Laub and Sampson's (1995) sampling plan for using quantitative data to select revealing cases. Case 1, David, exhibits the highest ratings on both the IMSA and the GAF. Case 2, Arnold, has the lowest IMSA and GAF ratings. According to Laub and Sampson (1995), it is also important to select cases that do not fit the model and to discuss possible reasons for the discrepancies. Case 3, Bob, exhibits a relatively high GAF rating, but low IMSA. Case 4, Ella, has a low GAF rating, but high IMSA. In the latter two case studies, we will examine the reasons for these discrepancies.

Case 1: David's GAF rating of 95 indicates "superior functioning in a wide range of activities, life's problems never seem to get out of hand, is sought out by others because of his or her many positive qualities. No symptoms. Extraordinary functioning in all areas." David is a 43-year-old happily married man, a highly engaged father of two children in college, and a university professor who expressed great satisfaction with his life. He balanced his work, women's health research, and family life with consistent cultivation of his own and his children's musical interests, a photography hobby, and what he termed his "intellectual development," which included active investigation of and participation in equal rights issues. Finally, David actively supported his community in a variety of ways.

David's model, rated 8 on the IMSA, also falls into the highest third. All of his goals are adaptive, well explicated, and well supported. For example, David supported his primary family goal, "to assure my children a good life," by arranging to be home when his young children returned from school. He also actively participated in their development by engaging their thinking skills to solve their problems, discussing values, and encouraging their musical talents.

What makes David's model better than most other parents' models is that, although most of the parents wanted their children to do well in life, most did not verbalize a set of assumptions that supported their goals. For example, David assumed that helping his children attain their goals would require extra time and effort on his part. He also thought carefully about what he should do to help his children if he wanted them to do well. Other parents simply set goals for their children, but did not support their goals, and often expressed disappointment that their children did not live up to their wishes for them. David was also one of the few parents who represented his children in terms of their interests and talents, which did not always match his own.

David's primary work goal, equally well considered, elaborated, and supported, was to "contribute something to the world." During the interview, David gave many examples of how he supported this goal: Choosing an area of research he felt would benefit elderly women and extensive involvement in university and neighborhood concerns. David's assumptions and self-descriptors also related to and supported his goals. During his interview David repeatedly mentioned his belief that he should pass on the values provided to him from his family. His self-descriptors included: "I am reflective," "I am [the sort of person who] feels an obligation to my family, neighbors, and the world," and "I am a tinkerer—I like to find out why things work the way they do."

Throughout his interview David exhibited a metacognitive orientation. One major assumption, "I think it is important to reflect and give consideration to my roles," supports metacognition, allowing David to change in response to different demands. For example, he frequently mentioned having to re-evaluate his role as a father as his children matured and their needs changed.

Case 2 is at the opposite extreme. Arnold's GAF rating of 41 is indicative of "serious psychological symptoms" and "impairment in social, occupational, or school functioning." Arnold is a 37-year-old married alcoholic man with an erratic school and work history. Although Arnold reported that he scored high on aptitude tests, he never performed well in school. As an adult, he rarely stayed at a job for more than one or two years, which he attributed to dissatisfaction with his supervisors.

Arnold also received a low (1.25) IMSA rating of his model of self. Arnold mentioned only a few, poorly explicated goals, expressed little verbal or behavioral support of his goals, and displayed many serious contradictions. One of Arnold's primary goals, for example, was to "search for a set of rules, but NOT DOGMA." Although Arnold marginally explicates what he doesn't want (dogma), he never explicated the kind of rules he did want. Arnold said he wanted rules, but only gave examples of his disdain for rules. His second primary goal, "Try to dream up an alternative" (to his present work), was equally poorly represented and unexplicated.

Further, Arnold's most frequently voiced assumption, "My work is meaningless," was very maladaptive and conflictual. As poor performers in other domains, Arnold does not seem to notice or be concerned about central contradictions. He claimed later in the interview that his work is important to him: "It shores up my weak ego."

Arnold's other major assumptions are similarly poorly represented and conflicted. He wants guidance, but Arnold discounts the helpers he finds because he believes no one can help him except "someone who has done his homework to provide answers—BRUTALLY (emphasis in transcript) done his homework." Again, this assumption is not explicated. Arnold never explains what it means for someone to have done "his homework."

Virtually all of Arnold's self-descriptors ("Something of me is missing"; "I'm an active alcoholic"; and "I have a very weak ego structure") are extremely negative. Neither does Arnold exhibit any evidence of metacognition. He recognizes that his drinking adversely affects him ("What have I done? Not much. My drinking interferes with everything"). However, Arnold never questions his strategies for solving his problems, e.g., whether his search for rules and "someone who had done his homework" had ever helped him.

The following two cases ostensibly represent discrepancies in the model. Case 3, Bob, an advantaged participant, had fairly high ratings on the GAF (78.5), but was rated in the lowest third of the IMSA E-N Assessment in both relationship (2.8) and work (3). Bob, a single man in his early thirties, had grown up in an intact upper-middle-class family, graduated from a prestigious university, and worked in an engineering firm. His relatively high GAF score reflects adequate functioning and the absence of significant psychological symptoms. "If symptoms are present, they are transient and expectable reactions to psychosocial stressors (e.g., difficulty concentrating after family argument); no more than slight impairment in social, occupational, or school functioning (e.g., temporarily falling behind in schoolwork." However, his model of self is represented by poorly explicated, conflictual goals, assumptions, and self-descriptors.

For example, Bob stated that he wanted to get married, but reported no significant relationships with women. During his interview, Bob did not define the type of woman he wanted to marry, nor did he mention any assumptions that might help him either find or develop a relationship with a woman. Moreover, the behavior he described did not support his goal. Most of his free time was spent with male friends and working on his car.

Bob also stated that he wanted to advance in his career, but again his goals were poorly defined and conflicted. At some points in the interview he stated that he wanted to progress in his field. At other points he said he was considering changing fields entirely. Further, Bob's assumptions and behavior did not support his goals. He implied that he was dissatisfied because, with only a B.S., he had reached a ceiling at work. Yet he had dropped out of graduate school twice, citing poorly articulated reasons, such as, "they do not accommodate working students." Finally, Bob's primary self-descriptor did not match his actual position. Bob had a B.S., but described himself as a "physicist," a term normally associated with a graduate degree.

Although his GAF score indicated psychological health, by his own standards, Bob felt he was not functioning as well as he could and expressed deep dissatisfaction both with his personal life and his employment. IMSA better explains why: Despite all his advantages, Bob's model is too poorly defined to help him resolve his relationship or work dilemmas.

Ella, Case 4, represents the opposite situation. Her GAF rating (69) falls in the lowest third whereas her IMSA ratings (8 in Family and 7.5 in Work) fall in the upper third. Ella, a woman in her mid-thirties, came from a severely disadvantaged background. She grew up in public housing projects in an extremely chaotic family. Abandoned by her mother when she was very young, Ella was reared by a grandfather who sexually abused her and an extremely neglectful, rejecting grandmother. Her grandmother used Ella to help care for a number of foster children, but exhibited little concern for Ella. When a school nurse identified a heart murmur, Ella's grandmother refused to take her for medical treatment. Although Ella loved her father, he was absent most of the time. Her descriptions of him also suggest that he was quite impulsive. Ella related an incident when her father shot the toilet out of the wall trying to kill a rat that had come out of it.

During her interview, Ella indicated that she had always wanted to have a better life. When she was young this goal centered on her assumption that her life would be better if she could only find her mother. After a considerable search during her adolescence, Ella finally found her mother, a prostitute who stole from Ella and interfered in her relationships. Still determined to find a better life, Ella rejected her mother and then established a relationship with a drug dealer.

Ella first shows evidence of metacognition when she describes how she began to question her previous choices. Ella saw how drugs hurt people and decided that she did not want her children exposed to that kind of life. Ella made profound changes after this point, but it is difficult to determine exactly what helped her to do so. Some cognitive scientists suggest that a reciprocal relationship exists between the quality of goals and the ultimate utility of models (Ashby 1970). That is, as goals become clearer and more functional, they better define the problem space, helping to organize and improve the search for solutions. Other cognitive scientists believe that metacognition is pivotal in the development of expertise (Bransford et al. 1983). What is clear is that

Ella increasingly engaged in higher-order metacognition. She described a process in which she increasingly evaluated her goals, assumptions, and self-descriptors and altered them in ways that helped her create a more satisfying life.

In terms of goals, Ella radically redefined her goal of finding someone to give her a better life to ones she could accomplish for herself. Carefully considering what having a better life meant to *her,* Ella decided that she wanted a job that paid well enough for her to buy a house in the suburbs and sustain a life there. Ella also actively challenged her previous assumption that other people were the best way to change her life. Her new assumption ("I can care about myself even if no one else does") helped her to work more directly toward what she wanted. Further, redefining herself as a "person," rather than as "just a woman," supported her efforts to make enough money to have what she wanted. She looked for and obtained a "male," better-paying job in the steel industry. Finally, throughout her interview, Ella continually emphasized the importance of planning ("Life be what you desire when you plan it"). She also spoke of her efforts to pass this assumption on to her children, relating how she constantly reminded her son why it was important for him to plan his life.

Although Bob and Ella ostensibly do not support the model, in many ways they illustrate the advantages of including assessments of implicit models of the self using personal goals, assumptions, and self-descriptors rather than only socially defined criteria or symptoms to determine higher-level functioning. However, one could also argue that the differences between the GAF and IMSA ratings were questionable. When examined carefully, the GAF ratings seem arbitrarily high for Bob and low for Ella.

To reiterate, we would not have chosen the GAF if other, more objective measures of functioning had been available in the original data set. Because the GAF is a global, general measure with few explicit criteria with which to rate functioning, it may be more easily affected by rater biases. Ella's rating of 69 indicates "Some mild symptoms (e.g., depressed mood and mild insomnia) OR some difficulty in social, occupational, or school functioning." Although Ella reported no psychological symptoms, the GAF raters questioned Ella's occupational functioning, noting that she was "litigious." Ella frequently fought the union to obtain jobs women were ordinarily not granted. Conversely, the raters did not give much weight to Bob's career and life dissatisfaction. When questioned about their ratings, both raters mentioned Bob's university degree and assumed that Bob's problems would be transient. To test whether the differences were due to the comparative inexperience of the graduate-student raters, we asked an experienced diagnostician and clinician to rate the two narratives as well. The psychiatrist's ratings suggest a slightly different bias. Although his GAF ratings were virtually identical to the student raters, the psychiatrist believed that he may have underestimated Ella's psycho-pathology. Given her early life experiences, he felt Ella would have exhibited more significant pathology had she been given a psychiatric evaluation.

IMSA ratings, on the other hand, may be less subject to rater biases because they rely more heavily on evaluating the quality and organization of information and on immanent critiques (Heidegger 1977 [1962]). That is, the utility of the model is evaluated both in terms of inherent structure and how well it helps the person achieve his or her own goals. Individuals can have relatively re-stricted goals, assumptions, and self-descriptors, as does Ella, yet receive high ratings if they are adaptive, well considered, and concordant. Bob's goals and self-descriptors are loftier than Ella's, but his assumptions do not correspond to or support them. Although Ella's goals and accomplishments are modest compared to Bob's, her better-explicated model helped her to create a satis-fying life while Bob's did not. Bob illustrates how a poor model inhibits de-velopment while Ella illustrates how a good model can dramatically improve a life.

Although we did not identify cases in this study where real differences oc-curred, we can imagine an individual who functions adequately despite a poor model and a person with a good model with limited functioning. In the first case, environmental support might compensate for an inadequate model. For example, a woman in the sample who was depressed had a model that fell in the lowest category. Dora's primary assumption, "I'm more comfortable at home," and her primary self-descriptor, "I'm not the social type" conflicted with her primary goal, "I don't want to be alone." Her GAF score of 55 re-flected Dora's depression and problems functioning: "Moderate symptoms . . . moderate difficulty in social, occupational, or school functioning."

Dora was a widow at the time of her interview. If she had been interviewed when her husband was alive, we can imagine that Dora might have scored higher, between 81 and 90, on the GAF: "Absent or minimal symptoms" and "generally satisfied with life." As long as Dora could depend on her hus-band for companionship, her inadequate model wouldn't have been a seri-ous problem. She didn't have to be alone. Once Dora became a widow, how-ever, her model interfered with her making new friends and contributed to her depression.

We can also imagine an individual with a very good model whose function-ing might be impaired by external circumstances. Václav Havel, president of the Czech Republic, has an extraordinary model that sustains his extraordinary functioning (Caire 1990). However, during his incarceration as a political pris-oner, Havel obviously could not function as proficiently as if he had been free. Nevertheless, given his limited circumstances, Havel's model certainly helped him to function better than most people in prison. Havel (1989) was still able to create a remarkable personal self-analysis in the only writing he was allowed: one four-page letter a week to his wife that could not refer to anything political or literary.

A fourth advantage of IMSA is its reliance on participants' own verbal productions. In most schema studies, the constructions are made by the researchers and presented to participants to elicit reactions (e.g., Muran et al. 1993) or imposed upon their responses (e.g., Horowitz 1991). Although this IMSA lacks the "real time" verbal productions of thinking processes during problem solving (e.g., Ericsson and Simon 1993), it takes a step closer to representing spontaneous constructions by featuring individuals' relatively unconstrained discussions about their lives.

Fifth, this construct of mental models provides a simpler, more parsimonious explanation of behavior than many other concepts used to explain development, such as ego defense mechanisms. Vaillant (1985, 1986) defines defense mechanisms as unconscious, based on processes outside of voluntary control, and of indeterminable origins. Mental models, on the other hand, are implicit, but not unconscious. Under the right conditions, people can make their tacit knowledge explicit (Ericsson and Simon 1993). Further, the capacity to model arises from recognized cognitive capacities that can be educated.

Finally, the greatest advantage of a modeling approach is its emphasis on functionality and modifiable factors. We develop, teach, and learn models every day. Research suggests that we can teach individuals to construct better models in many domains (e.g., Bransford et al. 1982) and that if we teach individuals better models, we can improve their performance in a wide variety of domains (e.g., Bruer 1993, Gentner and Stevens 1983). Cognitive behavior therapy research also suggests that we can alter mood and behavior of clinically depressed individuals by teaching them metacognitive techniques that help them to alter their assumptions (e.g., Rush et al. 1977). What remains to be seen is whether better models of the self can be taught and, if so, whether they do produce better general functioning. If we can explicate these models and develop strategies for improving them, it is expected that enhanced functioning will follow.

References

American Psychiatric Association. 1987. *Diagnostic and Statistical Manual of Mental Disorders.* 3d ed. rev. Washington, DC: American Psychiatric Press.
———. 1994. *Diagnostic and Statistical Manual of Mental Disorders.* 4th ed. rev. Washington, DC: American Psychiatric Press.
Ashby, W. R. 1970. "Analysis of the System To Be Modeled." In *The Process of Model-Building in the Behavioral Sciences,* ed. R. M. Stogdill, 95–114. Ohio: Ohio State University Press.

Bandura, A. 1977. "Self-Efficacy: Toward a Unifying Theory of Behavioral Change." *Psychological Review* 84: 191–215.

Battista, J. R. 1982. "Empirical Test of Vaillant's Hierarchy of Ego Functions." *American Journal of Psychiatry* 138: 356–57.

Baumeister, R. F. 1994. Introduction to "Symposium: Samples Made of Stories: Research Using Autobiographical Narratives." *Personality and Social Psychology Bulletin* 20: 649.

Beck, A. T. 1991. "Cognitive Therapy: A 30-Year Retrospective." *American Psychologist* 46: 368–75.

Bédard, J., and M. H. C. Chi. 1992. "Expertise." *Current Directions in Psychological Science* 1: 135–39.

Bransford, J. D., B. S. Stein, N. J. Vye, J. J. Franks, P. M. Auble, K. J. Mezynski, and G. A. Perfetto. 1982. "Differences in Approaches to Learning: An Overview." *Journal of Experimental Psychology: General* 111: 390–98.

Bruer, J. T. 1993. *Schools for Thought: A Science of Learning in the Classroom.* Cambridge, MA: MIT Press.

Caire, J. B. 1981. "A Holographic Model of a Psychosomatic Pattern: Freud's Specimen Dream Re-interpreted." *Psychotherapy and Psychosomatics* 36: 132–42.

———. 1993. "Toward a Science of Self: The Self as a Mental Model." Manuscript.

———. 1990. "Vaclav Havel: Hero or Expert?" Manuscript.

Caire, J. B., and S. M. Cosgrove. 1995. "An Expert-Novice Approach to the Self." *The Behavior Therapist* 18: 137–40.

Cantor, N., W. Mischel, and J. Schwartz. 1982. "A Prototype Analysis of Psychological Situations." *Cognitive Psychology* 14: 45–77.

Ceci, S. J., and J. K. Liker. 1986. "A Day at the Races: A Study of I.Q., Expertise, and Cognitive Complexity." *Journal of Experimental Psychology: General* 115: 255–66.

Chi, M. T. H., R. Glaser, and M. J. Farr. 1988. *The Nature of Expertise.* Hillsdale, NJ: Erlbaum.

Colby, A., and W. Damon. 1992. *Some Do Care: Contemporary Lives of Moral Commitment.* New York: The Free Press.

Craik, K. 1943. *The Nature of Explanation.* Cambridge: Cambridge University Press.

Derry, P. A., and N. A. Kuiper. 1981. "Schematic Processing and Self-Reference in Clinical Depression. *Journal of Abnormal Psychology* 90: 286–97.

Dweck, C. S. 1991. "Self-Theories and Goals: Their Role in Motivation, Personality, and Development." In *Nebraska Symposium on Motivation, 1990: Perspectives on Motivation,* ed. R. A. Dienstbier, 199–235. Lincoln: University of Nebraska Press.

Endicott, J., R. L. Spitzer, J. L. Fleiss, and J. Cohen. 1976. "The Global Assessment Scale: A Procedure for Measuring Overall Severity of Psychiatric Disturbance." *Archives of General Psychiatry* 33: 766–71.

Epstein, S. 1973. "The Self-Concept Revisited: Or a Theory of a Theory." *American Psychologist* 28: 404–16.

Ericsson, K. A., and H. A. Simon. 1993. *Protocol Analysis: Verbal Reports as Data.* Rev. ed. Cambridge, MA: MIT Press.

Gentner, D., and D. R. Gentner. 1983. "Flowing Waters or Teeming Crowds: Mental Models of Electricity." In *Mental models,* ed. D. Gentner and A. L. Stevens, 99–129. Hillsdale, NJ: Erlbaum.

Gentner, D., and A. L. Stevens, eds. 1983. *Mental Models.* Hillsdale, NJ: Erlbaum.

Gergen, K. J. 1971. *The Concept of Self.* New York: Holt, Rinehart, and Winston.

Gobbo, C., and M. Chi. 1986. "How Knolwedge Is Structured and Used by Expert and Novice Children." *Cognitive Development* 1: 221–37.

Havel, V. 1989 [1983]. *Letters to Olga,* trans. P. Wilson. New York: Henry Holt.

Hayes, J. R., and L. S. Flower. 1986. "Writing Research and the Writer." *American Psychologist* 41: 1106–13.

Heidegger, M. 1977 [1962]. *The Question concerning Technology and Other Essays.* New York: Harper and Row.

Henry A. Murray Research Center: A Center for the Study of Lives. 1993. Character and Competence Research Program Brochure.

Higgins, E. T. 1987. "Self-Discrepancy: A Theory Relating Self and Affect." *Psychological Review* 94: 319–40.

Horowitz, M. J., ed. 1991. *Person Schemas and Maladaptive Interpersonal Patterns.* Chicago: University of Chicago Press.

Horowitz, M. J., and N. Zilberg. 1983. "Regressive Alterations of the Self Concept." *American Journal of Psychiatry* 140: 284–89.

Johnson-Laird, P. N. 1983. *Mental Models.* Cambridge, MA: Harvard University Press.

Kelly, G. A. 1955. *The Psychology of Personal Constructs.* New York: Norton.

Laub, J. H., and R. J. Sampson. 1995. "Integrating Quantitative and Qualitative Data: Illustrations from the Glueck Data Archives." Manuscript.

Linville, P. W. 1987. "Self-Complexity as a Cognitive Buffer against Stress-Related Illness and Depression." *Journal of Personality and Social Psychology* 52: 663–76.

Luborsky, L. 1962. "Clinicians' Judgments of Mental Health." *Archives of General Psychiatry* 7: 407–17.

Markus, H. 1977. "Self-Schemata and Processing Information about the Self." *Journal of Personality and Social Psychology* 35: 63–78.

————. 1990. "Unresolved Issues of Self-Representation." *Cognitive Therapy and Research* 14: 241–53.

Muran, J. C., L. W. Samstag, Z. V. Segal, and A. Winston. 1993. "The Development of Interpersonal Scenarios as an Idiographic Measure of Self-Schemas." Manuscript.

Neisser, U. 1976. *Cognition and Reality: Principles and Implications of Cognitive Psychology.* San Francisco: Freeman.

Newell, A., and H. A. Simon. 1972. *Human Problem Solving.* Englewood Cliffs, NJ: Prentice-Hall.

Norman, D. A. 1983. "Some Observations on Mental Models." In *Mental Models,* ed. D. Gentner and A. L. Stevens, 7–14. Hillsdale, NJ: Erlbaum.

Palincsar, A. S., and A. L. Brown. 1984. "Reciprocal Teaching of Comprehension-Fostering and Comprehension-Monitoring Activities." *Cognition and Instruction* 1: 117–75.

Rogers, T. B., N. A. Kuiper, and W. S. Kirker. 1977. "Self-Reference and the Encoding of Personal Information." *Journal of Personality and Social Psychology* 35: 677–88.

Rush, A. J., A. T. Beck, M. Kovacs, and S. Hollon. 1977. "Comparative Efficacy of Cognitive Therapy and Imipramine in the Treatment of Depressed Outpatients." *Cognitive Therapy and Research* 1: 17–37.

Segal, Z. V. 1988. "Appraisal of the Self-schema Construct in Depression." *Psychological Bulletin* 103: 147–62.

Simon, H. A. 1973. "The Structure of Ill-Structured Problems." *Artificial Intelligence* 4: 181–201.

———. 1992. "What Is an Explanation of Behavior?" *Psychological Science* 3: 150–61.

Vaillant, G. E. 1977. *Adaptation to Life.* New York: Little, Brown, & Company.

———. 1985. "An Empirically Derived Hierarchy of Adaptive Mechanisms and Its Usefulness as a Potential Diagnostic Axis." *Acta Psychiatrica Scandinavica* 71: 171–80.

———. 1986. "An Empirically Validated Heerarchy of Defense Mechanisms." *Archives of General Psychiatry* 43: 786–94.

Whitbourne, S. K. 1986. *The Me I Know: A Study of Adult Identity.* New York: Springer-Verlag.

Whitbourne, S. K., and W. D. Dannefer. 1986. "The 'life drawing' as a Measure of Time Perspective in Adulthood." *International Journal of Aging and Human Development* 22: 1986.

PART TWO

Character

CHAPTER SIX

Family Values about Education and Their Transmission among Black Inner-City Young Women

NAOMI B. FARBER AND
ROBERTA REHNER IVERSEN

Despite the accumulation of decades of research on persistent poverty in American society, scholars continue to debate about why black families are poor at rates well above national averages. A considerable body of work suggests that abridged education contributes to long-term poverty (Tucker and Mitchell-Kernan 1995, Wilson 1996). However, inadequate attention is paid to the significant variability that exists among the urban poor and to what factors influence their more positive outcomes in such important areas as education.

Values and the Poverty Debate

Central to the current debate about poverty is the historically enduring question of what role values play in behavior patterns as observed in chronically impoverished families and communities. Insofar as some groups of poor people are more likely to behave in ways that are considered by most citizens to be negatively nonnormative, we are led to question whether there is something characteristic and different about their definitions of desirable conduct and positively valued ways of living.

Values represent a collective definition of human ideals, the ends toward which its members strive; values define what a good life is. Kroeber and Kluckhohn assert that values are "of the essence of the organization of culture. It is true that human endeavor is directed toward ends; but those ends are shaped by the values of culture; and the values are felt as intrinsic, not as means. . . . Finally, values . . . are 'intangibles' which are 'subjective' in that they can be internally experienced, but are also 'objective' in their expressions, embodiments, or results" (1969: 60).

Research about poverty tends to fall on one end or another of a theoretical dichotomy, increasingly often associated with political positions, with each side positing different views about values and their significance among the urban poor. On the one hand, it has been difficult to explain the wide variations among different groups' patterns in such basic areas as sexuality, family formation, education, and work within our society in general, and especially among the long-term poor. This fact suggests to some the existence, somewhat like a Venn diagram, of multiple subcultures within a complex society.

Oscar Lewis's formulation of the culture of poverty, though not the first, strongly influenced a tradition of research that analyzes life among the poor as the expression of a distinct set of norms and values that guide behavior and possess internal logic and integrity that are both adaptive to the present and self-reproducing across generations. Though there are many theoretical variations on the theme of poverty culture, there is a basic assumption that poverty begets poverty primarily because, "By the time slum children are six or seven, they have usually absorbed the basic values and attitudes of their subculture and are not psychologically geared to take full advantage of the changing conditions or increased opportunities that may occur in their lifetimes" (Lewis as cited in Rainwater 1987: 26).

On the other hand, if most members of our society share a central core of values and norms, what accounts for the many discrepancies between ideal and real culture? What is the relationship between stated values (ideal) and observable behavior (real)? Responding, however implicitly, to this question, many other scholars assume that while the poor share the central values of the larger society, the convergence of race and the structure of social and economic institutions offer people differential access to resources, thus to legitimate means for acting on their values (Rainwater 1970, Wilson 1987, 1996). In this structural view, each person, in each generation somewhat independently, devises strategies for survival, but these strategies are not based on any distinct cultural imperatives per se that deviate from mainstream society. Scholars in this tradition have variously tried to explain through such concepts as "value stretch" (Rodman 1971) or "shadow values" (Liebow 1967) how poor individuals essentially rationalize behaving in ways that deviate so clearly from their ideal—or conventional—values about, for example, marriage, employment, or education.

Poverty and Education

We know that education is not the only factor necessary for economic mobility in American society, but we know also that it provides a critical foundation. The weight of research suggests consistently that family background is one of the most salient influences on children's educational achievement (Schneider and Coleman 1993). Murnane (1994: 290) reported that recent research exploring the impact of family poverty on children's education finds that

. . . family stresses and the lack of learning resources that accompany poverty reduce children's cognitive skills and the likelihood that children will complete high school (McLanahan 1985, Schorr 1988). These effects are particularly severe for children who live in areas of concentrated poverty where they encounter few, if any, successful role models (Wilson 1987). Moreover, effectiveness of schooling depends on the quality of the home environment, and this condition becomes more important as children grow older (Snow et al. 1991).

Many such studies suggest also that families' values, their communication processes, and children's outcomes are related. However, we know less from this research about *how* they are related, which is our focus here. As with many questions about complex behavior, the answers are best sought in the concrete details of individuals' lives. We employ a microlevel perspective to examine the connections between the home environment and educational attainment among poor, young black women. In so doing, we build on Clark's (1983) seminal study of how differential academic achievement among poor black youth is related to their families' beliefs, attitudes, and behaviors. We analyze the perceived family values about education, the ways in which the young women's families acted on those stated values with the intention of influencing their daughters' educational outcomes, and how these values and transmission processes are related to the young women's educational attainment.

Framework

We focus here on two aspects of the home environment in relation to educational attainment: the parents'[1] values about formal education and the intra-familial transmission of those values. Transmission of values is defined generally as the processes over time by which children learn from family members, particularly adults who have both responsibility for and authority over them, what is important in their lives and toward what ends they should set goals and direct their activities.

Theories about human and social capital offer a useful way to conceptualize the transactional nature of intra-familial processes of value transmission as they relate to educational attainment among young women. Human capital, specifically the education and training individuals possess relative to labor market success, is "created by changing persons so as to give them skills and capabilities that make them able to act in new ways" (Coleman 1990: 304). Families influence the accumulation of their children's human capital partly through their ability to generate social capital, or "the set of resources that inhere in family relations . . . that are useful for the cognitive or social development of a child or young person" (Coleman 1990: 300). McLanahan and Sandefur describe social capital as an "asset" that "functions as a conduit of information as well as a source of emotional and economic support, and it can be just as important as financial capital in promoting children's success" (1994: 3).

Social capital develops within social structures, the forms of which vary. The social structure of primary interest here is the family, with secondary attention paid to relations between the young women and school personnel and other adults. We focus on two aspects of relations between young women and adults specifically as they are directed toward the young women's educational attainment: (1) the intensity of relations between adult and child: for example, emotional contact, intimate feelings, demonstrations of excitement about tasks, depth of commitment to goals, help in overcoming obstacles and internalized parent goals; and (2) the interactions between two or more adults who have relations of intensity with the child such as a mother and a father, a parent and other adult family member, and parents and school personnel.

A salient characteristic of the generation of social capital is that it facilitates certain actions of individuals within the social structure. Thus it can contribute independently to different outcomes at the level of individual action, specifically here the young women's attainment of formal education.

The analysis is organized to highlight both a comparison between adolescent parents and their non-parent peers and differences within each group. Becoming a teen-parent is widely regarded as being a critical, if not determining event in the life trajectory of a young woman, especially if she is poor and black. Therefore, the comparison of families' values and their transmission processes in relation to educational attainment both by and within parent status group contributes to our understanding of how adolescents who do have children might differ from other teens and from one another in these dimensions.

Methods
Sample Description

These data are part of a set of focused life histories based on intensive interviews with 74 young black women aged fifteen to twenty-three at the time of the interviews who resided in the inner city of Milwaukee, Wisconsin. Half of the respondents had a child as an adolescent; the remainder were non-parent peers from the same impoverished community. This chapter reports on data from a subset of 50 randomly selected participants: 24 teen mothers and 26 non-parent peers.

From a core of teenage mothers who had participated in an earlier study of AFDC (Danziger and Radin 1990), snowball sampling was used to get referrals of other potential participants. We recruited the majority of participants through personal referrals rather than through formal organizations such as social-service agencies in order to avoid any systematic bias introduced by professional intervention and to enhance the comparability of experience in the neighborhood and community-level environment.

The city of Milwaukee was of particular interest at the time of the study because it had the highest rate of teenage pregnancy in the United States (Moore 1991). In addition, during the 1980s, when the women in the study would be in secondary and post-secondary educational institutions and entering the labor market, Milwaukee experienced a large increase in ghetto poverty (Jargowsky 1994). Thus, although there are problems with including younger teens in the non-parent peer category because they were still potentially teen mothers, that concern was weighed against an interest in environmental similarity and a focus on individual differences.

Data Collection and Analysis

Interviews were conducted between 1987 and 1989 by the first author and two graduate research assistants from the University of Wisconsin–Madison School of Social Work. Sixty respondents participated in two intensive interviews in their homes and fourteen respondents participated in one such interview.

The larger study examined the relationship of teenage-parent status to educational attainment, occupation, and selected psychosocial outcomes in late adolescence/early adulthood. What, if anything, about young women's family characteristics and environment, ideals, sense of self, and attitudes contributed to the critical choices they made, from the perspective of the young women themselves? The intensive interviews focused on the women's ideals and actual experiences in relation to their family, educational, vocational, peer, and community environments. Elsewhere we report findings about family transmissions of values about work and welfare and occupational attainment (Iversen and Farber 1996) and findings about the range of educational resources available to the study respondents (Danziger and Farber 1990). Here we report on the analysis of family transmissions of educational values and educational attainment as experienced by poor urban black women in general and also in relation to teen-parent status.

Interviews were audio-taped and transcribed verbatim. The data for this report were analyzed through a process of coding the interviews in terms of individual and family characteristics and behaviors. Individual characteristics included age, teen-parent status (teen-parent/non-parent peer), number of children, age at first birth, performance problems in school such as repeating a grade, finding work too hard, having serious problems with teachers (yes/no), and educational attainment (dropout/in school/completed twelfth grade/beyond twelfth grade). Family characteristics included mother's educational attainment (dropout/completed twelfth grade/beyond twelfth grade/dropout with later GED), parent supervision of daughters' school efforts (yes/no; also coded as none/low/medium/high), parents' marital status (never married/separated or divorced/married), family history of welfare receipt (never/ever), and current family welfare receipt (none/AFDC/SSI). Descriptive categories included families' stated values about education (importance and purpose); families' behaviors related to school (direct and indirect); and aspects of parent-child relations (for example, kinds and quality of communication, closeness with parents, supportiveness). The interviews were coded by the two authors. Inter-rater reliability of the coded interviews was .93 for category and .99 for content.

Findings
Description of the Women

Many aspects of the young women's experiences are consistent with those reported in other studies about childbearing, educational, and family domains among their cohorts (Iversen 1995, Upchurch and McCarthy 1990, Jarrett 1994) (See Table 1; some data not shown).

None of the women in the study was ever married and three-quarters of those who had children had a single child. Over half of the women completed high school and over one-third of the graduates pursued some post-secondary education or training. Of the remaining women, 13 were still in high school and 9, all of them teen mothers, dropped out of school. Four teen mothers dropped out of school well before becoming pregnant; 5 dropped out in conjunction with their pregnancies. Fifteen women reported academic performance problems in elementary or middle school while the remaining 35 did not. Twenty of the 24 teen mothers received some income from AFDC. For half of these women, AFDC was their only source of income. None of the peers received AFDC directly, per program definition.

The young women's parents were unlikely to have intact marriages: over half were married at some point, but fewer than one in five remained married. Nearly half of the women's mothers dropped out of school, although five returned later for a GED. Most of the families had received AFDC but relatively few of them experienced long-term dependence. The families of 1 in 4 non-parent peers and 1 in 5 teen mothers received AFDC for the respondent's entire life. Three-quarters of the families received governmental financial assistance at some time, but slightly less than half of the families (n = 21) received such assistance at the time of the interview. Two-thirds of this current assistance was AFDC and one-third was SSI.

Individual and Family Characteristics and Educational Attainment

The two characteristics that differed by teen-parent status were educational attainment ($\chi^2 = 17.7, p = .003$) and parent supervision of education ($\chi^2 = 11.4$, $p = .01$) (Table 1). As our interest was not only the possible influences of a teen birth but also the relative influences of parental characteristics and be-

Table 1

Demographic Characteristics of the Women According to Teen Childbearing Status

Characteristics	Non-parent peers (n = 26)	Teen mothers (n = 24)
Age		
Range (Mean ± SE)	15–23 (18.4 ± 0.36)	15–22 (19.1 ± 0.38)
Number of children		
Range (Mean ± SD)		1–4 (1.3 ± 0.8)
Age at first birth		
Range (Mean ± SD)		14–20 (16.8 ± 1.7)
Educational attainment* (n, %)		
School dropout	0	9 (38%)
In school (pre-high school graduation)	10 (38%)	3 (13%)
Completed 12th grade	8 (31%)	8 (33%)
More than 12th grade	8 (31%)	4 (17%)
Academic performance problems		
No	21 (81%)	14 (58%)
Yes	5 (19%)	10 (42%)
Respondent's mother's education (n, %)		
Dropout	7 (30%)	12 (60%)
Completed 12th grade	7 (30%)	4 (20%)
More than 12th grade	5 (22%)	3 (15%)
Dropout/later GED	4 (17%)	1 (5%)
Parent school supervision**		
No	5 (19%)	12 (50%)
Yes	21 (81%)	12 (50%)
Parent marital status (n, %)		
Never married	7 (28%)	12 (50%)
Separated/divorced	11 (44%)	10 (42%)
Married	7 (28%)	2 (8%)
History of family welfare receipt (n, %)		
Never	5 (22%)	5 (24%)
Ever	18 (78%)	16 (76%)

*ANOVA $\chi^2 = 17.7, p = .003$ **ANOVA $\chi^2 = 11.4, p = .01$

haviors on children's educational attainment, we examined other sociodemographic characteristics generally cited in the research literature as influences on children's educational attainment (see, for example, Hayes 1987) (Table 2).

Academic performance problems in elementary or middle school and parent supervision of school efforts both were associated with the young women's educational attainment in the expected directions. Eight of the 9 women who dropped out of school were among the 15 who reported earlier performance problems. Eleven of the 12 who completed more than twelve years of education were among the 35 who reported no earlier school problems. This is consistent with other study findings that early school performance problems are associ-

Table 2
Analysis of Variance of Selected Individual and Family Characteristics on Educational
Attainment

Characteristics (χ^2, p)	Educational attainment			
	Dropout	In school (pre-H.S. grad)	Completed 12th grade	More than 12th grade
Teen parent status ($\chi^2 = 17.7, p = .003$)				
Teen mother	9 (38%)	3 (13%)	8 (33%)	4 (17%)
Non-parent peer	0	10 (38%)	8 (31%)	8 (31%)
Academic performance problems ($\chi^2 = 18.4, p = .0003$)				
No	1 (3%)	10 (29%)	13 (37%)	11 (31%)
Yes	8 (53%)	3 (20%)	3 (20%)	1 (7%)
Respondent's mother's educational background ($\chi^2 = 12.5, p = .37$)				
Dropout	6 (32%)	4 (21%)	5 (26%)	4 (21%)
Completed 12th grade	2 (18%)	2 (18%)	4 (36%)	3 (27%)
More than 12th grade	0	2 (25%)	2 (25%)	4 (50%)
Dropout/later GED	0	2 (40%)	3 (60%)	0
Parent supervision of education ($\chi^2 = 11.4, p = .01$)				
No	7 (41%)	2 (12%)	6 (35%)	2 (12%)
Yes	2 (6%)	11 (33%)	10 (30%)	10 (30%)
Levels of parent supervision of education ($\chi^2 = 23.5, p = .009$)				
None	7 (41%)	2 (12%)	6 (35%)	2 (12%)
Low	1 (13%)	2 (25%)	5 (63%)	0
Medium	1 (6%)	7 (44%)	3 (19%)	5 (31%)
High	0	2 (22%)	2 (22%)	5 (56%)

ated with higher rates of dropout and, sometimes, teen pregnancy (Upchurch
and McCarthy 1990). Similarly, 7 of the 9 who dropped out of high school
were among the seventeen who reported no parental school supervision. In
contrast, 10 of the 12 with post-secondary educational attainment were among
the 33 who reported medium to high levels of parental supervision for their
school efforts.

Not surprisingly, since socioeconomic status was relatively uniform according to the study design, family welfare history was not associated with
the young women's educational attainment. However, somewhat surprisingly,
mother's education and parents' marital status were not associated either
(welfare and marital data not shown in Table 2). Upon further examination,
although not statistically significant, we found that while 24 of the young
women's mothers were school dropouts, only 9 of their daughters dropped out

of school. The mothers of the young women in the study attended high school in a historical period when pregnancy or marriage resulted in automatic expulsion from school. While we have first birth information for only 31 of the mothers of the teens, 22 had their first child as teenagers. Thus the levels of education attained by the older women may have been affected by school policies.

Further analyses of variance showed that the respondents' mother's level of education was just short of significant association with the daughters' academic problems in school ($\chi^2 = 10.6$, $p = .06$). While the daughters of mothers who dropped out of school were split about equally between having and not having earlier school problems, the daughters of mothers who completed twelfth grade, beyond twelfth grade, or returned for GED were less likely to have had performance problems in school. Similarly, although also short of significance ($\chi^2 = 6.5$, $p = .10$), the level of a respondent's mother's education showed the following pattern of association with her supervision of her daughter's education. Respondents' mothers who dropped out of high school and did not return for a GED were split about evenly among parents who did and did not supervise their daughters' school efforts while 80% of the mothers in all higher educational categories did supervise their daughter's efforts. These findings were further evidence of the need to examine family processes to understand more fully the complex intergenerational influences on children's education.

We conducted one additional examination of the relative importance to educational attainment of teen-parent status, levels of parent supervision, and performance problems (data not shown). Regression results indicated that these three variables explained 36% of the variance in education (F = 8.54, $p = .0001$). Proportionately, however, teen-parent status explained less than 1%, parent supervision explained 18%, and performance problems in school explained a further 17%. In addition, as parent supervision and performance problems were added to the model, each supplanted teen-parent status as the significant influence on education. In the final model, both parent supervision and performance problems were significant and teen-parent status was not.

These findings directed us to intensive examination of the processes of interaction among the young women of teen-parent status, school problems, and forms of parent supervision—what we call here the transmission of values about education. Since educational differences were associated with teen-parent status, educational background, and family behaviors, we compare patterns and processes of transmission by teen group. At the same time, since the descriptive categories suggested directions of association but did not help us understand *how* parent characteristics influenced children's educational attainment, we report on the range and complexity of the value-transmission processes, both by teen group and within each group.

Education: Family Values and Their Transmission
Educational Status: Non-parent Peers and Teen Mothers

One of the most striking findings about the non-parent peers was their high degree of similarity to one another on a number of dimensions: their educational attainment, perceived family values, and the specific ways in which those values were transmitted by parents. All 26 of the nonparents could be considered to be on course in their educational careers. All either graduated from high school or attended high school full-time and could project when they expected to graduate. Three young women were older than is usual at their grade level. However, none who was currently in school considered herself at risk of not graduating. Eight of the young women completed a post-secondary degree or certificate or attended a post-secondary program ranging from law school to secretarial training. Two non-parent peers experienced serious performance problems in high school and three others reported behavior or academic problems in elementary school, but none of the problems were so daunting that young women left before graduating from high school.

In significant contrast to their non-parent peers, over one-third of the teen parents were not on course with their education. A total of 10 teen mothers (42%) reported problems with earlier academic performance compared with 19% of their non-parent peers. Nine of the 24 teen mothers (38%) dropped out before finishing high school. Three of these women participated in a GED program but none had finished. Of the other 15 teen mothers who did not drop out, 10 remained in school after giving birth (3 of them were in post-secondary educational programs), while 5 had their first child as teenagers but after graduating from high school. These findings are consistent with other research showing considerable heterogeneity in the educational attainment of black adolescent mothers (Furstenberg, Brooks-Gunn, and Morgan 1987). Despite the undeniable challenges of early motherhood to educational achievement, those teenagers who remain in school after having a baby are equally likely to graduate as those who have no children (Upchurch and McCarthy 1990).

Also consistent with other research that finds that many teen mothers experience difficulties in school before conceiving (Upchurch and McCarthy 1990, Harris 1993), there were notable within-group differences between the teen mothers who dropped out and other teen mothers in their histories of academic performance. All but one of the 9 dropouts reported having serious academic problems in school independent of and usually pre-dating becoming pregnant; 4 of the 9 failed at least one grade earlier in their educational careers.

A few teen mothers believed that they were "slow" because of the great academic difficulties they encountered, although it is troubling that none reported being officially tested or diagnosed as learning disabled: "I was always a grade or two behind . . . I didn't want to go any more." In sharp contrast to those who dropped out, only two teen mothers who remained in school reported having academic problems.

In a few instances young women who dropped out attributed their problems to school friends who encouraged them to "skip" school, use drugs, and engage in other problematic behaviors. In general, this behavior occurred as they entered high school: "They was the wrong crowd. That's why I dropped out. I was with them." Even if their own behavior was not affected, other teen mothers found the transition to high school difficult because of the new—and often rougher—environment.

> The [school] change because the people change—being around different people and the way they act. That's probably why I didn't go to high school cause after I got out of [junior high] I didn't, you know, I don't know, the school here they really don't teach you much or something, you know, and then people come to school and they play and you try to learn, they stop you from all that.

Family Values about Education: Non-parent Peers and Teen Mothers

None of the young women reported that their parents did not value formal education. The non-parent peers uniformly reported that their parents communicated strongly positive messages about education. Twenty-one teen mothers' parents told them, both before and after their daughters' pregnancies, that education was important. Three teen mothers described family lives so full of violence and neglect that they reported having virtually no communication about education at all. The following excerpts illustrate the uniform valuation of education and the range in form and substance of the family messages about the importance of education among both peers and teen mothers.

A few of the parents' messages about education could be considered to be implicit:

> Tops, it was tops. They never really had to say anything. It was just more like, you know, school was a part of life . . . You're supposed to go to school.

Many parents used more explicit and instrumental terms to describe the importance of going to school, for example, getting "that piece of paper" to be qualified for a "nice" or a "good" job, one that will permit the young woman to achieve economic stability and independence. To these parents of both peers and teen mothers, education was primarily a means to having choices in the future:

> Finish school, go to college, and get my education. And then I can become anything that I want to be. [Mother] told me there's nothing that I can't be.

[My guardian aunt] always encouraged us to go to school and so when we get out of school, when we graduate and stuff, we can get a good job and be something in life.

Some young women's parents valued high-school graduation not only for its practical use, but also as symbolic of the possibility of upward mobility and movement away from their own hard youths of poverty—many from the world of sharecropping in the south. This idea was suggested by the non-parent peers' and teen mothers' parents who hoped to see at least one of their children "walk across the stage" to receive the high-school diploma, in many cases as the first member of their family ever to do so.

[Mother] didn't finish her education, so she wanted to see all of us finish our education.

Like the families of the teen mothers, the majority of the non-parent peers' families had been dependent on AFDC as their primary source of income for some time. These parents viewed education as one way to help their daughters avoid early motherhood and the attendant risk of long-term welfare dependence. One nonparent who attended law school said of her mother and grandmother, both of whom had been single teen mothers:

There's this, this fear [in them] that it was going to be a continuous cycle. And in all likelihood, but it could have been, had it not been for, you know, my mother letting me know how important education was, always being there for me.

Another peer's mother told her children "about school":

How, when she was young, it was a privilege to go to school. And if you didn't go [to school], you'll wind up just out there pregnant, on welfare, and not able to do anything.

Most peers reported that their parents wanted them to go as far in school as they could. However, two peers whose parents were Jehovah's Witnesses said that higher education explicitly was not valued:

They don't pressure their kids to go to college. Well, they feel that this world wouldn't stay that long for us to get involved with a career or anything.

Although this finding represented the view of a small minority of families in this study, it raises questions about the relationship between religious and educational values, at least in this particular religious sect, that bear further study.

Several teen mothers' parents emphasized that it was important for their babies' futures to achieve enough education to be able to support them and also to be a "model" for them.

> [Mother] says, you better get an education, you got to take care of
> these kids, they your kids now, and you got to provide for them.

Transmission of Educational Values

The processes of transmission of educational values, coded as levels of parent
supervision of education, differed between the non-parent peers and teen mothers (see Table 3). While short of statistical significance, perhaps because of the
number of categories in relation to the size of the sample, we considered the
pattern of the results to be highly suggestive, particularly since parent supervision was associated with both teen-parent status and educational attainment
when it was coded dichotomously. Thus, we describe here the processes of
transmission, or the behavioral means by which families transmitted values
about education, separately by teen-parent status group. We also describe how
these processes differ within each group.

Non-parent Peers

Twenty-one of the 26 peers (81%), compared to 12 of the 24 teen mothers
(50%), reported active parental supervision or transmission processes, and educational attainment varied accordingly. That parent involvement contributes to
the generation of social capital and influences children's educational attainment
finds consistent support in the educational research literature (Lee 1993). Most
frequently such involvement is considered to be an intervening variable between family background and children's education (Muller 1993).

Few peers' parents (19%) left to chance their children's educational performance or level of achievement. Most parents (81%) tended to be active and
direct in their efforts to monitor, supervise, and guide their daughters' education, consistent with other research findings that African-American parents
have relatively high levels of involvement with their children's education, both
in home and school contexts (Muller and Kerbow 1993). Thus, the following
excerpt from our study further corroborates previous research:

> My grandmother taught my mother and my aunt values about their
> education and she had them instilled into their kids—that's me.

Table 3
Analysis of Variance of Teen Parent Status and Levels of Parent Supervision of Education

| Teen parent status | Levels of parent supervision of Education | | | |
$(\chi^2 = 5.8, p = .13)$	None	Low	Moderate	High
Non-parent peers	5 (19%)	5 (19%)	11 (42%)	5 (19%)
Teen mothers	12 (50%)	3 (13%)	5 (21%)	4 (17%)

These parents facilitated the development of social capital through intense adult-child relations and through reinforcing relationships with other adults and/or teachers.

There was a range in the intensity of involvement by parents of the 21 peers who reported active family support of their education. The least actively involved parents, 5 of the 21, frequently checked their daughters' report cards and inquired about homework, assuming that all was well at school unless they saw grades drop. In each instance, if they observed a decline in their daughters' grades, they took swift action to correct the situation such as asking for "daily reports" from teachers or increasing their own participation by ensuring that homework was completed.

A moderate level of parent involvement, which was the case in 11 of the 21 respondents, included a variety of supervisory actions, usually on a daily basis. These parents helped with or checked homework:

> [Mom] would just sit down and help me with my homework almost every night. And tell me to study more . . . And it helped, too.

They also required their daughters to maintain regular daily routines, especially on school days, that included strictly enforced curfews to facilitate completion of homework:

> Well, if I have homework, the first thing I do, my mama likes me to come home. If you have homework, get it out of the way. Usually I don't go anywhere on school days.

These rules contributed to a home environment that was conducive to doing school work, getting enough rest to function well at school, and generally to carrying out the tasks necessary to being a student.

These moderately active parents also attended parent-teacher conferences, parents' nights, and other regular events held at school. Findings from national surveys indicate that these particular kinds of parent actions are associated with children attaining higher grades and achievement test scores (Muller 1993).

In a few instances, parents visited school unexpectedly to see that all was as it should be with their daughters:

> It's [family involvement] so strong, you know, they, everything, all kinds of support . . . whatever you needed or thought would help you or whatever they thought would help, you know, they did the best they could do to have it like that for you. . . . Mom's at this school one day, at this school another, Dad's at one school.

Other forms of moderate and direct involvement in education included parents paying children for good grades and taking them to school if they were late or were not comfortable traveling alone.

At the highest or most intense level of involvement were the parents of 5 non-parent peers who, in addition to the above kinds of actions, also chose the schools their daughters attended. Several parents whose daughters attended inner-city schools selected the one in the school district that they thought was academically best and safest. Other parents took the initiative to enroll their daughters in suburban schools when they entered high school or even moved their families out of the inner-city school district in time for high school. These parents explicitly wished their daughters to avoid the myriad problems of inner-city education, such as "hanging around with the wrong kind of people" like "gang members and drug users," and to have the advantages of attending a public school in a more affluent district. Although young women who went to predominantly "white" schools described racial tensions, the shock of higher academic expectations, and complex issues of racial identity that cannot be examined here, each agreed with her parents that she received a better education away from her home neighborhood that justified any personal discomfort.

Not all of these parental actions designed to encourage education were in the form of rewards. However, as Coleman (1990) notes, short of extreme abuse, strong relations—whether positive or negative—are potential sources of social capital that contribute to a child's development. Many peers reported that no matter what grades they brought home, their parents insisted they try to do better. One young woman's parents gave her "whippings" for poor grades because:

> [My parents] knew that I could do better than that. But I just didn't try. But then I started trying hard. Set my grades always to be on the honor roll.

About half of the non-parent peers reported that their parents used various forms of punishment to reinforce their expectations about school attendance and performance: "First [mother] will talk to us and then give us a whooping." In addition to being "whooped," typical punishments for unacceptable grades or behavior included being "grounded" and not being permitted to watch television or talk on the telephone:

> You did not bring home bad grades. You did not cause problems with the teachers. You went to school to learn, period. [Because] after you dealt with my mother, you had to deal with my father!

Even the peers who described active levels of parental involvement and received physical punishment did not appear to resent the strict discipline. Several young women believed that their parents were motivated by a desire to protect them from dangers outside of the home, such as violence and unwholesome peers, and from making the same "mistakes" they had made:

> Well, when I first got in high school, it was something new. So I kind
> of let my hair down. But then I realized this was, you know, as time
> progresses, that I'd have to change. I cut classes a couple of times.
> But I was never really, you know, wow, wow, cause my Mom, she
> knows how I sneak. And she basically wanted you to go to school and
> get your education and everything. Got in trouble for it. . . . She al-
> ways says she wants us to be better. She wants us to have more [than
> she had].

Some young women even expressed gratitude for the discipline they received:

> I think we got the best raising and discipline anybody could have.
> Kids who drop out need parents like mine.

In addition to receiving explicit messages about education, non-parent peers
learned from their parents general lessons about life that provided them a base
for making decisions in the often difficult circumstances they faced. The ways
parents structured family life to enhance their influence over their daughters'
behavior was appreciated by those peers who valued being able to talk openly
with their parents. Some peers explicitly asserted that the quality of their communication with their parents motivated them to "listen" to their advice and
try to please them:

> [The most important thing is] having a relationship with your parents.
> Being able to talk with them. If you haven't any communication, or
> your parents act like they don't care what you do, then, you know,
> you're going to do things to try to get attention.

Other examples suggested how even young women who did not feel "close"
to their parents looked to them for guidance and granted them legitimate authority over them:

> You know, my mother, she said education and go to school and all
> that. And it make sense to me. I think if I was a child that didn't listen
> to my mother, probably would be pregnant. But you have to listen
> because they're telling you stuff for your own good. They wouldn't
> tell you nothing bad, give you bad advice.

Many peers believed that their parents provided them with important beliefs,
attitudes, and skills that contributed to their success. The most commonly mentioned of these beliefs was the value of being an active agent in accomplishing
personal goals—for example, achieving an education. One peer whose mother
intervened when her grades fell appreciated the help, but also was motivated
herself to improve because:

> I wasn't brought up to be sitting in class when you could be doing
> something else. Just sitting there doing nothing.

Another peer was one of the few black students in a predominantly white school who avoided racial antagonism:

> My mother didn't bring me up like that. . . . She say you better get the best out of it because ain't nobody going to help you unless you want to learn. You just can't sit back and expect for everything to come [to] you. You got to go out there and you got to work hard for it. And that's what I tried to do.

In one tragic case, the young woman's mother was murdered trying to protect her daughter from a rapist. Yet the young woman's plans to pursue post-secondary education suggest that she internalized some of her mother's values about the importance of education:

> [Mother] always told me, you know, sometime life may not be the things you want it but you got to make life what you want it [to be]. She taught us we should be nice people, how to take care of ourself, not to be dependent on other people.

Another peer said she was different from teenagers who get pregnant and drop out of school because:

> My background, just that's the most important . . . and it's just that it—wanting something for yourself. . . . If you don't care nothing, or you don't care about your future, then you are going to do what you please. But just look in the future, and say, "Well, a couple of years from now, I'm almost grown. I'm gonna have to have, to go to college, or do something." I don't want to be on welfare. I want to make something of myself.

The patterns of family involvement described above did not vary significantly by family characteristics such as marital status of parents (the vast majority of whom were not married), educational attainment of parents, or history of welfare receipt. However, in a recent analysis of several major surveys, McLanahan and Sandefur (1994) found that living in a single-parent family can have negative consequences for children's academic achievement. They attribute this effect primarily to the lower levels of social capital that are generated when only one parent is available, in contrast to the benefits of being raised by two biological parents. In another study, Lee concluded that educational outcomes within "non-traditional" family structures are explained by their characteristically "lower levels of parent involvement as well as . . . lower family income and student psychological well-being" (1993: 66).

In our study, a few young women did suggest the negative impact of living with a single mother. One young woman whose parents separated when she was eight noticed that she and her sister had a lot more "freedom" at home after their father left:

> When I was living with my daddy and my mother, they used to make
> us go in to the room and just study. Study for tests and stuff. . . . We
> had to be in be like at 8:00.

However, it was noteworthy in our study that 12 non-parent peers reported having a strong positive relationship with their fathers, regardless of whether or not he lived with them, and 10 of these 12 believed that his interest had a significant impact on their education. This observation is congruent theoretically with Coleman's emphasis on the potential impact on children's development of having consistent, reinforcing relationships with more than one concerned adult. The particular importance of transmission of values from fathers to children is documented in other research (Parcel and Menaghan 1994), but most of the studies include only children in intact, two-parent families.

Lee (1993) also suggests that any parent's increased involvement in their children's education can compensate for the disadvantages of living with only one biological parent. This latter point is consistent with our finding that the perceived influence of educational value transmissions of even nonresident fathers can be important to their daughters' educational attainment. For example, for some peers, their fathers represented an independently strong source of support for their education:

> [Dad] wants us to go to college. As far as high school and my morals
> and the respect that I have for myself [and] that I want others to have
> for me, I'd say my mother [has greatest influence]. But as far as going
> to college and looking toward the future, I'll say my father.

Other non-parent peers indicated the importance of consistent and unified parental messages to their educational accomplishments:

> I had to listen to them, you know. They had their hold on me. . . . I
> couldn't get away with a lot of things, you know, like some parents
> would probably look over, my mother and father looked at me step
> for step; they'd make sure I didn't do, you know, anything that was
> out of line.

In contrast to the 21 peers described above, the 5 peers who reported no active parental involvement in their education also described home lives characterized by some combination of family members using drugs and/or alcohol, physical abuse, emotional abuse, neglect, and a generally high level of chaos. Two young women, both of whom had physical disabilities, were in foster care for some time. How did these 5 young women manage to remain in school despite a severe lack of family care and support? They all reported having a significant relationship with a caring teacher and/or possessing a special talent that was nurtured by an adult, usually at school. This finding points to the potential for adults outside of the family to contribute to the development of social capital when the parent-child relationship is weak or destructive.

Moreover, the absence of parental support did not mean that young women were not motivated at all by their parents to fulfill their educational expectations. Four of the 5 peers whose family environments were deeply unhappy characterized their motivation to achieve in school as wanting to "show" their parents they can "do something," or even to "prove wrong" parents' grim prophesies for their daughters. Like several peers who experienced active parental involvement, 3 of these young women explicitly wanted to be different from people, in this case their families, who "got all these babies and they on welfare." They also saw their parents as reference points, however negative, for their educational and vocational aspirations. Unfortunately, the data do not permit meaningful analysis of these complicated emotional dynamics but do suggest great complexity in the process of social capital development within the family.

Teen Mothers

While the teen parents described family values about education and modes of transmission that were substantively similar to those described by non-parent peers, significantly fewer teen mothers than their non-parent peers—12 of the 24 (50%)—reported that their parents were actively involved in their schooling. The remaining half reported no active parent involvement. Thus, although nearly all of the teen mothers perceived that their parents had positive values about education, the degree to which their families' actions intensively and consistently supported those values varied widely within the group. The capacities of families to generate education-related social capital thus varied both by parent status of the adolescent and in relation to the young women's school status.

Among the 9 teen mothers who dropped out of school, only 2 reported any consistent actions by their parents designed to keep them in school. These women were also the only two dropouts currently attending GED programs. In the accounts of the other 7 teen mothers, several common themes emerged.

Typically, the young women who dropped out perceived little positive encouragement by their parents to attend school. Most of their interactions concerning school were solely in the form of punishment and humiliation for failure. Several parents warned that they would be "dummies" if they did not go to school.

Although these young mothers tended to have continuing problems in school, they received little help at home. The example of one young woman, "Keisha," who dropped out in eighth grade after her first pregnancy, exemplified several aspects typical of this group. Keisha's mother "pushed" her daughter to go to school, mostly by "yelling" and physical punishment. "She always saying, 'Go to school, or else.' " But school was generally a problematic and aversive experience for Keisha:

> [I had problems with] most everything, the work, and the kids, and the teachers, and I just didn't get along with people or anything.

When Keisha's teachers called to report these academic and interpersonal problems, her mother's usual response was to "ground" her from the television for a week. Sometimes when a teacher called

> She'd come to school and I would get yelled at in the school. She used to say, um, "if you don't behave I am going to pull your pants down right here in the classroom and spank you in front of all these people." But thank God she never did.

Poor performance resulted in Keisha being held back for two years. Though she wanted to fulfill her mother's expectations for her education, she needed more help to do so than was available:

> I didn't have no help at all. Well, I asked [mother], but she just didn't have the time. . . . I did the best I could, but I didn't pass in school. . . . With all the problems, I couldn't do it.

Keisha's description suggested that while her mother's intention was to enhance her daughter's education, her actions were ineffective and perhaps even contributed to Keisha's problems in school.

Even among those families that were less harsh, the young women who dropped out believed that they were discouraged by the lack of active support. Some women wished that their parents had "pushed" them harder.

In contrast to the non-parent peers who had unsupportive families, the teen mothers who dropped out less frequently reported having strong relationships with teachers or other adults outside of the family. One young mother was "kicked out" of school and soon after attempted suicide. Her mother offered no help, but she felt she would have been able to return to school and to perform better had another adult paid more attention to her:

> [I wish] somebody [would] sit down and talk to me about something. Ain't nobody really never did that with me.

While the particulars of family life varied among the school dropouts as among any families, what they did share was a lack of structure and routine geared toward their daughters' educational activities. That is, many young mothers' parents imposed rules on them, but not rules that supported educational activity. For example, one young woman who dropped out after she had her child believed she had a baby in part to gain freedom from her mother's overwhelming demands at home:

> I felt like if I had a baby of my own I wouldn't have to worry about doing this, you know, the house chores and cooking because I had my own responsibility to look after. I had my baby to look after and therefore I wouldn't have time to clean up or cook.

Like their non-parent peers, although fewer in number, higher levels of educational attainment were associated with more active parental involvement in the teen mothers' schooling. The families of the young women who graduated from high school before their child was born were in clear contrast to the unsupportive families of the teen mothers who dropped out. Four of these 5 young mothers reported low to high levels of parental involvement in their education similar in form to that described by non-parent peers. For example, one young woman's proud mother took her daughter's report cards to work to show to colleagues. The families of the 4 teen mothers who pursued post-secondary education showed similarly supportive moderate or high levels of involvement.

All parents in these groups provided consistent supervision at home. One young woman who was wheelchair-bound since childhood said that her mother treated her with "no pity" and disciplined her as she did her other children:

> And I'm glad she did it like that, otherwise don't know where I would be right now. Probably somewhere helpless. . . . Well, [mother] did [go to parent-teacher conferences], and then she had to go to work too. . . . She made sure we went to school every day. She helped with the homework. Made sure everybody got it done.

These young women typically regarded their parents as crucial and positive sources of motivation to do well in school: "[Mother] pushed school hard and it stayed in my head."

In contrast to 12 non-parent peers, only 3 teen mothers reported strong involvement by their fathers which each characterized as significant for their education. One young woman's father died while she was in high school. Her performance suffered, but she recovered her commitment:

> And that's when I stopped going to school. And then I went back. Cause I, made me feel like, he looking down on me, see I'm failing. So I went back.

The 10 teen mothers who had a child before graduating and remained in school presented a more varied picture of kinds of family support for education. Three teen mothers were in high school at the time of the interview; the other seven graduated or were in post-secondary programs. Six reported active family involvement in their schooling.

In contrast to the teen mothers who dropped out, most of these young mothers who retained their attachment to school were good students and reported enjoying school before becoming pregnant. Only 2 of the 10 had earlier academic problems. Many were involved in extracurricular activities and most had firm attachments to school:

> Basically, I just did my work, and you know, paid attention in class, and never really got into any, you know, groups that's misbehaving. . . . Like, we emphasized getting good grades, and we make bets and everything on getting good grades.

Despite the multiple and constant demands of motherhood, these young women maintained adequate levels of performance and even attendance at school (one young woman won an attendance award upon graduation). Although having a baby radically changed their lives, the young mothers in this group retained their primary identity as students and struggled not to let the demands of motherhood simply replace the demands of school:

> The baby, it was like, her periods of sleeping was off and stuff. So, I would have to try to get my housework done, and things washed when she was asleep. Cause if she wasn't asleep, I would have to take care of her, and watch every move she makes. But I believe that it's not her fault that my grades slipped. . . . I feel that I let other things come before my school work, which I shouldn't have. . . . I really feel that, you know, I should have a better GPA (grade point average). But, I'm going to have to work harder at getting it. But, I feel that next year, I should be able to do better.

That these teen mothers were so successful in school appeared to be in part because their families provided much time and effort toward that end. The types of actions taken by parents of these teen mothers both before and after their pregnancies were virtually identical to those reported by their non-parent peers. These actions included choosing what schools their daughters attended, monitoring homework, strictly supervising their time and activities, attending school functions, and having frequent contact with teachers.

Most of their home environments were highly structured, closely supervised and emotionally close. The range of these common elements was described by one young woman who missed no school during her pregnancy and gave custody of her son to his father so that she could pursue her education:

> My mother trained us. . . . We were children that were brought up to know right from wrong and you were punished when you did the things that were wrong. . . . We were not allowed to leave the house and stay out until dark and then come back. You had a certain time that you had to be in and there was only so far from the house you could go. Discipline, you discipline your child, you don't let them run

wild. . . .You get a grateful spirit after, once you get old enough to see what's going on.

These elements seemed to help the family absorb some of the tumult that comes with a new baby and also to help their daughters continue working toward the adolescent task of finishing secondary school.

Three young mothers' own mothers provided full-time care for the baby so that their daughters could finish school. A rather dramatic example of this action was the young woman whose mother took temporary legal custody of the baby so that her daughter could participate in a military program in high school leading to ROTC at college.

Those teen mothers who remained in school and who reported no active involvement commonly described parents who did not invest heavily in their daughters' education. One young woman whose mother "tried to make me stay home sometimes" to help care for younger siblings believed she might have avoided the difficulties of early motherhood and done better in school with more guidance:

> [Mother] didn't talk to me. I more or less grew up my self. . . . I learned a lot of things from her, but not as much as a kid should learn from their parent.

Another young mother graduated from high school, but barely. Her thoughts on her mother's part in her education revealed common features of other teen mothers' experiences in this group:

> [My mother] wasn't a real pusher about grades, you know, as long as you went. And my grades were bad, she never fussed at me about that. . . . Maybe if she had I would have did a little extra. . . . You know, I think my mother, because she didn't graduate, it was enough for her just for me to go. . . . I was not motivated to learn. And I think that comes from your parents. My parents, my mother, she, she told me to go to school, she wanted me to go to school, but she was never like, "Well, if you don't get this grade, you don't go outside." It was never an enforcement on having good grades.

Discussion

The experiences of the teenage mothers and their non-parent peers in this study suggest that not only what but *how* one learns about the importance of education in the family can significantly help or hinder a poor young woman's ability to achieve in school. Our study finds that among the 50, poor black young women from the same inner-city community, nearly all were told by their parents that formal education was important and that they should attend school; no participant reported receiving any direct messages at home implying otherwise. This finding is important theoretically because it supports other research on poverty suggesting that poor, black inner-city families share the mainstream American value of education rather than any alternative or deviant view.

However, we also find that holding positive values about education is not sufficient for adults to enhance their children's educational attainment: the values must be transmitted to children and reinforced concretely and repeatedly in ways that substantively influence their education-related behavior. The patterns of parental involvement in relation to educational attainment found here closely correspond with Clark's (1983) analysis of the impact of families of black male and female "high achievers" and "low achievers" living in poverty. In our study, the importance of parents' involvement in their children's education is evident both in the significant differences in the education attained by teen mothers and their non-parent peers and also among the teen mothers themselves.

Young women who did not have children expectedly attained higher levels of education than did teen mothers, and significantly more non-parent peers than teen mothers report active parental involvement in their education. Yet, nearly all teen mothers who delayed childbearing beyond high school and the majority of those teen mothers who remained in school after having a child report levels and types of parental involvement similar to those of their non-parent peers. Conversely, nearly all of the teen mothers who dropped out of school report little or no parental action supporting their stated value of education. Thus, the educational attainment of the teen mothers, who potentially are at such high risk for poor educational outcomes, seems to be mediated by their parents' direct involvement in their education.

The fact that so many poor parents in our study were able to enhance their children's educational attainment argues against a cultural position about persistent poverty that does not include the possibility for change from one generation to the next. We note particularly that while 24 mothers of the teens did not complete high school, only 9 of their daughters dropped out. At the same time, those who imply that economic and social institutional structures are monolithic in preventing poor Americans from advancing would also deny families the ability to mediate the sometimes disabling circumstances of impoverished inner-city neighborhoods and their usually inferior schools. Families can sometimes mitigate the tremendous difficulties of being simultaneously a young mother and high-school student, even difficulties stemming from earlier academic problems, by providing concrete assistance and emotional support, day by day, in a community environment that holds discouragingly few educational resources and too few models for conventional achievement.

Findings of this study suggest that even though parents may have few material resources, they can create family environments that generate sufficient social capital for children to attain education that is so important for later economic achievement. This raises a central question about what conditions enhance or detract from a parent's ability to provide meaningful assistance to a child in school. Our study does not support the research suggesting that a parent's own level of education has independent significance for children's educational attainment. The findings do suggest, however, the possibility that the mother's education indirectly influences her children's educational attainment through parental supervision and mediation of children's earlier problems in academic performance. It is important to emphasize that the respondents' mothers' educational attainment may not correspond to their commitment to education because earlier policies prevented pregnant teenagers from remaining in school. Overall, the ways in which parents' education—as one aspect of their own experience, in combination with other individual and social characteristics—affects family dynamics and individual outcomes deserves careful attention. Also, while in our study the parents' marital status did not directly affect their children's education, the substantive influence of fathers—resident or not—on their daughters' education suggests an additional research direction.

A notable aspect of the 50 young women's histories is the very fact of their heterogeneity. We did find differences between the teen mothers and the non-parents and among the teen mothers, both in their level of educational attainment and, relatedly, in the degree of active involvement by their parents in education. However, we believe that the strong association between parents' actions and educational attainment should direct attention for research and intervention toward the importance of the family environment for education and should direct the formation of policy away from a deterministic view of the impact of early childbearing. While some poor people may not be able to help their children take advantage of their often limited educational or vocational opportunities, others, for reasons we do not yet understand fully, are able to garner and direct their internal and external resources for the benefit of their own and their children's futures. Further research should continue to examine the sources of such diversity in parental involvement in children's education.

The experiences of the young women in this study suggest that the parent who provides close supervision of a young woman's daily life as a student can help her set and reach her educational goals, creating social capital to aid her movement toward a more productive future. Nevertheless, full development of children's educational potential depends also upon the availability of social capital resources beyond the family, including the quality of schools and other community institutions.

Note

1. In a few instances the young women's primary family caretakers were not biological parents but were grandmothers or another adult relative. We use the term parent to mean any adult who was identified as the respondent's primary caretaker.

References

Clark, R. 1983. *Family Life and School Achievement: Why Poor Black Children Succeed or Fail.* Chicago: University of Chicago.

Coleman, J. S. 1990. *Foundations of Social Theory.* Cambridge, MA: Harvard University, Belknap Press.

Danziger, S. H. and N. Radin. 1990. "Absent Does Not Equal Uninvolved: Predictors of Fathering in Teen Mother Families." *Journal of Marriage and the Family* 52: 636–42.

Danziger, S. K. and N. B. Farber. 1990. "Keeping Inner-City Youths in School: Critical Experiences of Young Black Women." *Social Work Research and Abstracts* 26: 32–39.

Furstenberg, F. F. Jr., J. Brooks-Gunn, and S. P. Morgan. 1987. *Adolescent Mothers in Later Life.* New York: Cambridge University Press.

Harris, K. M. 1993. "Work and Welfare among Single Mothers in Poverty." *American Journal of Sociology* 99: 317–52.

Hayes, C. D., ed. 1987. *Risking the Future, Vol. 1.* Washington, D.C.: National Academy Press.

Iversen, R. R. 1995. "Poor African-American Women and Work: The Occupational Attainment Process." *Social Problems* 42: 554–73.

Iversen, R. R. and N. B. Farber. 1996. "Transmission of Family Values, Work and Welfare among Poor Urban Black Women. *Work and Occupations* 23: 437–60.

Jargowsky, P. A. 1994. "Ghetto Poverty among Blacks in the 1980's." *Journal of Policy Analysis and Management* 13: 288–310.

Jarrett, R. L. 1994. "Living Poor: Family Life among Single-Parent, African-American Women." *Social Problems* 41: 30–49.

Kroeber, A. L. and C. Kluckhohn. 1969. "General Features of Culture." In *Man in Contemporary Society,* ed. Columbia University Staff, 60–70. New York: Columbia University Press.

Lee, S-A. 1993. "Family Structure Effects on Student Outcomes." In *Parents, Their Children, and Schools.* Ed. B. Schneider, and J. S. Coleman, 43–76. Boulder: Westview.

Liebow, E. 1967. *Tally's Corner.* Boston: Little Brown.

McLanahan, S. 1985. "Family Structure and the Reproduction of Poverty." *American Journal of Sociology* 90: 873–901.

McLanahan, S. and G. Sandefur. 1994. *Growing Up with a Single Parent: What Hurts, What Helps.* Cambridge, MA: Harvard University Press.

Moore, K. A. 1991. *A State-by-state Look at Teenage Childbearing in the U. S.* Flint, MI: Charles Stewart Mott Foundation.

Muller, C. 1993. "Parent Involvement and Academic Achievement: An Analysis of Family Resources Available to the Child." In *Parents, Their Children, and Schools,* ed. B. Schneider and J. S. Coleman, 77–114. Boulder: Westview Press.

Muller, C. and D. Kerbow. 1993. "Parent Involvement in the Home, School, and Community." In *Parents, Their Children, and Schools,* ed. B. Schneider and J. S. Coleman, 13–42. Boulder: Westview Press.

Murnane, R. J. 1994. "Education and the Well-Being of the Next Generation." In *Con-*

fronting Poverty, ed. S. H. Danziger, G. D. Sandefur, and D. H. Weinberg, 289–307. New York: Russell Sage Foundation.

Murray, C. 1984. *Losing Ground.* New York: Basic Books.

Parcel, T. L. and E. G. Menaghan. 1994. "Early Parental Work, Family Social Capital, and Early Childhood Outcomes." *American Journal of Sociology* 99: 972-1009.

Rainwater, L. 1970. *Behind Ghetto Walls.* New York: Aldine.

———. 1987. *Class, Culture, Poverty and Welfare.* H.H.S. Contract No. OS-100-86-0021. Washington, D.C.: U.S. Department of Health and Human Services.

Rodman, H. 1971. *Lower-class Families: The Culture of Poverty in Negro Trinidad.* New York: Oxford University Press.

Schorr, L. B. 1988. *Within Our Reach.* New York: Doubleday.

Schneider, B. and J. S. Coleman, eds. *Parents, Their Children, and Schools.* Boulder: Westview Press.

Snow, C. E., W. Barnes, J. Chandler, L. Hemphill, and I. Goodman. 1991. *Unfulfilled Expectations: Home and School Influences on Literacy.* Cambridge, MA: Harvard University Press.

Tucker, M. B. and C. Mitchell-Kernan. 1995. *The Decline in Marriage among African Americans: Causes, Consequences and Policy Implications.* New York: Russell Sage Foundation.

Upchurch, D. M. and J. McCarthy. 1990. "The Timing of a First Birth and High School Completion." *American Sociological Review* 55: 224–34.

Wilson, W. J. 1987. *The Truly Disadvantaged.* Chicago: University of Chicago Press.

———. 1996. *When Work Disappears.* New York: Alfred A. Knopf.

CHAPTER SEVEN

Exploring American Character in the Sixties Generation

CONNIE FLANAGAN

The kind of life we want depends on the kind of people we are—on our character. (Bellah et al. 1985: vi)

More than a century has passed since the French political theorist, Alexis de Tocqueville, reflected on the character of *Democracy in America* (Tocqueville 1966 [1848]). An astute foreign observer, Tocqueville wrote about the ardent commitment of the average American to the freedom, rights, and independence of the individual. However, he warned that rabid individualism, unfettered by group commitments and social tolerance, could undermine civil liberties. In this chapter I explore the theme of character by focusing on values that form the foundation of democracy in America: the right to think freely and dissent; the commitment to civil liberties and to tolerance of diversity. Rather than discussing character as a trait of individuals, I concentrate on these qualities that distinguish us as a nation and do so by looking at a cohort of youth who came of age as the decade of the sixties closed.

Focusing on youth as they made the transition from high school to college in 1969 has several theoretical benefits for the study of character. First, because issues of free speech, social tolerance, and civil rights were among the defining elements of the student movements of that period, it raises the very principles that define the American character. Second, from a developmental perspective, the period between late adolescence and early adulthood appears to be an optimal time for reflecting on questions of character. On the threshold of adulthood youth face questions of who they are, how they fit in society, and where they stand on various social and political issues. Finally, this developmental perspective can be extended to highlight the unique role of the college experience as an opportunity to develop character.

The word character, derived from *charassein* or *charattein,* means to engrave. It suggests a distinctive mark, quality, or trait, something etched indelibly. The decade of the sixties left such an indelible mark on the political landscape of America and on a generation of her citizens. Longitudinal studies suggest that values and commitments youths adopted during that period endured into their middle adult years. For example, activists from the Civil Rights movement remained committed in midlife to the needs of minorities and disadvantaged groups (Marwell, Aiken, and Demerath 1987). Twenty-five years after Mississippi Freedom Summer, participants in that movement for civil rights were more likely than nonparticipants to be active in politics in their local communities and in movements for women's rights, peace, and the environment (McAdam 1989).

Other work documents the positive role family values played in motivating young people's participation in the movements of that era. For example, activism in the peace movement showed a stronger relationship to the family milieu than it did to coming of age (Roberts and Lang 1985). Antiwar protesters were more likely than their non-activist peers to come from families where disagreement and debate about current events were common (Haan, Smith, and Block 1968), suggesting not only that politics was a salient topic in those families but that an attitude of open-mindedness and a willingness to hear alternative views prevailed. The political positions of activists and their parents, especially mothers, were more liberal than those of their agemates during the height of student activism as well as fifteen years later (Dunham and Bengston 1992).

Still other studies point to the intergenerational transmission of values from parents to their activist children and from the activists in later years to their own children. Wood and Ng (1980) found that fathers of activists tended to have radical ideas and their mothers humanitarian ones. Franz and McClelland (1994) followed up student activists at midlife and found that not only were they more altruistic and rebellious than non-activists but, as a group, they had taught their children the importance of understanding others and of serving the common good. And finally, in a 1990s study of college-student views, Duncan and Stewart (1995) found that college students' attitudes towards the Persian Gulf War were highly correlated with the views their parents had held toward the war in Vietnam.

The sixties clearly had an impact on the character formation of many youth who were students at the time. But the decade is also noteworthy for having left a distinctive mark on the cultural norms and social practices of America. According to Delli Carpini (1989), the generation that came of age in that decade altered the political landscape, not by charting a clear direction on the political spectrum, but by enlarging the perspectives and increasing the tolerance of the American middle class.

The Transition to Adulthood

The stage between late adolescence and early adulthood is a prime time to engage in discussions and reflect on questions of character. Typically the early adult transition is a period when an individual makes decisions about the direction of his or her life. Because identity consolidation is a core developmental task of this period, the way an individual grapples with and resolves the salient political and social issues of his or her early adult years becomes an integral part of personality thereafter (Stewart and Healy 1989). Regardless of the historical period in which an individual comes of age, the political events of the early adult years appear to act as a marker, shaping broad ideological commitments and attitudes for the rest of the life span (Glenn 1980, Schuman and Scott 1989). Fendrich and Lovoy's (1988) longitudinal studies suggest that it is not historical events per se but how individuals negotiate those events that is associated with their political activities and positions in adulthood. They followed students from the same university who responded to the Civil Rights movement in distinct ways: radical activists who confronted the system; institutional activists who worked within the system in a consensual mode; and non-activists. In adulthood, both the radical and institutional activists were more politically engaged compared to their non-activist peers, but their affiliations were quite different. Whereas the radicals were more likely to identify themselves as Democrats, to be active in local community politics, and to participate in humanitarian causes, the institutional activists tended to be conservative, patriotic, and affiliated with the Republican Party.

Although political activists were, in fact, in the minority among college students of the sixties, the decade is synonymous with political change. And whether or not students actually engaged in the Civil Rights, free speech, antiwar, or women's movements, they would have been hard-pressed to escape the public discourse on issues raised by these movements or to avoid taking a personal stand. The fact that youth had to grapple with political and moral issues of this period makes this era an interesting focal point for an examination of character. Character is exhibited when one is faced with a dilemma and must make some kind of commitment, deciding between alternatives with certain risks and consequences. Youth is an ideal time for such reflection and commitment. Because they are not yet fully integrated into adult society and have relatively few responsibilities, young adults are free to experiment, search, and define their relationship to the social order (Erikson 1968, Mannheim 1952). According to Mannheim, they may experience a "fresh contact" with their society if they perceive that values learned while growing up are at odds with the ethos of the social order. Not only does this period afford an opportunity for individual growth, it can also benefit society by fostering a civic ethic:

> To be sure, those who have had a youth—who have seriously questioned their relationship to the community that exists, who have a self and a set of commitments independent of their social role—are never likely to be simple patriots, unquestioning conformists, or blind loyalists to the *status quo*. (Keniston 1968: 272)

The Transition to College

The opportunity to spend this time in college has several advantages for the development of character. College offers an atmosphere in which the kind of Socratic dialogue that nourishes character can take place. For many, college literally offers a "time away" from home and family. Removed from familiar surroundings and norms, young people enjoy greater autonomy to decide what they value and what direction their life might take. An example is provided in Newcomb's studies of undergraduates in the late 1930s attending Bennington College, a progressive women's college in Vermont. Exposure to the young faculty's perspectives on public issues—perspectives that departed from their parents' conservative convictions—was related to a shift in the women's positions towards greater identification with the New Deal (Newcomb, Koenig, Flacks, and Warwich 1967). This realignment with a new reference group showed a remarkable continuity thereafter, affecting their political attitudes even into the late adult years (Alwin, Cohen, and Newcomb 1992).

What is it about the undergraduate experience that may be related to more reflective thinking and a reconsideration of perspectives on social issues? Rest (1988) answers this question as it applies to the growth in moral judgment during the college years. He contends that "the growing awareness of the social world and one's place in it seems to be more important than specific moral crises or educational programs" (192). Of course some youth take advantage of the intellectual stimulation of college more so than others, and Rest goes on to list the individual characteristics of people who show gains in moral judgment. These include a love of learning, risk-taking and seeking challenge, and taking responsibility for oneself and one's environs. Although Rest's work was based on the role of the college environment in the development of moral judgment, similar inferences can be made about the opportunities college presents for the development of political attitudes and social tolerance. In Haan, Smith, and Block's (1968) study of students of the sixties, those who were active in political protests were more likely to be principled moral reasoners compared to non-activists, who tended to think more conventionally.

Perry (1970) contends that college attendance promotes reflectiveness because students are likely to encounter a meaningful "pluralism of ideas" (214) there. He argues for extending Piaget's model into the college years and refers to this stage as a "period of responsibility" (205). Faced with social and political dilemmas for which there are no easy answers, students must, nonetheless, make commitments and live with the consequences of their decisions. From a developmental perspective, the challenge of having to make commitments when there are no easy answers, when the world cannot be broken down into simple dichotomies of right and wrong, could be considered a test of character. College life also offers opportunities for student leadership and interaction with faculty from a wide range of disciplines. In their study of more than 10,000 students attending 487 colleges and universities during the 1970s, Pascarella, Ethington, and Smart (1988) found that these opportunities had a significant impact on the development of humanitarian and civic values, independent of students' pre-college characteristics.

In summary, the college environment is a setting where youth are likely to encounter different perspectives on social, political, and moral questions. At the same time, they are at a stage in life when they must make certain commitments—deciding who they are, what they value, what direction their lives should take, and what kind of society they want to live in.

Hypotheses

In her work on social movements, Freeman (1983) notes certain conditions that facilitate the emergence of a new social movement. At the top of her list is the importance of an infrastructure and pre-existing communications network, one that is potentially co-optable to the ideas of the movement. The college campus of the 1960s certainly met that criterion and empirical work has documented the key role of the college infrastructure in facilitating involvement in political protest (Fernandez and McAdam 1988, Sherkat and Blocker 1994). I will argue that attending college during a period when topics such as the egalitarian treatment of minorities and women, issues of free speech, and the ethics of American involvement in Vietnam were salient in public discourse, put young adults in a setting where they had to grapple with questions of personal and national character. Moving from a familial to a college environment should be associated with a change in students' reference groups and should have a liberalizing impact on their attitudes. Therefore, the transition from high school to college should be associated with an increase in tolerance, commitment to the rights of oppressed groups, and support for democratic dissent.

Gender Differences

After examining changes in the attitudes and political engagement of youth between high school and college, I explore what might account for such changes. Toward that end, I look separately at women and men for the following reasons. First, empirical work suggests that women were less involved in some of the movements of that era (McAdam 1992), perhaps due to their lower sense of political efficacy, stronger religious beliefs, or lower rates of college attendance when compared with men (Sherkat and Blocker 1994). Furthermore, 1969–1970 was a period of intense focus on the Vietnam War and draft resistance, a political movement that illustrated the social inequities of the sexes (Freeman 1983). Thorne (1975) contends that women in the draft-resistance movement experienced a contradiction between the egalitarian themes of the antiwar movement and their own subordination from within the ranks of that movement, leading to their awareness of sexual inequality as a political issue. In short, an awareness was growing of the second-class status of women in society as well as in the antiwar movement in these early days of the modern women's movement. Because the political issues of the moment were highly gendered with distinct implications for women and men, one would expect to find different developmental processes at work in the negotiation of issues of character.

Methods
Data Set

The data are drawn from a three-wave study conducted by Allen Berger in 1969 and 1970. Berger followed youths from the end of their senior year in high school (Wave 1) through their first two semesters at the University of Illinois (Waves 2 and 3). Unlike many of the studies of the sixties that focus primarily on political activists, these data are more broadly representative of college students of the era. Although this was a historical period of political upheaval, the University of Illinois is not memorable as a hotbed of student unrest. However, Chicago was the site of the Democratic National Convention in the summer of 1968, the year prior to data collection for this study. Events that occurred during the convention should have made issues of the Bill of Rights, free speech, and the antiwar movement salient in the minds of the youth in the sample. There were large demonstrations in the streets of Chicago and the police, sanctioned by then Mayor Richard Daley Sr., responded with physical beatings and arrests, all televised on the nightly news. As already noted, these were also the early days of what has been referred to as the second major wave of the women's movement in the United States, and Chicago was the site of one of the stronger chapters in that movement (Freeman 1983).

Measures

Measures are based on students' self-reports. I have organized the measures into the following theoretically meaningful sets: Attitudes towards social movements; beliefs about civil liberties; activism or participation in social movements; attitudes towards countercultural trends and sex roles. In addition, students reported their perceptions of the faculty's attitudes towards political issues and drug use as well as on their own religiosity. Measures are listed in Table 1.

Before continuing, it should be noted that it was common in studies of the sixties to treat such things as experimentation with drugs, involvement in coun-

Table 1
Description of Constructs

Dependent Measures	
Attitudes toward social movements	
Pro student movements	Support of students' rights to protest or dissent
Pro racial integration	Support civil equality of racial minorities
Reject civil disobedience	Only lawful means, not civil disobedience, are justifiable actions
Attitudes toward civil liberties	
Support civil liberties[a]	Support articles from the Bill of Rights
Active in social movements	
Likely to participate in political movements[b]	Campaigns, communities, ecological, student, or women's movement
Likely to participate in antiwar protests[b]	In demonstrations against war or draft
Attitudes toward countercultural trends	
Opposition to extramartial sex	Sex outside marriage is bad, disrespectful, even unnatural
Tolerance towards alternative lifestyles	Approve of people experimenting with drugs and communal living
Support male dominance	It is more appropriate that men, not women, be in positions of authority
Restrict women's roles	Women's roles should be restricted to home and family
Homophobic attitudes	Belief that homosexuals should be ostracized from society

Independent Measures	
Faculty attitudes towards drug use[c]	Attitudes toward experimentation
Faculty attitudes towards political issues[c]	Attitudes toward war, draft, civil rights, social welfare
Religiosity	How religious student was

Note: Except when noted, scales of: 1 = strongly disagree, 4 = strongly agree; or 1 = not at all likely, 4 = very likely
    a. Scale is sum of 8 (yes/no) items
    b. Time 2 and 3 indicators changed from "how likely" to "how active are you"
    c. Scale: 1 = more liberal than mine to 3 = less liberal than mine

tercultural lifestyles, antiwar, or civil rights activities as if they were all aspects of the same behavioral structure (Whalen and Flacks 1989). For example, in Jessor's (1968) research on problem behavior, involvement in political activism as well as marijuana and alcohol use were each considered departures from regulatory norms and therefore studied as part of the structure of problem behavior. I would argue that, without departures from regulatory norms and, in particular, without political challenges to the status quo, we would not have passed a Civil Rights Act in this country and racial segregation would still be law in the United States. In this spirit I will distinguish students' attitudes towards sociopolitical movements from their attitudes towards countercultural lifestyles, although I would agree that both tap a common theme of tolerance towards diversity and nonconformity.

Data reduction via factor analyses was used to derive constructs. Scales were typically based on the mean of the item scores (exceptions are noted within the tables). Following data reduction, Cronbach's alpha was computed on each scale at each wave to determine its internal consistency. Most scales were composed of three to four items and internal consistency ranged from a minimum of .68 to a maximum of .89.

Analyses

To assess the implications of the transition to college on students' attitudes and engagement, repeated measures analyses of variance were run with gender as a between-subjects factor and time of measurement (senior year of high school, first and second semesters of the freshman year at college) as the repeated measure. Following these analyses of change over time, gender differences were assessed. Finally, multiple regressions were conducted separately for women and men to identify the extent to which the following factors contributed to change in their attitudes and behaviors during the first year of college: (1) residential status, i.e., whether the student lived with or away from family while attending college; (2) how the student compared his or her attitudes (more or less liberal) vis-à-vis those of the faculty; and (3) how religious the student felt he or she was.

Results
Trends during the Transition from High School to College

The results in Table 2 suggest an increase after the transition to college in tolerance of diversity and in support of the rights of free speech and dissent. In addition, compared to their attitudes in high school, by the end of their freshman year in college, young people were more supportive of student movements and more willing to condone civil disobedience as a means of effecting social policy. Although aging and context are confounded in these data, the precipitous change would hardly be expected within a period of six months were it not for a change in setting. The increase in support for racial integration, civil liberties, and citizens' rights of free speech and dissent suggest that something about the college climate made a difference.

The most dramatic changes occurred in students' attitudes towards sexual experimentation and life-style issues. Opposition to extramarital sexual relationships and to experimentation with alternative lifestyles and living arrange-

Table 2
Students' Political Attitudes During the High School to College Transition

	Spring 1969 High School	Fall 1969 College	Spring 1970 College	F Stat
Attitudes toward social movements				
Pro student movements	2.80 (.46)	2.91 (.46)	2.95 (.45)	68.74***
Pro racial integration	2.83 (.57)	2.93 (.58)	2.97 (.57)	49.61***
Reject civil disobedience*a*	2.90 (.84)		2.55 (.82)	149.85***
*Support civil liberties*a*	13.83 (1.58)		14.12 (1.49)	42.37***
Active in social movements				
Likely to participate in political movements	1.94 (.55)	1.85 (.58)	1.84 (.57)	20.86***
Likely to participate in antiwar protests	1.94 (.92)	1.96 (.89)	2.00 (.88)	3.07*
Attitudes toward countercultural trends				
Opposition to extramarital sex	2.12 (.63)	1.96 (.60)	1.83 (.63)	131.90***
Tolerance towards alternative lifestyles	2.23 (.62)	2.41 (.64)	2.55 (.63)	168.65***
Restrict women's roles	2.00 (.48)	1.92 (.47)	1.86 (.49)	48.96***
Support male dominance	2.09 (.50)	1.99 (.52)	1.92 (.54)	68.87***
Homophobic attitudes	2.30 (.56)	2.18 (.53)	2.08 (.56)	71.86***
Comparisons with faculty				
Faculty attitudes towards drug use	2.26 (.53)	2.17 (.49)	2.21 (.50)	11.05***
Faculty attitudes towards political issues	2.25 (.47)	2.12 (.46)	2.19 (.43)	31.72***

*p < .05   **p < .01   ***p < .001
a. measured only at waves 1 and 3

ments declined across the three waves. In addition, during their first year in college, students became more committed to the civil rights of gay people and women. However, the latter change was not as significant as that for tolerance of extramarital relationships and alternative lifestyles. Finally, high-school students' expectation that "most faculty at their college would be more conservative than the students themselves were" declined after the transition, suggesting that a pre-college stereotype may have been moderated by the opportunity to interact with members of the faculty.

Gender Differences

Table 3 summarizes gender differences in mean levels across the three waves in students' attitudes and engagement. On most of the indicators of tolerance, women in this sample had significantly higher scores than men. Not surprisingly, they were more supportive of equality between the sexes. But women were also more supportive of civil rights for gay people, minorities, and students and were more likely than men to be active in a range of political movements. The only instance in which men were more open-minded than women

Table 3
Gender Differences in the Political Attitudes of the Sixties Generation

	Men N = 459	Women N = 391	F Stat
Attitudes toward social movements			
Pro student movement	2.85 (.40)	2.91 (.39)	4.09*
Pro racial integration	2.86 (.53)	2.97 (.50)	8.83**
Reject civil disobedience	2.36 (.64)	2.50 (.64)	10.26**
Support civil liberties	13.90 (1.42)	14.08 (1.36)	3.69
Active in social movements			
Likely to participate in political movements	1.80 (.46)	1.96 (.51)	20.87***
Likely to participate in antiwar protests	1.99 (.83)	1.93 (.75)	.92
Attitudes towards countercultural trends			
Opposition to extramarital sex	1.96 (.53)	1.99 (.56)	.66
Tolerance toward alternative lifestyles	2.48 (.55)	2.30 (.59)	20.21***
Restrict women's roles	2.05 (.38)	1.78 (.44)	91.87***
Support male dominance	2.15 (.42)	1.82 (.46)	118.80***
Homophobic attitudes	2.26 (.47)	2.11 (.47)	20.32***
Comparisons with the faculty			
Faculty attitudes toward drug use	2.20 (.41)	2.21 (.40)	.09
Faculty attitudes toward political issues	2.20 (.36)	2.17 (.37)	.99

Note: Means reflect scores averaged over 3 waves, or—in two measures—2 waves
*$p < .05$ **$p < .01$ ***$p < .001$

was in their attitudes toward alternative lifestyles (i.e., experimentation with drugs and communal living). The fact that women were more likely than men to endorse civil rights for a broad range of groups and to be active in a range of political causes is consistent with the gender differences noted in Franz and McClelland's (1994) work on sixties' activists. Whereas activist men in their sample protested specifically against the draft, women protested for the rights of blacks, the poor, women, and draft-resisters.

The absence of gender differences on several measures is also noteworthy. Women were just as likely as men to approve of extramarital sex, support civil liberties, and participate in antiwar demonstrations. Fewer women than men attended college in that era, thus it is possible that these results reflect a selection bias in terms of the women who were in college at the time. Interestingly, despite the greater egalitarian and tolerant attitudes women reported when compared to men, they were more cautious about civil disobedience, preferring lawful means to effect change.

Thus far, although the empirical trend at the transition to college is clear, explaining that trend is less clear. In the next set of analyses I control for development prior to college entry and look at some of the processes that may have been implicated in the change during the freshmen year.

What Accounts for Change during the First Year of College?

Table 4 presents the results of the multiple regressions predicting outcomes at the end of the freshman year. Looking first at the control variables at Time 1, it is no surprise that attitudes in high school were highly predictive of those same attitudes one year later. In fact, entering such control variables at Wave 1 is a very stringent test of factors related to change in the first year of college. In addition, political involvement in high school was positively associated with liberal attitudes toward social movements as well as toward alternative life-styles one year later. Family background as measured by parents' average education had little effect either on students' political attitudes or involvement.

Controlling for these predictors in high school, consistent gender patterns emerged in the freshman year. Among men, feeling that they were more liberal than the faculty was associated with greater support for student movements, racial integration, women's and gay rights, civil liberties, and alternative lifestyles. Men who felt more liberal than the faculty were also more active in political movements and antiwar protests. This use of social comparison with faculty is interesting in light of Perry's (1970) research on change in students' intellectual and ethical development during the college years. He found that students were better able to deal with uncertainty and still make commitments when they felt a sense of community with faculty and other students who were grappling with the challenges of pluralism. The results for males in this study also echo the findings of Pascarella et al. (1988), i.e., that interactions with faculty were positively related to the importance college students attached to civic and humanitarian values. The fact that male but not female students' attitudes were sensitive to social comparison with the faculty may reflect the preponderance of male faculty in the universities of the 1960s.

For women, religiosity was a more consistent predictor of change during the first year of college. Controlling for attitudes prior to college entry, religiosity was related to *less* support of civil liberties, *less* tolerance of gay people, of alternative lifestyles, and of extramarital sex, and *more* support of male dominance and traditional roles for women. For men, religiosity was related to some outcomes, for example, to *less* tolerance of student movements and extramarital sex and to *more* participation in protests against the war. Finally, only in a few instances and for women was the student's residential status (i.e., living away or at home) important. Not surprisingly, women who moved away from home were more tolerant of extramarital sex and experimentation with alternative lifestyles. However, those who stayed at home were more politically active than their peers on campus, in part because such activity implied community involvement in partisan politics, a local connection that may have been lost with a move to campus.

These gender differences offer some interesting insights into the process of

Table 4

Regression of Political Attitudes and Engagement at the End of the Freshman Year, Holding Constant Indicators in High School

Outcome at Wave 3	Predictors in college			High School predictors		
	Residence[a]	Faculty attitudes[b]	Religiosity[c]	H.S. political involvement	Parent education	Time 1 indicator
Males						
Pro student movements	.05	.13**	−.08*	.18***	−.07	.42***
Pro racial integration	−.03	.13***	.03	.15***	−.02	.61***
Support civil liberties	−.03	.17***	.07	.08	.05	.56***
Participate in political movements	.06	.10**	−.01	.06	−.04	.54***
Participate in antiwar protest	.03	.20***	.09*	.11*	.03	.50***
Oppose extramarital sex	−.02	−.07	.09*	−.04	−.02	.58***
Tolerate alternative lifestyles	.06	.12**	−.06	.04	−.001	.63***
Restrict women's roles	.07	−.10**	−.07	−.05	−.01	.57***
Support male dominance	.08	−.19***	−.03	−.08*	−.04	.54***
Homophobic attitudes	.02	−.12**	−.03	−.07	−.03	.55***
Females						
Pro student movements	−.07	.16***	−.06	.05	.01	.53***
Pro racial integration	.03	.05	−.03	.06	−.01	.71***
Support civil liberties	.07	.01	−.11*	.06	−.02	.59***
Participate in political movements	−.09*	.11*	.06	.21***	.01	.44***
Participate in antiwar protests	−.05	.17***	−.001	.18***	.001	.49***
Oppose extramarital sex	−.15***	−.07*	.11**	−.03	−.02	.63***
Tolerate alternative lifestyles	.14***	.07	−.14***	.07	.002	.60***
Restrict women's roles	−.02	−.05	.10**	−.04	−.02	.67***
Support male dominance	−.04	−.01	.11**	−.08*	−.02	.62***
Homophobic attitudes	−.04	−.01	.11**	−.08*	−.02	.62***

$*p < .05$ $**p < .01$ $***p < .001$

a. High score = live away from home

b. High score = Most faculty at the school are more conservative than me

c. High score = Very religious

consolidating a political identity. It appears that in their first year of college, men who became more supportive of civil and social equality used the faculty as a basis for social comparison and sharpened their own positions on issues by comparing their "stand" relative to that of their professors. In contrast, for women, religion was like a bedrock of tradition in the face of radical political and social change. One might speculate that religion served a protective function for women who were uneasy about sexual experimentation. However, religiosity also served an exclusionary function, i.e., the more religious women were, the more they endorsed the exclusion of women and gay people from full membership in society. The association of religiosity with conservatism and traditional views among women in this sample is consistent with other work from that era. According to Sherkat and Blocker (1994), religious fundamentalism was negatively related to participation in protest activities for both sexes, and Rohrbaugh and Jessor (1975) reported that religiosity functioned as a personal control against problem behavior for high-school and college males and females in the late sixties.

However, in the data reported in this chapter religiosity played a somewhat different role in men's when compared to women's development. Although there were no gender differences in the likelihood of participating in antiwar protests, religiosity increased the likelihood that college men would participate. In light of the gendered implications of antiwar and especially antidraft activities, taking a stand on the war may have posed a spiritual dilemma for men and, in this sense, presented a test of character.

Discussion

Bellah and his colleagues (Bellah et al. 1985) argue that representative characters provide both a focal point where a society encounters its problems as well as a set of cultural understandings for resolving those problems. The generation that came of age in the sixties is one such representative character. From a historical perspective, 1969 marked the end of a decade of utopian thinking, a period of heady optimism about resolving some of America's deepest social problems. By contrast, the seventies ushered in several decades of political cynicism, social isolation, and, some would contend, retreat from our moral dilemmas. Juxtaposing the collective spirit of the sixties against the personalist trends of subsequent decades can help us raise questions about the content of our character and the direction we are headed as a nation. The data discussed in this chapter suggest that college attendance in 1969 may have increased students' tolerance and commitment to broad-based human rights. In part that was a function of the times but undoubtedly it was related to being in a college setting as well. Because the transition from adolescence to adulthood is a period for reflecting on the direction of one's life, it is a prime time for raising questions of personal character and civic virtue.

The changes associated with the transition to college could be interpreted as nothing more than the result of pressures toward collegiate norms. However, in terms of the effects of college on moral judgment, Rest (1988) dismisses "social pressures" explanations as too simplistic. Furthermore, although college attendance had a liberalizing influence on the opinions of the average student in this sample, attributing all of this change to social pressures alone implies passivity on the part of these freshmen and suggests that they didn't think about the issues before them. McAdam (1989) estimates that no more than 2 to 4 percent of the sixties generation actually took an active part in the social movements of that period. Yet the college campus was the site of a great deal of discussion and debate of the social issues of the time and students would inevitably have been pulled into these discussions. Thus, at least some of the change in students' attitudes must have been due to their exposure to new reference groups and sociopolitical perspectives. Furthermore, in the analyses controlling for students' political attitudes and participation during their senior year in high school, there were identifiable factors associated with the process of attitude change in the freshman year at college, factors that differed for men and women.

The sixties began with movements advocating for the civil equality of minorities and for freedom of speech among students. They closed with massive, conscientious objection to American involvement in Vietnam, with a recognition of how deeply embedded gender inequities were in our culture, and with growing numbers of young people longing for some deeper meaning in life than that which "the system" offered. According to Miller (1971, cited in Nicgorski 1987), universities were not responsive to the challenges of students at the time:

> The university can train students to make a living and to contribute to the smooth functioning of the system. It cannot guide their deliberations about the best way of life for man and society because it is largely indifferent to questions about the goodness or justice of things. Students have charged, quite properly, that American higher education is "one-dimensional," that it trains young people to accept things as they are without imparting a vision of a higher good. (214)

The challenge for higher education to foster character development is even greater today. Concerns have been raised that the marketplace has become the arbiter of values in America and that self-interest has eclipsed commitments to the commonwealth (Bellah et al. 1985). Among our youth, self-interest and materialism have been on the increase for the past two decades while, during the same period, the desire to contribute to society has declined (Astin et al. 1986; Johnston, Bachman, and O'Malley 1986). A century ago, Tocqueville was impressed with the American tendency to form and join associations. But in the last few decades scholars have become concerned that the social integuments that hold civil society together may be jeopardized by trends toward isolationism (Putnam 1995). The social movements of the 1960s were anything but isolationist in character. Focusing on the values those movements espoused may help us think about, paraphrasing Bellah et al., the kind of life we want and the kind of people we are.

In addition, centering attention on students in college forces us to look at ways that higher education can both train intellect but also challenge character (Coles 1995). Although citizenship figures prominently in the mission statements of most universities, higher education has been lax in achieving that mission. College students' interest in politics is at an all-time low (Astin 1995), as is that of the American public (Dionne 1991). In their report on the role that higher education should play in our nation's service, Boyer and Hechinger (1981) observe:

> Education's primary mission is to develop within each student the capacity to judge wisely in matters of life and conduct. The center holds because the search for truth leads to the discovery of larger meanings that can be applied with integrity to life's decisions. This, we conclude, is higher learning's most essential mission in the nation's service. (9)

Acknowledgment

Work on this manuscript was supported by a William T. Grant Faculty Scholars Award.

References

Alwin, D. F., R. L. Cohen, and T. M. Newcomb. 1991. *Political Attitudes Over the Life Span: The Bennington Women after Fifty Years*. Madison: University of Wisconsin Press.

Astin, A. W. 1995. "The Cause of Citizenship." *The Chronicle of Higher Education,* 6 October 1995, pp. B 1–2.

Astin, A. W., K. C. Green, and W. S. Korn. 1987. *The American Freshman: Twenty Year Trends*. Los Angeles: UCLA Higher Education Research Institute.

Bellah, R. N., R. Madsen, W. M. Sullivan, A. Swidler, and S. M. Tipton. 1985. *Habits of the Heart: Individualism and Commitment in American Life*. Berkeley: University of California Press.

Boyer, E. L., and F. M. Hechinger. 1981. *Higher Learning in the Nation's Service*. Washington, DC: Carnegie Foundation for the Advancement of Teaching.

Coles, R. 1995. "The Disparity between Intellect and Character." *The Chronicle of Higher Education* 22 September 1995, p. A 68.

Delli Carpini, M. X. 1989. "Age and History: Generations and Sociopolitical Change." In *Political Learning in Adulthood: A Sourcebook of Theory and Research,* ed. R. Sigel, 11–55. Chicago: University of Chicago Press.

Demartini, J. R. 1985. "Change Agents and Generational Relationships: A Reevaluation of Mannheim's Problem of Generations." *Social Forces* 64: 1–16.

Dennis, J., and C. Webster. 1975. "Children's Images of the President and of Government in 1962 and 1974." *American Politics Quarterly* 3(4): 386–405.

Dionne, E. J., Jr. 1991. *Why Americans Hate Politics.* New York: Simon and Schuster.

Duncan, L. E., and A. J. Stewart. 1995. "Still Bringing the Vietnam War Home: Sources of Contemporary Student Activism." *Personality and Social Psychology Bulletin* 18: 147–58.

Dunham, C., and V. Bengston. 1992. "The Long-Term Effects of Political Activism on Intergenerational Relations." *Youth and Society* 24: 31–51.

Erikson, E. H. 1968. *Identity: Youth and Crisis.* New York: W. W. Norton.

Fendrich, J. M., and K. L. Lovoy. 1988. "Back to the Future: Adult Political Behavior of Former Student Activists." *American Sociological Review* 53: 780–84.

Fernandez, R., and D. McAdam. 1988. "Multiorganizational Fields and Recruitment Contexts." *Sociological Forum* 3: 327–82.

Flacks, R. 1967. "The Liberated Generation: An Exploration of the Roots of Student Protest." *Journal of Social Issues* 23: 52–75.

Franz, C. E., and D. C. McClelland. 1994. "Lives of Women and Men Active in the Social Protests of the 1960's: A Longitudinal Study." *Journal of Personality and Social Psychology* 66: 196–205.

Freeman, J. 1983. "On the origin of Social Movements." In *Social Movements of the Sixties and Seventies,* ed. J. Freeman, 8–30. New York: Longman.

Glenn, N. D. 1980. "Values, Attitudes, and Beliefs." In *Constancy and Change in Human Development,* ed. O. G. Brim and J. Kagan, 596–640. Cambridge, MA: Harvard University Press.

Haan, N., M. B. Smith, and J. Block. 1968. "Moral Reasoning of Young Adults: Political-Social Behavior, Family Background, and Personality Correlates." *Journal of Personality and Social Psychology* 10: 183–201.

Jennings, M. K. 1989. "The Crystallization of Orientations." In *Continuities in Political Action,* ed. M. K. Jennings et al., 313–48. Berlin: DeGruyter.

Jessor, R., T. D. Graves, R. C. Hanson, and S. L. Jessor. 1968. *Society, Personality, and Deviant Behavior: A Study of a Tri-Ethnic Community.* New York: Holt, Rinehart, and Winston.

Johnston, L. D., J. G. Bachman, and P. M. O'Malley. 1986. *Monitoring the Future: Questionnaire Responses from the Nation's High School Students, 1985.* Ann Arbor: University of Michigan, Institute for Social Research.

Keniston, K. 1968. *Young Radicals: Notes on Committed Youth.* New York: Harcourt, Brace, and World.

Mannheim, K. 1952 [1928]. "The Problem of Generations." In *Essays on the Sociology of Knowledge,* ed. P. Kecshevich, 276–322. London: Routledge and Kegan Paul.

Marwell, G., M. T. Aiken, and N. J. Demerath III. 1987. "The Persistence of Political Attitudes among 1960's Civil Rights Activists." *Public Opinion Quarterly* 51: 359–75.

McAdam, D. 1989. "The Biographical Consequences of Activism." *American Sociological Review* 54: 744–60.

McAdam, D. 1992. "Gender and the Activist Experience: The Case of Freedom Summer." *American Journal of Sociology* 97: 1211–40.

Newcomb, T. M., K. E. Koenig, R. Flacks, and D. P. Warwich. 1967. *Persistence and Change: Bennington College and Its Students after 25 Years.* New York: Wiley.

Nicgorski, W. 1987. "The College Experience and Character." In *Character Development in Schools and Beyond,* ed. K. Ryan and G. F. McLean, 328–57. New York: Praeger Publishers.

Pascarella, E. T., C. A. Ethington, and J. C. Smart. 1988. "The Influence of College on Humanitarian/Civic Involvement Values." *Journal of Higher Education* 59(4): 412–37.

Perry, W. G., Jr. 1970. *Forms of Intellectual and Ethical Development in the College Years: A Scheme.* New York: Holt, Rinehart, and Winston.

Putnam, R. D. 1995. "Bowling Alone: America's Declining Social Capital." *Journal of Democracy* 6: 65–78.

Rest, J. R. 1988. "Why Does College Promote Development in Moral Judgment?" *Journal of Moral Education* 17: 183–94.

Roberts, C. W., and K. Lang. 1985. "Generations and Ideological Change: Some Observations." *Public Opinion Quarterly* 49: 460–73.

Rohrbaugh, J., and R. Jessor. 1975. "Religiosity in Youth: A Personal Control against Deviant Behavior." *Journal of Personality* 43: 136–55.

Schuman, H., and J. Scott. 1989. "Generations and Collective Memories." *American Sociological Review* 54: 359–81.

Sherkat, D. E., and T. J. Blocker. 1994. "The Political Development of Sixties' Activists: Identifying the Influence of Class, Gender, and Socialization on Protest Participation." *Social Forces* 72: 821–42.

Sigel, R., and M. Hoskin. 1981. *The Political Involvement of Adolescents.* New Brunswick, NJ: Rutgers University Press.

Stewart, A. J., and J. M. Healy. 1989. "Linking Individual Development and Social Changes." *American Psychologist* 44: 30–42.

Thorne, B. 1975. "Women in the Draft Resistance Movement: A Case Study of Sex Roles and Social Movements." *Sex Roles* 1: 179–95.

Tocqueville, A. 1966 [1848]. *Democracy in America.* New York: Harper and Row.

Whalen, J., and R. Flacks. 1989. *Beyond the Barricades: The Sixties Generation Grows Up.* Philadelphia: Temple University Press.

Wood, J. L., and W. C. Ng. 1980. "Socialization and Student Activism: Examination of a Relationship." In *Research in Social Movements, Conflict, and Change,* vol. 3. ed. L. Kriesberg, 21–44. Greenwich, CT: JAI Press.

CHAPTER EIGHT

Family Structure and Political Participation of African-American Women

ERIC PLUTZER

More than thirty years after Lyndon Johnson "declared war" on poverty, black neighborhoods in America's largest cities remain poor and have high rates of crime victimization, substandard housing, infant mortality, and other problems. One problem seen as linked to many others—either as cause or effect—is the high incidence of single parenthood.

Urban poverty and the problems associated with it will not disappear of their own accord but will require conscious decisions and actions on the part of public officials and citizens, including those who are most disadvantaged. It is surely necessary and desirable for poor urban communities to be characterized by a norm of social responsibility that encompasses political participation in the broadest sense of the term.

Unfortunately, research is fairly consistent in showing that both being poor (e.g., Brady, Verba, and Schlozman 1995), and living in a poor neighborhood (e.g., Cohen and Dawson 1993) lead to lower levels of civic involvement. Moreover, low turnout by the disadvantaged has clear consequences for public policy, the quality of life, and opportunities to reduce hardship in future generations. In states where turnout is especially low among the poor, social welfare benefits are especially meager (Leighley and Hill 1995) and state educational spending is relatively inequitable (Wiefek 1997).

Of course, the barriers erected by low socioeconomic status can be countered by personal or community resources. In fact, for about two decades, research has shown that blacks' participation rates were higher than corresponding rates for whites with similar levels of education. A strong sense of race consciousness, combined with the belief that government action would improve the condition of blacks, apparently compensated for low levels of political resources such as education and income (Shingles 1981). But more recent research suggests that this compensation has disappeared (Bobo and Gilliam 1990) and

black electoral participation may be in the midst of a downward slide that began in 1984. Moreover, turnout rates are especially low among a group that has
grown in size over the last three decades: single mothers.

Single mothers represent an important group within the African-American
community. This chapter attempts to explain their low participation rate in
more general terms, examining factors that explain political participation
among middle-class Americans (e.g., socioeconomic status, mobility, and internalized norms of the "civic culture") as well as factors with special relevance to African Americans (e.g., extended family structure, compensating social networks).

Turnout as a Developmental Process

Figure 1 illustrates the turnout deficit associated with single parenthood. Using
data from the 1979–1980 National Survey of Black Americans, I have plotted
the probability of reported turnout for 252 married and 322 single mothers.[1]
The timing of the study requires that the analyses be based on women aged
twenty-two or older in order to ensure that everyone asked whether they voted
in the 1976 election was of voting age when the election occurred.[2]

Figure 1 reveals that although both groups start with similar levels of turn-

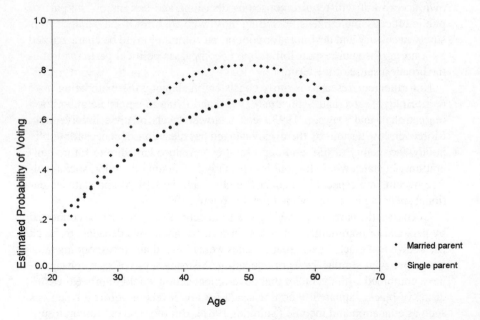

FIGURE 1. Probability of Voting in 1976 Election, by Age and Marital Status.

out, the developmental trends are strikingly different. Married parents' electoral participation increases rapidly with age. In contrast, single mothers' rate of voting increases gradually so that they fall further and further behind. Married women's turnout rates stop increasing at about fifty years old, with both groups converging at about age sixty-five.[3] This age trend is apparent in the larger American public as well (e.g., Milbrath 1965: 134; Verba and Nie 1972, chapter 7), with groups varying in the rapidity that their turnout rises in young adulthood. Although this study and other cited research is based on cross-sectional data, cohort analyses have found similar patterns (see, e.g., Miller and Shanks 1996).[4] Explanations for group differences are highly contested with three broad explanations relevant to the present study.

Political Character and the Psychology of Political Participation

Political philosophers and political scientists have divided into three (sometimes, but not always, opposed) camps on the question of political character.

Liberalism and Pluralism

The classic liberal view is derived from the social contract theories of Hobbes and Locke along with such later thinkers as John Rawls. The relationship of the citizen to the state is deemed to be *contractual*. In return for certain rights and protections, the citizen internalizes certain norms that govern the citizen's responsibilities. Responsibilities are viewed as a burden on the citizen that are justified by the benefits of residing in a liberal, democratic state.

From this perspective, certain personality traits are beneficial to the functioning of a democracy; these include habitual voting, deference to compromises reached by elected officials, adherence to the will of the majority, and valuing rights of conscience, speech, property, and other civil liberties. In the contractual framework, it makes sense for loyal citizens to ask what their country can do for them and to ask elected officials, "What have you done for me lately?" Yet for all this, one's identity as citizen makes up a tiny portion of the self. The citizen role is invoked infrequently and is rarely a major component of one's personality.

A distinctly American version of liberal democratic theory is *pluralism*. Pluralism has a number of versions, but at base it argues that political conflict is best undertaken by interest groups, that interest groups vie against one another in the political marketplace, and that the presence of many groups means that no group consistently wins or consistently loses. In this view, the ideal citizen delegates the responsibility for *direct* political involvement to numerous interest group and community leaders. Voting is desirable but additional activity is nonessential because the citizen is well represented in those arenas in which decisions are made and compromises forged. If the citizen is content with the pattern of political outcomes, there is no need to play an active citizen role so long as one plays an active role in community organizations. Citizens merely have the *right* to participate but need not continually exercise it to be competent citizens and to display mature political character.

More than three decades ago, Almond and Verba proposed that representative democracy would flourish when citizens internalized a complex of values and beliefs that they dubbed the *Civic Culture* (1963). A central characteristic of civic character is *trust*. Citizens must trust one another in order to respect the judgment of the majority when it differs from their personal opinions, trust community and interest group leaders to speak on their behalf, and trust politicians to respond to the will of the majority (at the very least because politicians are motivated to maximize their chances of re-election). Societies and subcultures low on survey indicators of interpersonal trust were among the least democratic (see also Banfield 1958). More recently, Inglehart has implicated subjective well-being and economic security as core values in the civic culture as well (1990, especially chapter 1).

Communitarianism

The second tradition has been referred to as communitarianism, sometimes associated with Aristotle's notion of civic Republicanism, and Rousseau's version of the social contract. More recent expressions of the communitarian philosophy can be found in Benjamin Barber's notion of "strong democracy" and Lerner's "politics of meaning." Israeli *kibbutzim* may be viewed as modern laboratories of communitarian citizenship.

In the communitarian ideal, the division between public and private is blurred. Community interactions become the basis of political striving to advance "the public good." Participation is not only permitted but expected—for the good of citizen and community. Citizen rights become less salient than citizen duties and responsibilities, which are welcomed rather than avoided. The citizen role occupies a much larger component of the self, as it is invoked daily and cannot simply be partitioned off from economic, social, and family life.

From the communitarian perspective, the central components of civic character are solidarity and integration into primary and especially secondary institutions of the community. This integration leads to knowledge of community issues, a feeling that one is a stakeholder, a sense of efficacy, and the belief that the community values the input of all members.

Democratic theorists, whether contractual or communitarian, assume that the norms of good citizenship must ultimately be internalized by large numbers of people. In neither democratic utopia can individuals be continually forced or induced to be good citizens. And this leads to attempts to promote demo-cratic character—through citizenship and civics courses, through efforts of voluntary organizations, and through education by social workers, community organizers, or even public-service advertising.

Mobility and Resources

A third group of studies heavily discounts the role of political character. Ac-cording to this view, motivation to vote does not vary significantly across the American public and it is generally low. Most Americans express an interest in voting, and most citizens will eventually register to vote. However, 20% of the public moves each year and many moves will place citizens in a new elec-tion ward, county, or state. In states with strict registration rules, many moves within the same neighborhood may require re-registration. For those Ameri-cans who have lived in the same community for five or ten years, registration is very high. And among those registered, traditional variables such as edu-cation or expressed interest in politics make only very small differences (see Squire, Wolfinger, and Rosenstone 1987 for an elaboration of this position). The relevance to African Americans is potentially significant. Mobility is high-est among the young, the poor, and the unmarried.

A related stream of research focuses on individual resources that can be translated into the capital of political participation. Cognitive resources are es-pecially important because the ability to understand the issues of a campaign is enhanced by high levels of education and by frequent newspaper readership, for example. In addition, motivation to participate may be blunted by a lack of free time (see Brady, Verba, and Schlozman 1995).

All three traditions have been hampered by a rather static view of voting. In spite of widespread knowledge of the shifting levels of participation with age, few studies explicitly adopt a dynamic approach to theorizing or hypothesis testing. The present study attempts to remedy that by seeking to explain rates of growth rather than static levels.

Explaining Turnout in the 1976 Presidential Election

The National Survey of Black Americans was conducted in 1979 and 1980 over a seven-month period. With a total of 2107 interviews, it is by far the largest national sample of African Americans and the only survey that makes detailed comparisons among black women possible (in contrast, James Jack-son's *National Black Election Study* has a sample of only 872 in its 1984 post-election interview wave; black oversamples in the 1982 and 1987 General So-cial Surveys contain only 311 and 334 blacks, respectively).

The NSBA includes a retrospective question asking individuals if they voted in the most recent (that is, 1976) presidential election. Although three years prior to the interview, the variable nevertheless appears to be a valid and reliable indicator of actual turnout, although there is a tendency towards over-reporting.

The 1976 election represented a change from the two previous elections inasmuch as the Vietnam War, "urban unrest," and civil rights were not dominant issues. Both Jimmy Carter and President Gerald Ford were centrists and thus issues played less of a role than in previous or ensuing elections. Turnout among all Americans had been falling steadily since the 1950s and fell by 5 percent compared with 1972.

In terms of black voting behavior, election polls suggest a great deal of continuity. Black turnout was 49 percent, in comparison with 52 percent in 1972 and 51 percent in 1980 (Conway 1991: 28). Gallup polls indicate that the black vote for the Democratic nominee fluctuated between 85 percent and 87 percent for a twenty-year period beginning in 1968 (Stanley and Niemi 1988: 77). Although every presidential election has its unique features, there is little to suggest that black turnout patterns from 1976 would be atypical of those in other recent elections.

Single and Married Mothers: Differences and Similarities

The NSBA has an extensive set of demographic, socioeconomic, and attitudinal measures that allow us to generate a profile of typical single and married mothers. Table 1 shows how the two groups compare on sixteen variables suggested by previous research (details on question-wording are provided in Appendix A).

In terms of family structure and family ties, there was a very large difference in whether there was a second adult in the household. This was almost universally the case for married respondents, but true for only about a quarter of single mothers. However, being the lone adult in one's household does not necessarily translate into a broader sense of familial isolation: Single and married mothers were virtually identical in answering questions regarding frequent contact with family members and in subjective closeness to their family.

With respect to community ties, married parents report more frequent church attendance and are more rooted in the community, having made a third fewer major moves in the previous five years. There were no significant differences in whether the respondent reported having a best friend or whether she was a crime victim. There was a significant difference in activity in community groups, with single parents about 30 percent less likely to be involved in such an organization.

I examined a number of psychological variables, only one of which revealed significant group differences. No differences were found in scores on multi-

Table 1
Difference of Means on Potential Explanatory Variables

Variable	Married parents	Single parents
I. Family structure		
R is only adult in household	3.5%	76.4%*
Frequency of contact with relatives (Likert)	2.07	2.05
Is R's family close (Likert)	1.55	1.61
II. Community ties		
Attends church weekly or more	50.0%	38.0%*
A crime victim	6.6%	8.7%
Has a "best friend"	72.2%	78.4%
Made inter-city move in last 5 years	12.5%	19.3%*
Member of community group(s)	12.4%	17.3%*
III. Social psychological variables		
Personal efficacy scale	6.11	6.33
R feels overworked often (Likert)	2.66	2.92
Self worth scale	1.42	1.39
How happy is R (Likert)	1.86	2.10*
IV. Socioeconomic status		
High-school diploma and beyond	70.0%	62.0%*
Currently employed	63.4%	55.0%*
On welfare	1.9%	14.0%*
Family income in 1978 (scale 1–13)	12.7	8.77*

*$p < .05$

item scales tapping personal efficacy and self-worth, nor were there differences in the frequency with which respondents report feeling overworked, which might have reflected time available to devote to politics. In contrast, single parents were slightly, though significantly, less likely to report they felt happy.[5]

Finally, I examined four indicators of socioeconomic status. On all four, single parents lag behind: They are less likely to have graduated from high school and less likely to be employed; their families are far more likely to be on welfare; and family income is substantially lower. The category means translate into approximately $6,700 for single mothers and $11,500 for married mothers.

Explaining Differences between Married and Single Mothers
Methodological Concerns

Explaining different trajectories is a little more complicated than simply explaining away main effects of variables. The latter is quite straightforward, as statistical controls representing intervening variables should render the main effect equal to, or close to, zero.

But the differences in trajectories represent complex differences in intercepts, main effects, and the curvilinear portion of the model. Table 2 reports the logistic regression model that corresponds to Figure 1 above. The variable "age" has been "centered" around the point where the two trajectories cross— at about 25.6 years old. Thus, the logistic regression model includes "centered age" (i.e., age -25.6), and the quadratic term of centered age^2 that adds a second inflection point to the logistic curve and permits proper modeling of the downward slope as respondents approach retirement age. Subtracting 25.6 years from each person's age means that when the modified age measure is zero, there is no difference between single and married mothers. And this allows dropping a main effect variable for marital status that otherwise would have generated substantial multi-collinearity (see Aiken and West 1991, for a useful discussion of the benefits of this type of centering).

The two interaction terms (variables 4 and 5) estimate the relative flatness of the single mothers' trajectory in comparison to the trajectory for married mothers. When the variable for single parenthood is zero, the last two terms drop out. Thus, the curve for married mothers is completely described by the intercept, age and age.^{2}

The crucial aspect of this model is the joint contribution of the last two terms. The lower panel of the table reports the fit of the model without the trajectory-single interactions, and then the fit of the model with these added. The difference in the likelihood ratio is distributed as χ^2 with two degrees of freedom. The difference of 8.66 is statistically significant and supports the hypothesis that the two trajectories are different (in the population from which the sample was drawn).[6]

Table 2
Logistic Regression of Voting in 1976 Presidential Election on Centered Age, Age Squared, and Relevant Interactions ($N = 574$)

Variable	b	SE(b)	sig
1. Constant	$-.7857$	.1483	
2. Age in years (centered)	.1925	.0350	*
3. Age (centered) squared	$-.0040$	.0014	*
4. Single parent X age	$-.0857$	.0395	*
5. Single parent X age^2	.0023	.0018	

Testing whether trajectories are significantly different

	χ^2	df	sig
-2(LLR) excluding variables 4–5	727.316	4	
-2(LLR) full model	718.656	6	
Net improvement in fit	8.660	2	.013

Explaining Different Trajectories

Earlier I showed that single and married mothers differed in social isolation, community ties, happiness, and socioeconomic status. I now move to see which of these differences can account for the large differences in the trajectories.

This is done by taking each of the variables that varied significantly across the two groups and seeing if its addition to the basic model reported in Table 2 substantially reduces the explanatory power of the interaction terms. Recall that the significance test for the two interaction terms yielded a χ^2 value of 8.66. Here we will examine the same test statistic but only *after* accounting for the effects of each explanatory variable. If the χ^2 test is substantially reduced by the addition of a variable, that variable has "explained" at least part of the differences.

We begin with the only family structure variable to yield significant group differences: Whether the mother was the only adult in the household. This variable was added to the model reported in Table 2 and the same analysis repeated. Table 3 reports summary statistics for this model in the first row. As predicted, this variable was a significant predictor of turnout with lower reported turnout among those who are the sole adult. Yet, when this variable is added, the two interaction terms representing the difference in trajectories continue to im-

Table 3
Improvement in Fit due to Single-Parent Status and Age Interactions after Controlling for Age, Age-Squared and Selected Explanatory Variables

Variable introduced into the model	χ^2 test for different trajectories	Reduction in improvement
Baseline model (from Table 2)	8.660	
I. Family Structure		
R is only adult in household	8.291	4.3%
II. Community Ties		
Church attendance*	7.747	10.6%
Inter-city move in last 5 years	7.996	7.7%
Member of community groups	7.182	17.1%
III. Social Psychological Variables		
Personal efficacy scale*	8.238	4.9%
How happy is R*	5.870	32.2%
IV. Socioeconomic Status		
Education (3 dummy vars)*	6.103	29.6%
Employment status*	6.664	23.1%
Currently on welfare*	5.779	32.1%
Family income in 1978*	2.042	76.4%

*Variable is significant predictor of turnout: $p < .05$

prove the fit of the model; the improvement in χ^2 has dropped 4.3 percent (as indicated in the last column) from 8.66 to 8.29. That is, the differences between single parents and married parents are very nearly the same as before we accounted for the possible effects of being the only adult at home. In addition, the difference remains statistically significant across the two degrees of freedom.

Thus, we can rule out social isolation as the primary explanation for the flatter trajectory of single mothers. For if this were the case, the differences between single and married mothers could be partially compensated for by the presence of other adults in the household, and their closeness to extended family members.

Among the community variables, similar results obtain. Participation in church services is related to participation in politics, but this does not explain the faster developmental pattern among married mothers. Furthermore, neither membership in community groups nor geographic mobility is related to turnout.

I then examined the possible effects of the psychological variables. Personal efficacy did not explain a large portion of the differences, but the single item asking about happiness reduces the group differences by 32.2 percent. This is consistent with the literature on the civic culture, which regularly finds happiness and life satisfaction to be part of this syndrome of civic character.

Finally, four indicators of SES were each introduced into the model. All explained away some of the differences between single and married parents. But the effect of family income was by far the most dramatic. After controlling for family income, the improvement in fit due to the interaction terms declines to an insignificant χ^2 of 2.042—a drop of 76.4 percent. That is, the relatively accelerated rate of increase of married mothers is almost entirely accounted for by their greater income.

Summary

To sum up the results, we can conclude that the relatively slow development of this one aspect of civic responsibility among single mothers is not due to social isolation, limited social and familial networks, or limited religious involvement. It is also not due to limited time or reported exhaustion. Nor is it due to low levels of personal efficacy. Many of these variables help determine average levels of turnout (averaged over all ages) but they do not explain why the association of turnout with age is so much stronger for young married mothers than it is for young single parents. The only measured psychological trait that even partially explains the flat developmental trajectory for single mothers is expressed personal happiness.

Among the socioeconomic variables, only income provides a statistical explanation. The effect of income was not mediated by education or mobility, nor was it spurious due to the prior cause of having a second adult earner in the household.

Making Sense of the Results: Some Informed Speculation

The results are in some ways surprising. There are no theories in political science suggesting a *direct* effect of income on voter turnout. To be sure, socioeconomic status is the most important concept in this field, but this is because socioeconomic variables presumably serve as indicators for the direct hindrances or facilitators of voting. It is for this reason that political scientists have begun to move "beyond SES" (Brady, Verba, and Schlozman 1995). Income, for example, is related to geographic mobility, which lowers the likelihood of being registered to vote (Squire, Wolfinger, and Glass 1987). Economic success might also increase the likelihood that one gets involved in commercial or consumer organizations. Yet we examined these and other factors and none explained the different developmental patterns of single and married mothers. When leading political scientists suggest that we should be moving "beyond SES" these results suggest we need to examine it more closely and rethink its possible role.

Let us now consider, then, why income is so important and why it might explain the relatively flat trajectory of single parents. That is, I want to speculate about how family income might function in the developmental process. In particular, I want to propose two possibilities: (1) low income leads to alienation from middle-class political institutions, and (2) the stability of single-parent income may result in a general pessimism that depresses turnout.

When family income is increasing, as it does early in the adult life course, it not only creates the ability to eliminate problems of poverty and to purchase consumer goods, but also changes the way that people think about the future and their political interests. The most conventional way that interests change is in a move from the left to the right as people get more affluent. Yet few African Americans become sufficiently affluent to share interests with conservative, free-market advocates.

Rather, they rise into the lower-middle, or middle-middle income range. This movement into the lower reaches of the middle class may increase interest in more "establishment" issues of conventional politics such as property rights, zoning regulations, tax policy, government assistance to small business, college loans, and so on. These are issues of little relevance or of low priority to the very poor. And these are issues addressed by elected officials in the conventional politics characterized by elections, interest-group lobbying, and legislation.

In this sense, income may be the precursor to a kind of middle-class civic awareness. It may also lessen people's enthusiasm for unconventional politics—including community activism, protest, and political violence. Owning property or feeling that one has a stake in the future may produce a shift in orientation in which conventional political involvement fits as a natural part of one's lifestyle.

If this speculation is true, then we should see a developmental pattern in family income that parallels the developmental pattern in voter turnout. In fact, this is exactly what we find. Figure 3 shows the predicted income levels at every age level, for both types of parents. Both groups get more affluent during their twenties and thirties. Yet the income levels of single parents may not cross a threshold that plunges them into the commercial and financial issues of their communities.

Yet not only do married mothers begin at a higher level of income, their rate of increase in income is dramatically faster. The income trajectory depicted in Figure 2 is not one to inspire optimism among single parents of any age. If marriage prospects are bleak, a lack of hope and optimism about one's financial future is a realistic response to single parenthood in the United States today— perhaps especially in the African-American community.

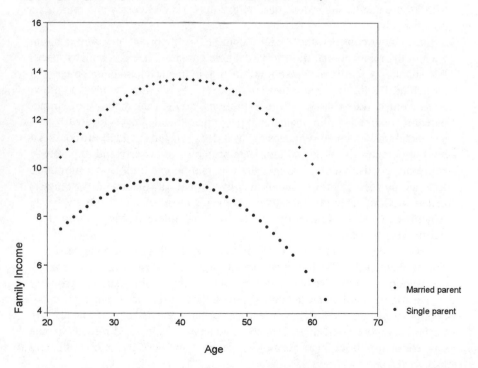

FIGURE 2. Family Income by Age and Marital Status.

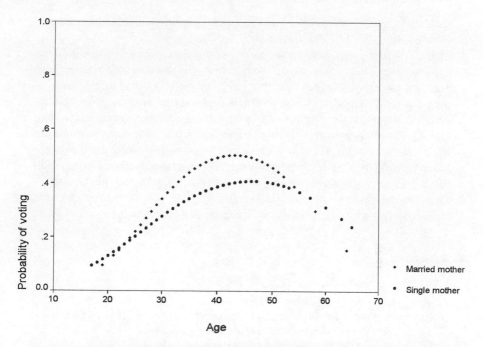

FIGURE 3.   Primary Turnout in 1984. (*Source:* National Black Election Study.)

Pessimism might suppress voter turnout through its impact on the future. Optimists might imagine that they will be in a position to benefit from government policies, but realistic pessimists may believe that most policies benefit the middle class the most. In short, electoral participation in the United States may be motivated far less by fear than by hope.[7] Those with little realistic chance of economic mobility may be difficult to mobilize politically—a theme implicit in Jesse Jackson's 1984 slogan, "Keep hope alive."

Finally this raises the question of whether patterns for an election that occurred twenty years ago constitute valid grounds for trying to understand contemporary politics. Unfortunately, no survey on the scale of the NSBA has since been attempted. However, the 1984 National Black Election Study's pre-election poll (with a sample of 1,150) allows replicating the analysis depicted in Figure 1 using self-reported vote in a presidential primary as the indicator of political involvement. Although the overall levels of participation are lower because primaries attract few voters, the pattern reported in Figure 3 is similar to what was observed eight years earlier.[8]

Moreover, the incidence of single parenthood in the black community has increased since 1979–80. Thus the consequences of depressed turnout among single mothers might well be amplified today, further limiting the electoral clout of America's black communities.

The results reported here do not necessarily weigh against traditional efforts such as voter-registration drives. Nor do they suggest that effort to increase personal efficacy and self-esteem will fail to increase political participation— they would have modest effects on single and married mothers alike. But the great divide in participation appears to be squarely rooted in economic status, and it will widen or narrow in response to levels of economic opportunity in the community at large. For it is economic opportunity, especially for young black men, that depresses marriage rates; and single parenthood offers such bleak prospects of upward mobility that optimism cannot easily be "manufactured" without real changes in opportunity. It is in this sense that opportunity, civic character, and civic competence are inseparably intertwined.

Appendix

I. Wording and response categories for single item scales

Frequency of contact with relatives
How often do your see, write, or talk on the telephone with family or relatives who do not live with you? Nearly everyday (coded 1), at least once a week (coded 2), a few times a month (coded 3), at least once a month (coded 4), a few times a year (coded 5) or hardly ever (coded 6)? Volunteered responses of "Never" are coded as 7.

Is respondent's family close?
Would you say your family members are very close (coded 1), fairly close (coded 2), not too close (coded 3), or not close at all (coded 4)?

Does respondent feel overworked often?
In general, do you ever feel overworked because of all the things you have to do?

How happy is the respondent?
Taking all things together, how would you say things are these days—would you say you're very happy (reverse-coded to 3), pretty happy (coded 2), or not too happy (coded 1) these days?

II. Wording and response categories for multi-item scales

Self-worth scale (all items were originally coded 1 = almost always true, 2 = often true, 3 = not often true, 4 = never true). Prior to scaling, three items were reverse-coded.
   I am a useful person to have around (reverse-coded).
   I feel that I am a person of worth (reverse-coded).
   I feel that I can't do anything right.

I feel that my life is not very useful.
I feel I do not have much to be proud of.
As a person I do a good job these days (reverse-coded).

Personal efficacy scale

Do you think it is better to plan your life a good ways ahead (coded 1), or would you say life is too much a matter of luck to plan ahead very far (coded 2)?

When you make plans ahead, do you usually get to carry out things the way you expected (coded 1), or do things usually come up to make you change your plans (coded 2)?

Have you been pretty sure your life would work out the way you want it to (coded 1) , or have there been times when you haven't been sure about it (coded 2)?

Some people feel they can run their lives pretty much the way they want to (coded 1), others feel the problems of life are sometimes too big for them (coded 2). Which are you most like?

Notes

1. "Mother" refers to women who have children under the age of eighteen living at home. Of course, women with adult children are also parents. In this analysis, however, I am interested in the effects of being responsible for children and the effect this might have on political involvement.

2. I also elected to restrict the analysis to women aged sixty-five and younger, since older women beyond the conventional retirement age may be quite different in many respects and have passed through an additional life transition which could fundamentally affect political participation and the meaning of several independent variables such as employment status.

3. It is important to emphasize that the estimates reported in Figure 1 are a simulation and not an actual representation of changes throughout the life course of real people. The data were all collected in 1979–1980 and therefore reflect the participation rates at each age only at that time. The curve is similar to those used in calculating life expectancy: It models what would happen for someone to age under the conditions in 1979–80. Of course, the thirty year olds of 1980 may encounter very different conditions when they reach age fifty than the fifty year olds surveyed in the NSBA.

4. In fact, it is possible to confound cohort and age effects in this type of analysis. In fact the fall-off in the fifties and sixties for both groups could well be an artifact of the fact that older women entered the electorate before the passage of the 1965 Voting Rights Act. Nevertheless, there is no reason to think that this would confound the *differences* between married and single parents.

5. Unfortunately, the NSBA does not contain a direct measure of interpersonal trust. Thus, an important component of the battery of civic culture variables was not available. Fortunately, Schuessler's massive analysis of social life feelings (1982) shows that interpersonal trust and personal efficacy are strongly correlated (his scales were correlated

at a level of .53). If his findings are generalizable to the black community, this suggests that the impact of a good scale of interpersonal trust should not differ substantially from the effects of the efficacy scale used in the current analysis.

6. The actual slope estimates have fairly straightforward substantive interpretations. The positive slope for age and the negative slope for age squared indicates that the odds of voting increase with age but decrease with age squared. After centering, the quantity age squared is zero at age twenty-six but increases rapidly, producing the sharp inflection among married parents at about age sixty. That is, these estimates make sense in the context of the trajectories depicted in Figure 1. The interactions have opposite signs. The slope for age among single parents is calculated by adding the main effect to the corresponding interaction—in this case .1925 minus .0857. That is, the slope for single parents is about half the size of that of married parents. Again, this is exactly what is depicted in Figure 1.

7. Again, Schuessler's (1982) comprehensive analysis of social life feelings is informative. He reports a correlation of .46 between his "Feeling up" scale and his scale of "Future outlook." Thus it is plausible that the NSBA's measure of happiness is functioning here as a rough indicator of optimistic future outlook.

8. The small number of cases (363) does not permit us to conclude that the two curves are significantly different across both parameters.

Bibliography

Aiken, L. S., and S. G. West. 1991. *Multiple Regression: Testing and Interpreting Interactions.* Newbury Park, CA: Sage.

Almond, G., and S. Verba, 1963. *The Civic Culture.* Princeton, NJ: Princeton University Press.

Banfield, Edward. 1958. *The Moral basis of a Backward Society.* New York: The Free Press.

Bobo, L., and F. D. Gilliam, Jr. 1990. "Race, Sociopolitical Participation, and Black Empowerment." *American Political Science Review* 84: 377–93.

Brady, H. E., S. Verba, and K. L. Schlozman. 1995. "Beyond SES: A Resource Model of Political Participation." *American Political Science Review* 89: 271–94.

Cohen, C. J., and M. C. Dawson. 1993. "Neighborhood Poverty and African American Politics." *American Political Science Review* 87: 286–302.

Conway, M. M. 1991. *Political Participation in the United States* Second edition. Washington: Congressional Quarterly Press.

Inglehart, R. 1990. *Culture Shift in Advanced Industrial Society.* Princeton, NJ: Princeton University Press.

Leighley, J. E., and K. Q. Hill. 1995. "Lower-class Mobilization and Policy Linkages in the U.S. States." *American Journal of Political Science* 39: 75-86.

Milbrath, L. W. 1965. *Political Participation.* Chicago: Rand McNally.

Miller, W. E., and J. M. Shanks. 1996. *The New American Voter.* Cambridge, MA: Harvard University Press.

Schuessler, K. 1982. *Measuring Social Life Feelings.* Jossey-Bass.

Shingles, R. 1981. "Black Consciousness and Political Participation: The Missing Link." *American Political Science Review* 75: 376–91.

Squire, P., R. Wolfinger, and D. Glass. 1987. "Residential Mobility and Voter Turnout." *American Political Science Review* 81: 45–65.

Stanley, H. W., and R. Niemi. 1988. *Vital Statistics on American Politics.* Washington, D.C.: Congressional Quarterly Press.

Verba, S., and N. Nie. 1972. *Participation in America.* New York: Harper and Row.

Wiefek, N. 1997. "Electoral Participation of Low Income Groups and State Policy." Paper presented at Annual Meeting of the Midwest Political Science Association, April 10–12.

CHAPTER NINE

Adult Character: Agency, Communion, Insight, and the Expression of Generativity in Mid-life Adults

SHELLEY MACDERMID,
CAROL E. FRANZ,
AND LEE ANN DE REUS

Laments regarding the strength of the social fabric of societies have been common throughout human history; recent years in the United States are no exception. Cultural critics have mourned the increasing isolation of families from their communities and each other; others' voices have called for programs that will weave back together the essential strands of community health and well-being. In a recent book, Marion Wright Edelman (1992: 19–20), asserts:

> The greatest threat to our . . . future comes from no external enemy but from the enemy within—in our loss of strong, moral, family, and community values and support. Parent by parent, youth by youth, voter by voter, professional by professional, congregation by congregation, club by club, city by city, county by county, state by state—all Americans must commit personally and as voters to a national crusade of conscience and action.

The threat to which Edelman refers—the "enemy within"—has been given many labels in cultural discussions. Its essence is a lack of attention to nurturing society's institutions so that they in turn will nurture succeeding generations. Many years ago, Erik Erikson included in his theory of adult development a single concept that has at its core this notion of sustaining the world: Generativity.

The seventh and longest of Erikson's eight stages, the stage of generativity versus stagnation comprises the period between early adulthood and old age[1] (Erikson 1963). During adolescence and early adulthood, persons typically become involved with establishing their own identities and intimate relationships. Mature adults then face the task of sustaining the world as their life cycles become more enmeshed with the life cycle of the next generation (Erikson 1963). This expanding concern for future generations may occur because of social and biological demands that are unique to adulthood—for instance, the birth and development of one's children, the expectations of the workplace that one become a mentor, the call to become a leader in one's community. The psychological essence of generativity is a shift from self-focus to other-focus. Generative adults become concerned with meeting the physical, social, psychological, and emotional needs of others, above and beyond their own needs (Franz and White 1985). At the core of generative character is caring. Erikson defines his broad view of caring: "I use 'care' in the same sense which includes 'to care *to do* something,' to 'care *for*' somebody or something, to 'take care *of*' that which needs protection and attention, and 'to take care *not to*' do something destructive" (Erikson, in Evans 1967: 53).

Erikson emphasizes that expressions of generativity will vary widely from one person to the next. Thus we see outlets for generativity in the caregiving of Mother Teresa: "It is not how much we do but how much love we put in the doing—a lifelong sharing of love with others" (Teresa 1983). On the other hand, Vera Brittain, a turn-of-the-century British activist, reflects that "[I] never have been philanthropically-minded or felt that philanthropy is any good. What it does is make me more politically minded than I can bear—seeing that I'm a writer and it's no use trying to be otherwise. . . . The moral for me, I suppose, is to go on urging [social action] in books, articles & speeches until people care sufficiently to get something done" (Brittain, in Bishop 1986: 17). While both Mother Teresa and Vera Brittain are engaging in generative activity, one focuses her efforts toward individuals, while the other addresses change at the level of society. That some people struggle with or even flounder in the generative developmental task is also recognized by Erikson. Some persons, unable to give to others, stagnate and falter in their growth during this important developmental period.

Although great variability in generative expressions *over time* is compatible with Erikson's theory, he gives the topic little explicit attention. In fact, the debate as to whether meaningful change occurs during adulthood remains unresolved (Helson and Stewart 1994). Researchers studying personality, for example (see overviews by Lachman 1989, McCrae and Costa 1990), find considerable consistency in studies of five major personality traits over the life course: neuroticism, extraversion, openness to experience, agreeableness, and conscientiousness. However, these findings do not necessarily rule out the kinds of changes anticipated in adulthood by the change theorists. A shift in *orientation* from self to others, for instance, may require little "personality change." Erikson's theory is unique, then, in that it describes a subtle shift in character that is specifically linked with the aging process. The capacity to become generative (or not) develops across the life course; its richest manifestations, in terms of behavior (taking care of the next generation) and character, are placed most prominently in middle adulthood.

Other models of adulthood also discuss patterns of change and consistency

(Franz 1993). For example, shifts toward more interdependent ways of thinking and being, becoming less self-assertive, and increased involvement with the well-being of others during adulthood are reflected in the theories of Kegan (1982), Levinson et al. (1978), Schaie (1978), and White (1966). Several theorists also suggest that mature adults become more realistic and pragmatic about themselves and their strivings (Buhler 1968, Buhler and Goldenberg 1968, Franz 1994, Gould 1980, Levinson et al. 1978). Still other universalistic theorists propose that the mid-life adult's cognitions and emotions become more contextualized, differentiated, and complex (Jung 1972; Labouvie-Vief, Hakim-Larson, and Hobart 1987; Loevinger 1976), and more introspective (Lubin 1964, Neugarten 1970, Rosen and Neugarten 1964). Finally, maturity—defined differently depending on the theorist or researcher—is assumed to increase with age and change in quality (cf. Erikson 1963, Franz and White 1985, Helson and Wink 1992, Vaillant 1977). In general, then, a variety of theorists view middle adulthood as a time of potential change.

While universalistic theories such as Erikson's propose general patterns associated with the process of aging or increased maturity, other researchers and theorists propose that sequences of development and typical concerns or responses may be specific to gender or social roles. For instance, Gutmann proposed that men move from an active, assertive mode to a more dependent, passive interpersonal one at midlife, whereas women become more assertive (Gutmann 1975, Neugarten 1970). These changes occur because of predictable shifts in parenting roles for men and women; men and women function in line with different biological demands. The timing of these changes, though, will depend on the timing of particular events in a culture or group. Thus, a person's expression of generativity may be sex-linked: Women may be more likely to maintain the world through taking care of people, men through work or creativity (Erikson 1963, 1968, 1974).

Helson and Wink (1992) suggest that common social contexts may differ by cohort. Although changes may occur in a particular cohort in response to expectable changes in social roles, even the definition of roles may be specific to a cohort. For instance, the role definition of being a young mother in middle-class white America in the 1950s when the majority of mothers did not work is likely to differ substantially from that of a young mother in the 1990s when the majority of young mothers are working at least part-time. Other researchers (Elder 1979; Stewart and Healy 1989; Stewart, Lykes, and LaFrance 1983; Veroff 1986) have suggested that the life path or personality of a cohort may change due to commonly experienced major historical events. Elder (1979, 1993), for instance, has examined the way in which the Great Depression differentially affected development depending on age, gender, and social class. Without multiple cohorts in a study, however, universalistic/maturational changes cannot be distinguished from changes linked to normative events.

Complex patterns of change in generativity across the mid-life years, then, are theoretically (and empirically) possible. There is little theory, however, to guide predictions concerning the type or direction of idiosyncratic change, and developmental trends in generativity during middle adulthood have seldom been studied (exceptions are studies of men by Brim [1992], Snarey [1993], and Vaillant and Milofsky [1980]). A number of researchers have identified higher levels of generativity among middle-aged adults as compared to younger adults (Franz 1995; McAdams, de St. Aubin, and Logan 1993; Peterson and Kloehnen 1995; Peterson and Stewart 1993; Ryff and Heincke 1983; Ryff and Migdal 1984; Stewart, Franz, and Layton 1988; Whitbourne, Zuschlag, Elliot, and Waterman 1992). Other researchers have gone beyond the measurement of generativity to evaluate whether it is associated with social roles (see De Haan and MacDermid 1995; MacDermid, Gillespie, and Heilbrun 1992; MacDermid, Heilbrun, and De Haan 1997). McAdams, however, has found generative themes to be more of an individual difference and—when present—evident in persons at many different ages (McAdams, de St. Aubin, and Logan 1993). Most studies to date, though, are cross-sectional or do not include participants from multiple-birth cohorts, social classes, or both genders. In addition, data sets have rarely been large enough to identify different patterns of development or change through the middle adult years. Only by examining lives through time can such patterning be discerned.

Our purpose in this chapter is to examine three basic aspects of generativity during middle adulthood. First, we evaluate the degree to which individuals shift in relation to one another in terms of generativity over time—labeled "differential stability" by Caspi and Bem (1990). Second, we assess absolute stability, or the degree to which mean levels of generativity change over time, and how these changes vary by gender and cohort. We ask, for example, whether the disposition to be generative looks different in males and females: Do women exhibit a more communal form of generativity and men a more agentic one (Bakan 1966, Erikson 1974, Gutmann 1977)? Finally, we address ipsative stability, or patterns of intra-individual change.

We were fortunate to have available to us a highly unique sample for studying these questions: two groups of men and women studied in depth approximately every ten years, from age thirty to age sixty. These samples, known as the Institute of Human Development (IHD) samples (the Oakland Growth Study and the Berkeley Guidance and Control Studies) have been written about extensively (e.g., Block 1971, Clausen 1993, Eichorn et al. 1981, Elder 1974). Since the study participants were born approximately eight years apart, they comprise two different birth cohorts. The question of developmental change, then, can be examined with greater clarity through the inclusion of cohort differences.

Interlude: A Brief Description of the Study Participants

The Institute of Human Development study participants (the Oakland Growth, Berkeley Guidance, and Berkeley Control samples), represent two different birth cohorts of middle- and working-class men and women studied since the 1920s as part of an attempt to understand childhood dynamics and life-course development (Block 1971, Clausen 1993, Eichorn et al. 1981, Elder 1974). This sample, because of the longevity and extensivity of the data collected on it, provides a unique opportunity to examine generativity in depth.

Participants in the Oakland Growth Study were born in the early 1920s and were studied at six different life periods ranging from early childhood to late adulthood; three assessments occurred during the relevant middle adulthood years under study. The men and women of the Oakland Growth Study experienced the Great Depression as young teenagers and were young adults (about age twenty) during World War II; many of the men served in the armed forces. The Berkeley Guidance and Control samples (one in which the mothers received "counseling" regarding their children, and a control group in which the mothers received no counseling) were about eight years younger than the Oakland group. The Berkeley participants experienced the major events of the early part of this century as children, and as teenagers were too young to serve in World War II until it was almost over. The psychological and economic effects of these early experiences have been well documented elsewhere (Block 1971, Elder 1974). According to Elder, the Oakland men and women experienced a more secure early developmental period than the Berkeley participants; Berkeley men displayed developmental lags that did not dissipate until near midlife.

Thirty percent of the study participants had only a high school education, typical of their cohort. Historical time made some difference for the women in these samples; for instance, no women from the Oakland sample went on to graduate school but 20% of the Guidance sample did. Otherwise, the adult lives of these groups appear, on the surface, very similar: the vast majority of men and women got married and had children. Most of the men worked full time (and more); most of the women worked managing their home and children. These are the parents of the group we now call the "baby-boom" generation— an unusually large birth cohort embedded in the upward mobility of post–World War II Americans. About 40% of the families of origin were considered "working class." For most of these men and women, the upward mobility that marked American lives in the middle of this century was also apparent in theirs; as adults, 90% had become middle class (Clausen 1993).

The sample for the present research consists of 177 study participants: 106 from the Berkeley Guidance (32 women, 29 men) and Berkeley Control (30 women, 15 men) studies, and 71 from the Oakland Growth study (36 women,

35 men). Only respondents with complete data for the three occasions of data collection during adulthood were included. The proportion of study participants meeting this criterion was somewhat lower for the Oakland participants (33% of original subjects; 67% of age eighteen sample) than for those from Berkeley (42% of original subjects; 67% of age eighteen sample). Adult data were collected in 1958–59, 1969–70, and 1982 (see Table 1). Berkeley participants were age thirty to thirty-one (referred to as age thirty-one in the text and tables), age forty-one to forty-two (age forty-two), and age fifty-three to fifty-four (age fifty-four), respectively; Oakland participants were studied at ages thirty-seven to thirty-eight (age thirty-eight), age forty-eight to fifty (age fifty), and age sixty-one to sixty-two (age sixty-two). Interviews and data collection procedures varied somewhat according to the different samples and at different assessments; greater consistency was achieved by the adult data collections (though generally with slightly less detail for the "control" sample). Within-time data collection was comparable across subjects. The data reported here represent only a small proportion of those collected.

Preliminary analyses (and observations by other scholars, see Clausen 1993) suggest few, if any, meaningful differences between the Berkeley Guidance and Berkeley Control samples; thus, these two groups are combined for subsequent analyses. Henceforth we use location to refer to our groups: "Berkeley" and "Oakland," remembering that the primary superficial differences between the groups lie in their age differences (about eight years) and the natural interventions of major historical events at (perhaps) developmentally salient periods.

Over the years, data for each subject at every time had been Q-sorted,[2] a technique used to render diverse data more comparable. Expert raters (clinical psychologists and a psychiatric social worker) rated each study participant based on case files that included interview transcripts, case records, and observational notes. At least two judges, one of whom had interviewed the person at the time of measurement, rated each person. Combinations of judges were varied systematically, and no judge rated the same person at more than one

Table 1
Study Participation and Data Collections

	Birth years	Ages at Assessment Dates		
		1958–59	1969–1970	1982
Oakland Growth Study 36 women, 35 men	1921–22	37–38	48–50	61–62
Berkeley Guidance Study 30 women, 15 men	1928–29	30–31	41–42	53–54
Berkeley Control 32 women, 29 men	1928–29	30–31	41–42	53–54

time of measurement. Inter-rater reliabilities were calculated after two ratings; for the few cases that were not satisfactory, additional ratings were performed until reliabilities were satisfactory (above .65) Additional information about Q-sort procedures specific to this sample and data reduction can be found in Block (1971), Clausen (1993), Eichorn (1981), and Haan, Millsap, and Hartka (1986).

The Q-sort technique provided us with the tool we needed for studying generativity in the IHD samples. The Q-sort is distinctive as a research instrument in that it can reliably and validly render different materials (narratives, questionnaires) comparable, through the common language of its 100 personality items, ipsatively arranged (see Block 1978). Problems associated with having somewhat different data collected at different assessments, and variations in the questions asked within time to the different subsamples can be reduced by "translating" the data into the language of the Q-sort. Thus, the Q-sort approach opens the door to many avenues of research, especially in secondary analysis of longitudinal data by rendering the data sets equivalent over time through carefully trained, reliable judges.

A Measure of Mid-life *Character:* Generative Realization

Having identified an appropriate sample in which generativity could be examined across multiple adult years, our first task was to create a reliable and valid measure of generativity from the already collected data. Reviews of prior studies revealed several different conceptualizations and operationalizations of mid-life generativity; these approaches have included clinical judgments (Kotre 1984, McAdams 1988, Vaillant and Milofsky 1980), self-report, content analysis, and Q-sort techniques. Kotre and McAdams, in particular, through their detailed studies of individual lives, elucidate the multidimensional nature of generativity and its importance in mid-life adults' thinking about themselves and the future (Kotre 1984; McAdams and de St. Aubin 1992; McAdams, Ruetzel, and Foley 1986).

The most promising assessment strategy for our purposes was a Q-sort based measure of generativity. Peterson (1993) had eight experts generate prototypes of the "ideally generative person" using the California Adult Q-set (CAQ; Block 1971, 1978). Judges agreed strongly (alpha = .97) as to what personality qualities best represented the ideally generative person. A Generative Realization index was created based on the 13 items most characteristic of the generative prototype (see Appendix; Peterson 1993). Factor analyses revealed three underlying components of generativity: A caring component as represented by the items oriented towards nurturing other people (called the Communion scale); an instrumental component as represented by an orientation to be effective and productive (called the Agency scale); and an insight component. These components correspond well to the blend of caring, productivity, and self-awareness in Erikson's notion of generativity.

As can be seen from the items, the Generative Realization index assesses the extent to which individuals express qualities associated with generativity in ways that are tangible to an observer (that is, being giving, productive, responsible, sympathetic, and so on). The assumption behind the measure is that a person who is manifesting more of these qualities is more generative. Convergent and divergent validity of the measure was found in two groups of mid-life women (Peterson and Kloehnen 1995). Peterson's sample had generative realization data at only two time periods, was small, and only included women. Convinced by the validity and reliability of the Generative Realization index, which built on a measure that was available at the most assessments for the majority of participants, we decided to use the Peterson method for assessing generativity in the IHD samples.[3]

For the present study, Q-sort based Generative Realization (GR) index scores were constructed at each age using the items identified by Peterson (1993; Peterson and Kloehnen 1995; see Appendix). Principal components factor analyses of the Generative Realization index in these study participants yielded three components similar to those found by Peterson (1993): Communion (nurturance), agency (prosocial competence/productivity), and insight. These three dimensions, however, are not orthogonal. Confirmatory principal components factor analyses were conducted specifying a one-factor model, consistent with Peterson (1993) and Peterson and Kloehnen (1995). Based on eigen values and factor loadings, the data appear to most strongly support a unitary model of generativity, for both men and women, at each time of measurement. Two items (proffers advice and philosophically oriented) had low loadings in most analyses: both items are part of the agentic component of generativity.

Cronbach's alphas for total Generative Realization were .85 at Time 1, .87 at Time 2, and .86 at Time 3, reflecting the coherence of the construct; alphas did not vary as a function of sex or group. For the three components, communion also had high internal consistency, ranging from .85 to .91 for the total sample at each time of measurement. Internal consistencies for the other components were lower, ranging from .54 to .61 for agency, and .63 to .75 for insight. Although the alphas were not as strong as we would like for the components of generativity, we decided to retain the total and component scores (Generative Realization, and the three components: agency, communion, and insight) during preliminary analyses because of hypotheses predicting sex differences in different aspects of Generative Realization. Our strategy is consistent with that employed by Peterson (1993) and Peterson and Kloehnen (1995).

Scores for Generative Realization and its three components (agency, communion, and insight) were created by standardizing each of the 13 items. The Generative Realization index is the sum of the 13 standardized items; the components are created by taking the averages of the relevant items for that scale

Table 2

Nonstandardized and (Standardized) Means for Generativity Total and Component Scores

	Berkeley		Oakland	
	Women	Men	Women	Men
Communal				
Time 1	55.6 (50.5)	53.9 (49.3)	58.1 (52.5)	51.3 (47.2)
Time 2	61.7 (52.0)	51.1 (43.3)	64.3 (54.1)	57.5 (48.6)
Time 3	65.6 (53.2)	54.8 (45.1)	66.4 (53.8)	59.4 (48.5)
Agentic				
Time 1	55.1 (48.9)	56.4 (50.2)	56.1 (49.9)	58.8 (52.7)
Time 2	63.0 (51.4)	60.3 (48.5)	61.6 (49.9)	63.6 (52.1)
Time 3	62.3 (50.8)	60.6 (49.0)	61.2 (49.6)	63.7 (52.3)
Insight				
Time 1	47.9 (50.3)	45.9 (48.7)	47.8 (50.3)	46.6 (49.3)
Time 2	57.8 (52.8)	49.8 (46.6)	54.6 (50.3)	53.5 (49.5)
Time 3	56.7 (52.5)	52.8 (48.9)	53.6 (49.5)	53.5 (49.5)
Total				
Time 1	697.3 (649.3)	689.6 (644.3)	714.9 (659.1)	690.6 (644.3)
Time 2	796.5 (668.2)	706.6 (611.3)	793.0 (666.1)	766.3 (650.5)
Time 3	809.7 (670.8)	735.8 (623.6)	798.6 (663.2)	776.1 (649.9)

(see Appendix). Standardization of items has been recommended as a means of controlling for possible variability in Q-sorters at each time (e.g., the extent to which a group of sorters might be biased or different in a systematic way across times of measurement [Ozer 1993]). Items were standardized to a mean of 50 and a standard deviation of 10 (means and standard deviations are presented in Table 2). Standardizing all times of measurement to the same mean is an extremely conservative strategy that will ensure that any biases in the estimate of change over time will result in underestimates.

The Q-sort based generative realization index and its component scores can be used to examine generativity longitudinally and multidimensionally. Because the Generative Realization index can be broken into separate components, sex differences in the manifestation of generativity also can be evaluated. Are women more communal and men more agentic in their generativity during some periods of adulthood? Are there sex-differentiated changes in generativity or its components over time?

How Does Generativity Change Over Time?
Assessing Differential Stability

The extent to which Generative Realization (GR) scores were consistent over time relative to the scores of other sample members can be seen in the correlations presented in Table 3. The correlations are not corrected for attenuation

Table 3
Correlations of Generativity Totals and Components Across Decades

	4th decade (age 30–40)		5th decade (age 40–50)				6th decade (age 50–60)	
	Berkeley		Berkeley		Oakland		Oakland	
	Women	Men	Women	Men	Women	Men	Women	Men
Generative realization	.16	.29+	.37**	.29+	.66***	.42*	.35*	.66***
Communal	.21+	.35*	.25*	.40***	.45**	.30**	.18	.64***
Agentic	.30*	.38**	.51***	.29+	.58***	.44**	.35*	.58**
Insight	.10	.15	.35**	.09	.69***	.55***	.46**	.52*

+p ≤ .10   *p ≤ .05   **p ≤ .01   ***p ≤ .001.

and, as a consequence, conservatively estimate the associations over time. Among the Berkeley men and women, there was little relation between GR at ages thirty-one and forty-two. Generative Realization at age forty-two, however, was associated with GR ten years later. Among the Berkeley women, all three of the generative components were correlated across the fifth decade. For the men, however, only the component of communion was significantly correlated over time across the fifth decade of life.

Among the Oakland men and women, who were studied at older ages than the Berkeley sample, moderately high correlations were apparent in all aspects of Generative Realization across their fifth decade from age thirty-eight to age fifty. The extent to which Oakland cohort men and women were perceived as nurturant, agentic, and insightful was significantly correlated across two decades, with the sole exception of a nonsignificant correlation across the sixth decade for the communal component. Keeping in mind that these estimates have not been corrected for attenuation and are thus conservative, and that ten years elapsed between assessments, these correlations are particularly impressive. Evidence of differential stability in Generative Realization in these samples as a whole does *not,* however, rule out the possibility of change at other levels of analysis.

Evidence for Change

Even though examination of the over-time correlations reveals relative consistency in Generative Realization in these samples (especially during the fifth decade), these correlations were not so strong as to preclude the possibility of change in generativity across the middle adult years. We first examined absolute change through repeated measure manovas, exploring the relationship between sample, gender, time, and Generative Realization. A manova with the three component scores was performed separately. The second approach was to develop trajectories across the three adult time periods assessed that indicated intra-individual or ipsative patterns of change (see, for instance, Gustafson and Magnussen 1991, Shedler and Block 1989).

A 3 (Time 1, 2, 3) × 2 (women, men) × 2 (Berkeley, Oakland) anova design was used with total Generative Realization treated as a repeated measure. The same design was used for component scores, with the addition of a second repeated measure: component (communal, agentic, and insight). In the Oakland sample, assessed across its fifth and sixth decades of life, neither total Generative Realization nor the components changed significantly over time for the men or women, or between any of the time periods (see Figure 1: F [2, 172] = ns for Time).

In the younger Berkeley sample, men's overall Generative Realization *increased* from age thirty-one to age fifty-four; however, at the component level, Berkeley men decreased significantly in communion from ages thirty-one to forty-two. Berkeley women tended to be higher in Generative Realization and communion ($p < .10$) at age fifty-four than they had been at age thirty-one; agency tended to increase from age thirty-one to forty-two. Thus, changes in generativity were somewhat more evident in the younger Berkeley sample (F [4, 170] = 2.3, $p < .06$ for Time × Cohort × Component) than in the older Oakland cohort.

Manovas reveal other differences as well. As can be seen in the means presented in Table 2, women from both samples were higher in Generative Realization than the men later in life (at ages forty-two and fifty-four for the Berkeley women, at ages fifty and sixty-two for the Oakland women). Examination of the different component scores reveals in what aspects of Generative Realization men and women differed. At all times, women were more communal than men; somewhat surprisingly, men appeared to be no more productive or agentic than women. At age forty-two (Time 2), Berkeley women appeared more insightful than Berkeley men; no evidence for sex differences in insight was found in the Oakland sample. Perhaps the most dramatic change and sex difference, however, was the Berkeley men's steep decline in communion between ages thirty and forty—most likely key years of career consolidation for that cohort of men.

The results just reported are based on group means, however, and do not address within-individual change. If people are changing idiosyncratically—some struggling with the generative transition, others experiencing renewed vigor, still others hurtling along at the same high level of caring and productivity since early adulthood—then a manova-based data analytic strategy that focuses on group means might *obscure* more normative changes in generativity. Thus, we felt it was important to use a life-pattern approach to studying

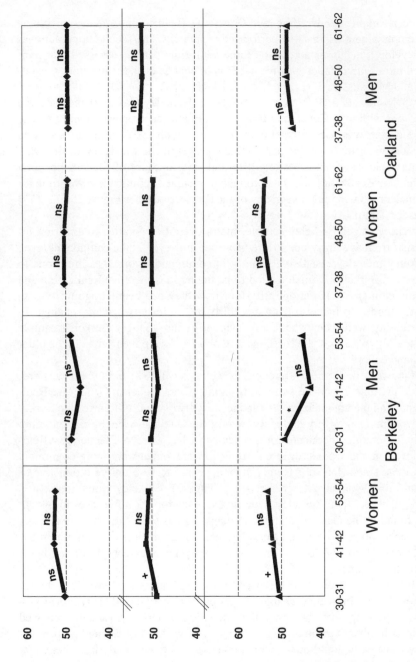

FIGURE 1. Multiple Dimensions of Generativity (from top to bottom: insight, agentic, communal).

change by creating trajectories reflecting patterns of consistency and change in generative realization over time.

Trajectory Groups as a Method of Analyzing Consistency and Change

For these analyses, we focused on the total Generative Realization Index across the three time periods for each cohort. Trajectory groups were created by assessing change in total Generative Realization across the three time periods; individual study participants were said to have increased or decreased between any two time periods if their scores at the later occasion were at least one-half a standard deviation greater than or less than their scores on the earlier occasion. Otherwise scores were considered consistent (no change). Change was assessed separately by sex and by sample. Nine possible patterns of change over time could be generated in this fashion for each cohort (e.g., consistent-consistent, consistent-increased, consistent-decreased, and so on). As can be seen in Table 4 and Figure 2, study participants displayed all possible trajectories of change over time. Although many of the cells are small, use of the trajectory approach highlights the inter-individual variability in paths through midlife.

Table 4
Trajectory Group Distributions

| Group | Berkeley (30–31, 41–42, 53–54 yrs.) | | Oakland (37–38, 48–50, 61–62 yrs.) | | |
	Women ($n = 62$)	Men ($n = 44$)	Women ($n = 36$)	Men ($n = 35$)	Total ($n = 177$)
1	19.4 (12)	4.6 (2)	11.1 (4)	17.1 (6)	13.6 (24)
2	12.9 (8)	11.4 (5)	19.4 (7)	5.7 (2)	12.0 (22)
3	8.1 (5)	18.2 (8)	22.2 (8)	8.6 (3)	13.0 (24)
4	4.8 (3)	2.3 (1)	0.0 (0)	2.9 (1)	2.8 (5)
5	16.1 (10)	18.2 (8)	8.3 (3)	22.9 (8)	16.0 (29)
6	19.4 (12)	2.3 (1)	19.4 (7)	11.4 (4)	13.0 (24)
7	3.2 (2)	2.3 (1)	0 (0)	5.7 (2)	2.0 (5)
8	3.2 (2)	13.6 (6)	5.6 (2)	14.3 (5)	8.0 (15)
9	12.9 (8)	27.3 (12)	13.9 (5)	11.4 (4)	16.0 (29)

Note: Figures in parentheses are base *n*s for the adjacent percentages.

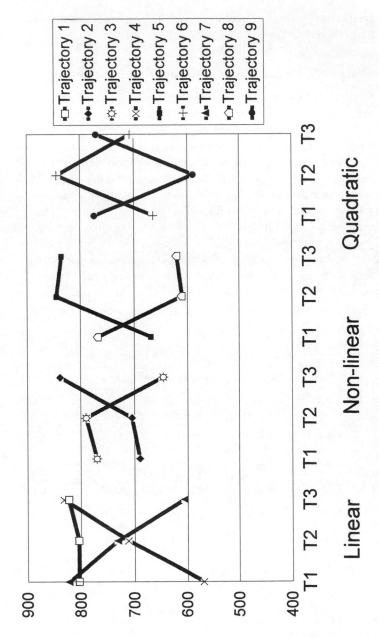

FIGURE 2. Trajectories of Change in Two Cohorts of Adults (T1 = 1958–59, T2 = 1969–70, T3 = 1982).

Table 5
Groupings Based on Total Generativity Change—Row Percent (frequency count)

	Net decrease	No change	Net increase	Curvilinear ($\vee$)	Curvilinear ($\wedge$)
Berkeley (Age 30, 40, 50)[a]					
Women	14.5 (9)	19.4(12)	33.9(21)	12.9 (8)	19.4(12)
Men	34.1(15)	52.3(23)	31.8(14)	27.3(12)	2.3 (1)
Oakland (Age 40, 50, 60)[b]					
Women	27.8(10)	11.1 (4)	27.8(10)	13.9 (5)	19.4 (7)
Men	28.6(10)	17.1 (6)	31.4(11)	11.4 (4)	11.4 (4)

Note: For total sample, χ^2 for sex by change group = 10.7, df = 4, p < .05.
  a. χ^2 for sex by change group = 17.6, df = 4, p < .001.
  b. χ^2 for sex by change group = 1.4, df = 4, p = ns.

To simplify describing the patterns of change over time, we collapsed the nine trajectories into five for each cohort. These five groups represent net decreases (or increases) in generative realization, relative consistency in generative realization, and the two quadratic patterns as represented by the v or inverted v (see Table 5). Here it is easier to see that the modal Berkeley woman became increasingly generative over two decades, from her early thirties to early fifties. The modal Berkeley man changed little from his thirties to his early fifties. The sex difference in patterning of generative trajectories is significant ($\chi^2 = 17.6$, p < .001, df = 4). The older cohort of Oakland men and women, however, were fairly similar to each other in their modal patterns of change: about a third of each sample increased in Generative Realization over the two decades from forty to sixty, and about a third decreased during the same period ($\chi^2 = 1.4$, ns, df = 4). Thus gender and age/cohort effects can be seen in the patterning of life in middle adulthood. It remains to be seen if these patternings are also associated with normative or idiosyncratic life events, or prior personality characteristics.

An obvious question arising from examination of the trajectory groups is "why": Why do individuals experience one pattern of change rather than another? As one way of exploring this question, we focused on change which occurred during the fifth decade of life for all respondents. Figures 3 and 4 summarize the demographic characteristics of the individuals whose levels of generativity increased, decreased, and remained stable during this period. Men (shown in Figure 3) whose total generativity increased during their fifth decade of life appeared to conform more to traditional family and role expectations than men whose total generativity decreased (and note that Block [1971; cited in Haan, Millsap, and Hartka 1986] tested for social desirability bias among the Q-sort judges, finding it in only 61 of 990 sorts). Men who increased in generativity were more likely than men who decreased in generativity to be employed, to be the only earner in their families, to have been married only

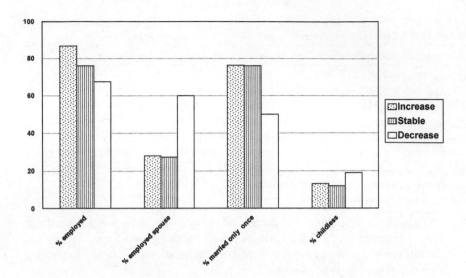

FIGURE 3. Demographic Characteristics of Men Based on Change in Total Generativity Across the Fifth Decade.

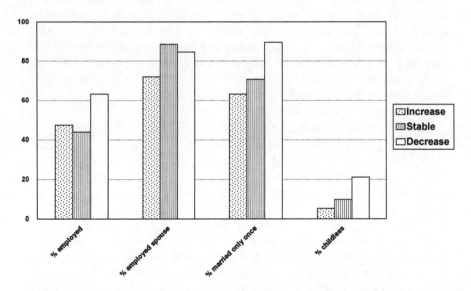

FIGURE 4. Demographic Characteristics of Women Based on Change in Total Generativity Across the Fifth Decade.

once, and to have children. Thus, for men, increases in generativity were associated with conventionality (note that small cell sizes precluded the accurate use of statistical tests for significance in these descriptive analyses).

Unlike men, increases in generativity for women across the fifth decade of life were not consistently associated with conformity. While women who increased in generativity were more likely than women who decreased to conform to traditional expectations for homemaking and motherhood, they were unconventional in that they were less likely to have an employed spouse or to have been married only once. The apparent importance of marital history and husbands' employment situations suggests that husbands' behavior may be important to their wives' trajectories of change in generativity.

Discussion

In recent years, theorists and researchers have discussed and evaluated whether there are certain kinds of change during adulthood. In particular, the question of whether adults expand their desires to maintain and nurture the world (here called generativity) has captured some researchers' attention. Increased interest in generativity parallels worries among cultural critics that the moral and social fabric of American culture is ripping at the seams. If the culture is at risk, who will safeguard the well-being of future generations? What kind of legacy are we leaving? Here, we examined the longitudinal patterning of generativity in two groups of adults over multiple decades of their lives. Because of the size of the sample, the clinical depth of the assessments, and the longitudinal nature of these assessments, we were able to explore previously unexamined issues related to generativity, such as gender and cohort differences, long-term trajectories, and developmental trends in the components of agency, communion, and insight. No other longitudinal analyses of Generative Realization across middle adulthood have previously been performed with such a large and diverse sample.

Only modest change trends in Generative Realization were observed. Most changes occurred between the ages of thirty and forty in the younger Berkeley cohort, where both men and women tended to be perceived as having increased in Generative Realization. No significant change over time was observed in the Oakland sample, on average. Gender differences were also apparent in the developmental trajectories of generativity. Women exhibited higher levels of generative realization than men in general. As was predicted, women were higher in communal aspects of generativity; that there were no sex differences in agency was unexpected. Our initial interpretation of these findings is that women's socialization towards caring may facilitate their negotiation of mid-life issues.

Evidence in these cohorts for both some consistency and some change in generativity during adulthood challenges the current bias in personality research toward identifying ways in which personality has often been conceptualized as being typified by consistency over time. According to McCall (1977: 338–39),

> I detect a tendency for our discipline to emphasize information on the stability of individual differences at the expense of data on the developmental functions. . . . I am appealing for an equally as rigorous attempt to describe and explain developmental change.

In response to McCall's appeal, we further explored more individualized patterns of change across two decades. Results from these exploratory analyses foster less conventional thinking concerning adulthood. Although generativity may be a relatively consistent personality characteristic, complex patterns of change in generative realization may occur during adulthood. Take as an example the patterns of overall change among the members of the Oakland cohort. During the twenty years of study, about one-third of these individuals experienced overall increases in Generative Realization while another third experienced overall decreases. Thus, the global averages that suggest consistency occur, in part, because the two contrasting patterns cancel each other out.

Nonetheless, the Berkeley cohort, as a group, displayed somewhat more change than the somewhat older Oakland cohort. Why might the patterns in these two cohorts be different? One possible explanation is that most generative change happens earlier in adulthood (e.g., as exhibited by the Berkeley cohort in its fourth decade) than is usually thought. The Oakland and Berkeley cohorts may appear different, then, because data were not gathered from the Oakland cohort in earlier adult years. From the perspective of "family time" instead of chronological age, the fourth decade of life was one in which both samples experienced their oldest children's transition to adolescence; lacking data for this decade from the Oakland sample, then, we are unable to test whether there were particular challenges for all of the adults to grow and develop during that decade. Some researchers have suggested that children's adolescence may *propel* parents into mid-life concerns (Silverberg 1989, Silverberg and Steinberg 1987); our data may be consistent with such a proposition.

The cohort differences in generative change may also be a function of systematic differences in life experience between the two cohorts (Elder 1993). Other researchers have established that the Oakland and Berkeley samples had meaningfully different early life experiences, and that the Berkeley men showed consistent developmental deficits at least until their forties (when compared with the Oakland men). Contrary to theoretical predictions and consistent with other researchers' findings of developmental lags, Berkeley men *decreased* significantly in the communal component of generativity during their fourth decade. Although one might anticipate, instead, an increase in agency (reflecting generative energy directed toward the workplace), agency did not change across the fourth decade. *Overall* generativity did increase, however, from the Berkeley men's early thirties to their fifties. It may be that the period from 1958/59 to 1969/70 was a difficult one for the younger Berkeley men: their sons were going to war (when they themselves had not); they were competing for higher level jobs with World War II veterans who (if they returned) came home to educational and career benefits; their large families were, perhaps, straining and constraining salaries and time. For the young Berkeley women, however, more opportunities for jobs and self-realization associated with advances made in the feminist movement may have opened more avenues of generative expression for them in their fourth and fifth decades.

These relatively large samples with multiple assessments at key age points provide new insights into the intersection of gender, age, and cohort in adult development. There was little support for the theoretical view that generativity increases *universally* toward midlife; analyses suggest, instead, multiple patterns of change. One way of reconciling these results with the various theoretical views is to attempt to distinguish adult development from personality change. The process of becoming generative may not call for a change in personality per se; rather the unique challenge of middle adult years may be the ability of the individual to respond to the socially and age-determined demands for other-oriented, world-sustaining, caring behaviors.

We see the strength of this work as locating a promising method of assessing Generative Realization in adults that can be used with these and other data to address a series of new questions about generativity as an important prosocial characteristic:

1. Can early personality characteristics predict what kind of generative trajectories a person might negotiate during middle adult years?

2. Given the sex differences in Generative Realization, are there further differences to be found in how generativity is manifested in competent behavior? How do men and women express their generativity in different domains of life?

3. Can we better understand what historical and social forces are involved with the development of Generative Realization? These analyses revealed cohort differences in generativity; the two samples, though, also differed along some other demographic dimensions that may or may not be cohort-related. What kinds of life experiences might be associated with different patterns of generativity?

4. Finally, we can move on to our next series of analyses on the relationship between generativity and behavioral competencies. To the extent that generative people invest energy in the needs of the next generation—by improving society or assisting younger and less experienced individuals—they also may be more likely to be socially responsible, to function well in the domains of work,

intimate relationships, and community involvement, and to display greater psychological health. Thus, we can test how and the extent to which psychologically generative persons manifest this generativity in practical, intellectual, social, and emotionally adaptive ways. Future work will examine these interrelationships, and perhaps will help us identify how individuals who are generative function in ways that nurture trust, hope, and optimism in the next generation, thus sustaining and maintaining the world.

Acknowledgments

Research for this chapter was supported by grants from the Character and Competence research program of the Henry A. Murray Research Center and by a grant from the Purdue Research Foundation. Assistance from Barbara Burek and Carol Huffine at the Institute of Human Development, University of California, Berkeley is gratefully acknowledged and especially appreciated.

Appendix

Generative Realization Q-sort Items

Communal Items
   Behaves in a giving way toward others
   Behaves in a considerate or sympathetic manner
   Is protective of those close to him
   Has warmth; has the capacity for close relationships; compassionate
   Is turned to for advice and reassurance

Agentic Items
   Is a genuinely dependable and responsible person
   Is productive; gets things done
   Behaves in an ethically consistent manner; is consistent with own personal
   standards
   Tends to proffer advice
   Is concerned with philosophical problems

Insight Items
   Has a wide range of interests
   Is socially perceptive of a wide range of social cues
   Able to see to the heart of important problems

Notes

1. Erikson is fairly adamant that age boundaries *not* be placed on his stages (Erikson 1968). Erikson's "generative" stage is placed between intimacy/young adulthood and

wisdom/old age. Current views place middle age as somewhere between ages thirty-five and sixty but these boundaries reflect the current life span among middle-class Americans and are an attempt to delineate the concept of midlife. In the context of this essay, any association between midlife and generativity should be read figuratively not literally.

2. The Q-sort will be discussed in greater detail in the methods section.

3. Other researchers have factor analyzed or created prototypes with the Q-sort that have some overlap with the generativity measure. An evaluation of Lanning's (1994) factor analysis of the CAQ into factors representing the five common personality factors (emotional lability, extraversion, conscientiousness, agreeableness, and openness), for instance, reveals that the thirteen generativity items fall across all five factors and tend to be among the strongest-loading items for a particular factor. In addition, communal items tended to fall on the agreeableness factor, agentic items on the conscientiousness factor, and insight onto the openness factor. Since Erikson's construct of generativity represented the individual's adaptation and coming into a form of healthy balance by midlife, this depiction of the generative person as agreeable, conscientious, open to experience, somewhat extraverted, and low in neuroticism is an appropriate description. Costa and McCrae's work on the association between the common five traits and the Q-sort items reveals a somewhat different placing of items from the work of Lanning. McCrae and Costa (1990) place six of the thirteen items; of these six items, any agentic items come from the conscientiousness factor; any communal items come from the agreeableness factor; and two of the insight items are placed on the extraversion factor. Trait approaches seem less useful to us for this chapter for several reasons: Some of the differences seen above between trait approaches occur because of variations in views of what comprises the common traits among different trait researchers; as yet, there is no agreed-on trait measure. Trait theory also lacks predictions for normative changes in personality during adulthood; the theory and its measurement strategies are primarily descriptive, predicated on stability, and are atheoretical concerning sex differences.

In recent years, the Block project has used a resiliency prototype to assess flexible coping during adolescence and young adulthood. In these young adults, scores on the generativity scale and resilience are highly correlated, indicating substantial overlap in the constructs. At the item level, Block defines the prototypically resilient person as most characteristically coping well, maintaining and sustaining good relationships, and as productive. Block reports high levels of consistency in resiliency across adolescence; the resilient person tends to stay resilient. Clausens' (1993) planful competence components are also based on the CAQ; planful competence represents Clausen's view of the adapted adult. Generativity items come from four of Clausen's six components: self-control, cognitive commitment, warmth, and dependability. Interestingly, several items appear on multiple components: dependable appears on three of these four; productive, sympathetic, and warm appear on at least two. This overlap suggests that these aspects of the individual may be superordinate in some way. While Block's and Clausen's analyses have yielded a portrayal of competent personality structures, our interests lay in testing whether personality development and sex differences in that development occur during adulthood; for these questions, the most clear and testable hypotheses arise from Erikson's theory.

References

Bakan, D. 1966. *The Duality of Human Existence: Isolation and Communion in Western Man.* Boston: Beacon Press.

Bishop, A., ed. 1986. *Chronicle of Friendship: Vera Brittain's Diary of the Thirties 1932–1939.* London: Victor Gollancz.

Block, J. 1971. *Lives through Time.* Berkeley, CA: Bancroft.

———. 1978 [1961]. *The Q-Sort Method in Personality Assessment and Psychiatric Research.* Springfield, IL: C. C. Thomas.

Brim, O. G. 1992. *Ambition: How We Manage Success and Failure throughout Our Lives.* New York: Basic Books.

Brim, O. G., and C. D. Ryff. 1980. "On the Properties of Life Events." *Life-span Development and Behavior,* vol. 3. New York: Academic Press.

Buhler, C. 1968. "The Developmental Structure of Goal Setting in Group and Individual Studies." In *The Course of Human Life: A Study of Goals in the Humanistic Perspective,* ed. C. Buhler and F. Massarik, 27–54. New York: Springer.

Buhler, C., and H. Goldenberg. 1968. "Structural Aspects of Individual's History." In *The Course of Human Life: A Study of Goals in the Humanistic Perspective,* ed. C. Buhler and F. Massarik, 54–63. New York: Springer.

Caspi, A., and D. J. Bem. 1990. "Personality Continuity and Change Across the Life Course." In *Handbook of Personality: Theory and Research,* ed. L. A. Pervin, 549–75. New York: Guilford.

Clausen, J. A. 1993. *American Lives: Looking Back at the Children of the Great Depression.* New York: The Free Press.

DeHaan, L. G., and S. M. MacDermid. 1995. "Is Women's Identity Achievement Associated with the Expression of Generativity? Examining Identity and Generativity in Multiple Roles." *Journal of Adult Development* 1: 235–47.

Edelman, M. W. 1992. *The Measure of Our Success: A Letter to My Children and Yours.* Boston: Beacon Press.

Eichorn, D. H., J. A. Clausen, N. Haan, M. P. Honzik, and P. Mussen, eds. 1981. *Present and Past in Middle Life.* New York: Academic Press.

Elder, G. H. 1974. *Children of the Great Depression.* Chicago: University of Chicago Press.

———. 1979. "Historical Change in Life Patterns and Personality." In *Life-span Development and Behavior,* vol. 2, ed. P. B. Balters and O. G. Brim, Jr., 117–59. New York: Academic Press.

———. 1993. "Studying Children in a Changing World." In *Children in Time and Place: Developmental and Historical Insights,* ed. G. H. Elder, J. Modell, and R. Parke, 3–22. Cambridge: Cambridge University Press.

Erikson, E. H. 1963 [1950]. *Childhood and Society.* New York: W. W. Norton.

———. 1968. *Identity: Youth and Crisis.* New York: W. W. Norton.

———. 1974. *Dimensions of a New Identity.* New York: W. W. Norton.

Evans, R. 1967. *Dialogue with Erik Erikson.* New York: Harper and Row.

Fiske, M. L., and D. A. Chiriboga. 1990. *Change and Continuity in Adult Life.* San Francisco: Jossey-Bass.

Franz, C. E. 1994. "Does Thought Content Change as Individuals Age? A Longitudinal Study of Midlife Adults." In *Can Personality Change?*, ed. T. Heatherton and J. Weinberger, 227–50. Washington DC: American Psychological Association.

———. 1995. "A Quantitative Case Study of Longitudinal Changes in Identity, Intimacy, and Generativity." *Journal of Personality* 63: 27–46.

———. 1997. "Stability and Change in the Transition to Midlife." In *Multiple Paths of Midlife Development*, ed. M. E. Lachman and J. B. James, 45–66. MacArthur Foundation Studies on Successful Midlife Development. Chicago: University of Chicago Press.

Franz, C. E., and K. M. White. 1985. "Individuation and Attachment in Personality Development: Extending Erikson's Theory." *Journal of Personality* 53: 224–55.

Gould, R. 1978. *Transformations: Growth and Change in Adult Life.* New York: Simon and Schuster.

———. 1980. "Transformational Tasks in Adulthood." In *The Course of Life: Psychoanalytic Contributions toward Understanding Personality Development*, vol. 3: *Adulthood and the Aging Process*, ed. S. I. Greenspan and G. H. Pollock, 117–27. Washington, DC: National Institute of Mental Health.

Gustafson, S. B., and D. Magnusson. 1991. *Female Life Careers: A Pattern Approach.* Hillsdale, NJ: Erlbaum.

Gutmann, D. L. 1975. "Parenthood: A Key to the Comparative Study of the Life Cycle." In *Life Span Developmental Psychology*, ed. N. Datan and I. H. Ginsberg, 167–84. New York: Academic Press.

———. 1977. "The Cross-Cultural Perspective: Notes toward a Comparative Psychology of Aging." In *Handbook of the Psychology of Aging*, ed. J. E. Birren and K. W. Schaie, 302–26. New York: Van Nostrand Reinhold.

Haan, N., R. Millsap, and E. Hartka. 1986. "As Time Goes By: Change and Stability in Personality over Fifty Years." *Personality and Aging* 1: 220–32.

Helson, R., and A. Stewart. 1994. "Personality Change in Adulthood." In *Can Personality Change?*, ed. T. F. Heatherton and J. L. Weinberger, 201–26. Washington, DC: American Psychological Association.

Helson, R., and P. Wink. 1992. "Personality Change in Women from the Early 40s to the Early 50s." *Psychology and Aging* 7: 46–55.

Jung, C. G. 1972. "The Transcendent Function." In *The Structure and Dynamics of the Psyche*, 67–91. Vol. 8 in *The Collected Works of C. G. Jung*, ed. H. Read, M. Fordham, G. Adler, and W. McGuire. 2nd ed. Princeton, NJ: Princeton University Press.

Kegan, R. 1982. *The Evolving Self.* Cambridge, MA: Harvard University Press.

Kotre, J. 1984. *Outliving the Self: Generativity and the Study of Lives.* Baltimore, MD: Johns Hopkins University Press.

Labouvie-Vief, G., J. Hakim-Larson, and C. Hobart. 1987. "Age, Ego-Level, and the Life-Span Development of Coping and Defense Processes." *Psychology and Aging* 2: 286–93.

Lachman, M. E. 1989. "Personality and Aging at the Crossroads: Beyond Stability versus Change." In *Social Structure and Aging: Psychological Processes*, ed. K. W. Schaie and C. Schooler, 167–90. Hillsdale, NJ: Erlbaum.

Lanning, K. 1994. "Dimensionality of Observer Ratings on the California Adult Q-Set." *Journal of Personality and Social Psychology* 67: 151–60.

Levinson, D. J., C. N. Darrow, E. B. Klein, J. L. Levinson, and B. McKee. 1978. *The Seasons of a Man's Life.* New York: Knopf.

Loevinger, J. 1976. *Ego Development.* San Francisco: Jossey-Bass.

Lubin, M. I. 1964. "Addendum to Chapter 4." In *Personality in Middle and Late Life: Empirical Studies,* ed. B. L. Neugarten, 102–4. New York: Atherton Press.

MacDermid, S. M., and L. K. Gillespie. 1992. "Generativity in Multiple Roles." In E. de St. Aubin (Chair), *Emerging Issues in Adult Development: Research concerning Generativity.* Symposium conducted at the meeting of the Midwestern Psychological Association, Chicago.

MacDermid, S. M., L. K. Gillespie, and G. Heilbrun. 1992. "Correlates of Generativity in Multiple Roles for Women during Midlife." Paper presented at the annual meeting of the National Council on Family Relations, Orlando, FL. November.

MacDermid, S. M., G. Heilbrun, and L. G. DeHaan. 1997. "The Generativity of Employed Mothers in Multiple Roles: 1979 and 1991." In *Multiple Paths of Midlife Development,* ed. M. E. Lachman and J. B. James. MacArthur Foundation Studies on Successful Midlife Development. Chicago: University of Chicago Press.

McAdams, D. P. 1988. *Power, Intimacy, and the Life Story.* New York: Guilford.

———. 1992. "The Five-Factor Model in Personality: A Critical Appraisal." *Journal of Personality* 60: 329–61.

McAdams, D. P., and E. de St. Aubin. 1992. "A Theory of Generativity and Its Assessment through Self-Report, Behavioral Acts, and Narrative Themes in Autobiography." *Journal of Personality and Social Psychology* 62: 1003–15.

McAdams, D. P., E. de St. Aubin, and R. L. Logan. 1993. "Generativity among Young, Midlife, and Older Adults." *Psychology and Aging* 8: 221–30.

McAdams, D. P., K. Ruetzel, and J. M. Foley. 1986. "Complexity and Generativity at Midlife: Relations among Social Motives, Ego Development, and Adults' Plans for the Future." *Journal of Personality and Social Psychology* 50: 800–807.

McCall, R. 1977. "Challenges to a Science of Developmental Psychology." *Child Development* 48: 333–44.

McCrae, R. R., and P. T. Costa. 1990. *Personality in Adulthood.* New York: Guilford.

Neugarten, B. L. 1970. "Adaptation and the Life Cycle." *Journal of Geriatric Psychology* 4: 71–87.

Ozer, D. J. 1993. "The Q-Sort Method and the Study of Personality Development." In *Studying Lives through Time: Personality and Development,* ed. D. C. Funder, R. D. Parke, C. Tomlinson-Keasey, and K. Widaman, 147–68. Washington, DC: American Psychological Association.

Peterson, B. E. 1993. "Two Measures of Midlife Generativity in a Longitudinal Sample." Ph.D. diss., University of Michigan.

Peterson, B. E., and E. Kloehnen. 1995. "Realization of Generativity in Two Samples of Women at Midlife." *Psychology and Aging* 10: 20–29.

Peterson, B. E., and A. J. Stewart. 1993. "Generativity and Social Motives in Young Adults." *Journal of Personality and Social Psychology* 65: 186–188.

Rosen, J. L., and B. L. Neugarten. 1964. "Ego Functions in the Middle and Later Years:

A Thematic Apperception Study." In *Personality in Middle and Late Life: Empirical Studies,* ed. B. L. Neugarten, 10–110. New York: Atherton Press.

Ryff, C. D., and S. G. Heincke. 1983. "Subjective Organization of Personality in Adulthood and Aging." *Journal of Personality and Social Psychology* 44: 807–16.

Ryff, C. D., and S. Migdal. 1984. "Intimacy and Generativity: Self-Perceived Transitions." *Signs* 9: 470–81.

Schaie, K. W. 1977–78. "Toward a Stage Theory of Adult Cognitive Development." *International Journal of Aging and Human Development* 8: 129–38.

Shedler, J., and J. Block. 1990. "Adolescent Drug Use and Psychological Health: A Longitudinal Inquiry." *American Psychologist* 45: 612–30.

Silverberg, S. B. 1989. "A Longitudinal Look at Parent-Adolescent Relations and Parents' Evaluations of Life and Self." Paper presented at the Tenth Biennial meetings of the International Society for the Study of Behavioral Development, Jyvaskyla, Finland.

Silverberg, S. B., and L. Steinberg. 1987. "Adolescent Autonomy, Parent-Adolescent Conflict, and Parental Well-Being." *Journal of Youth and Adolescence* 16: 293–312.

Snarey, J. 1993. *How Fathers Care for the Next Generation.* Cambridge MA: Harvard University Press.

Stewart, A. J., C. E. Franz, and L. Layton. 1988. "The Changing Self: Using Personal Documents to Study Lives." *Journal of Personality* 56: 41–74.

Stewart, A. J., C. E. Franz, E. P. Paul, and B. E. Peterson. 1991. "Revised Coding Manual for Three Aspects of Adult Personality Development: Identity, Intimacy and Generativity." Unpublished. University of Michigan, Ann Arbor. [Original manual by A. J. Stewart, C. E. Franz, and L. Layton, 1984.]

Stewart, A. J., and J. M. Healy. 1989. "Linking Individual Development and Social Changes." *American Psychologist* 44: 30–42.

Stewart, A. J., M. B. Lykes, and M. LaFrance. 1982. "Educated Women's Career Patterns: Separating Social and Developmental Changes." *Journal of Social Issues* 38: 97–117.

Teresa, Mother. 1983. *Words to Live By.* Notre Dame, IN: Ave Maria Press.

Vaillant, G. E. 1977. *The Adult Life Cycle in One Culture: Adaptation to Life.* Boston: Little, Brown, and Co.

Vaillant, G. E., and E. Milofsky. 1980. "Natural History of Male Psychological Health, IX: Empirical Evidence for Erikson's Model of the Lifecycle." *American Journal of Psychiatry* 137: 1348–59.

Veroff, J. 1986. "Contextualism and Human Motives." In *Frontiers of Motivational Psychology: Essays in Honor of John W. Atkinson,* ed. D. R. Bworn and J. Veroff, 132–45. Berlin: Springer-Verlag.

Whitbourne, S. K., M. K. Zuschlag, L. B. Elliot, and A. S. Waterman. 1992. "Psychosocial Development in Adulthood: A 22-Year Sequential Study." *Journal of Personality and Social Psychology* 63: 260–71.

White, R. W. 1966. *Lives in Progress: A Study of the Natural Growth of Personality.* New York: Holt, Rinehart and Winston.

AUTHOR INDEX

SUBJECT INDEX

Achievement, educational: influence of family background on, 142–43

Achievement, socioeconomic: influence of adolescent competence on, 109; as measure of competence, 93–101

Adolescent Health Care Evaluation Study (Earls), 57–58, 60, 62–68, 83

Adolescents: data collection for sexual decision-making analysis, 64–68; factors related to competent, 89–92; meaning of competence for, 59; sexual activity of, 61–62; sexual decision-making of female, 57–60. *See also* Competence, adolescent; Mothers, single teenage; Peer relationships

Adulthood: achievement in, 91; adolescent competence in transition to, 90–92; changes during middle, 206–7; Generative Realization analyses during, 221–22; generativity stage of, 205–6; research related to, 206–7; social and biological demands of, 205–6; theories of change and consistency, 206–7

Adults: adolescent competence related to adult outcomes, 96–110; optimal functioning requirements, 113; participants in Berkeley Guidance and Control Studies, 209–10, 219, 221–22; participants in Oakland Growth Study, 209–10, 219, 221–22; role in children's moral education, 10–11. *See also* Parents

African-Americans: comparisons of single and married mothers, 192–96; factors related to adolescent pregnancy, 60–64; National Survey of Black Americans, 191–92; sexual decision making of adolescent girls, 57–60; socialization goals, 16; voting behavior, 192; women in family values study, 145–46

Agape, 12–13

Agency, 212–13; in concept of competence, 16–20; exercise of human, 21; planfulness and self-efficacy of human, 20–23. *See also* Communion

Agents: moral, 13; socializing, 14

Altruism: defined, 20; reciprocal, 9

Apprenticeship, 36

Arete, 12

Attachment, as part of moral education, 10

Autonomy: as part of moral education, 10; of youth in college, 172–73, 182–83

Behavior, aggressive/delinquent: related to peer relations, 60–63

Behavior, prosocial: child's development of, 8–12; in competence, 14

Beliefs, self-efficacy, 21–23

Beneficence, as ethical strategy, 8

Berkeley Guidance and Control Studies, x, xiv, 91, 208–9

Blacks. *See* African-Americans

California Adult Q-set (CAQ), 211, 225 n.3

Caring: as component of generativity, 211; Erikson's perception of, 206